Cathy H. C. Hsu, PhD
Editor

Global Tourism Higher Education: Past, Present, and Future

Global Tourism Higher Education: Past, Present, and Future has been co-published simultaneously as *Journal of Teaching in Travel & Tourism*, Volume 5, Numbers 1/2/3 2005.

Pre-publication REVIEWS, COMMENTARIES, EVALUATIONS . . .

"A collection of works that profile tourism programs in different countries is always a pleasure to receive. This particular collection brings together 11 different chapters each of which profiles a country, group of countries or region. The intent to capture and compare each country's past with its present and (expected) future is a good model which makes it easy for the reader to follow. The countries that are profiled are important ones and each has an interesting story to tell with regard to its tourism education profile. A special emphasis is placed on Pacific Rim countries which should be of particular interest to readers who want to learn more about that region. This text would be a great addition to anybody associated with international tourism education."

Clayton W. Barrows, EdD
Professor
School of Hospitality
and Tourism Management
University of Guelph
Canada

More pre-publication
REVIEWS, COMMENTARIES, EVALUATIONS . . .

"As global tourism continues to grow, there is an increasing interest to understand how tourism and hospitality education has developed. This is not only of academic interest, but also of interest to those guiding tourism development and education policy. As tourism education matures and internationalises, there is also a need to understand how and why it has developed the way it has and what lessons and best practices can be adopted from each country. Consequently, the arrival of this book is most timely.

This international review of tourism education offers the reader an in-depth analysis, with each chapter focusing on a specific country—such as China, Canada, South Korea, Turkey and Israel. The wide-range of countries is drawn from around the globe with representation from Asia-Pacific, Europe and North America. This book also complements the recently edited book by David Airey and John Tribe "An International Handbook of Tourism Education," as together they reveal the enormous strides that have been made in developing tourism education over the last three decades.

While this book reveals the very different circumstances that have contributed to the development of tourism related education in each country, it also becomes clear to the reader that there are a number of common themes that emerge. These include: changes in government policy towards higher education; the relative economic importance of tourism to each country; the perceived status of tourism jobs in creating student demand for courses; the arrival of fee-paying overseas programmes in some countries; the varying levels of internationalisation of tourism and education; and also the various levels of involvement between the industry and education.

As with many edited books, the challenge is in keeping each individual chapter focused and ensuring the same basic details about each country, its education system and tourism related developments are all covered. Despite the widely varying national education systems, and the varying degrees of importance of tourism to each country, the various individual authors have all delivered on providing a comprehensive and as broadly comparable analysis as is humanly possible."

J. S. Perry Hobson, PhD
Director, International Centre
for Excellence in Tourism
and Hospitality Education (THE-ICE)
and Associate Professor
School of Tourism
and Hospitality Management
Southern Cross University
Australia

Global Tourism
Higher Education:
Past, Present, and Future

Global Tourism Higher Education: Past, Present, and Future has been co-published simultaneously as *Journal of Teaching in Travel & Tourism,* Volume 5, Numbers 1/2/3 2005.

Monographic Separates from the *Journal of Teaching in Travel & Tourism*™

For additional information on these and other Haworth Press titles, including descriptions, tables of contents, reviews, and prices, use the QuickSearch catalog at http://www.HaworthPress.com.

Global Tourism Higher Education: Past, Present, and Future, edited by Cathy H. C. Hsu, PhD (Vol. 5, No. 1/2/3, 2005). *A comprehensive examination of tourism education development in various regions and countries around the world.*

The Internet and Travel and Tourism Education, edited by Gary Williams, William Chernish, and Bob McKercher (Vol. 1, No. 2/3, 2001). *Discusses both the micro and macro aspects of using the Internet to contribute to your class objectives.*

Global Tourism Higher Education: Past, Present, and Future

Cathy H. C. Hsu, PhD
Editor

Global Tourism Higher Education: Past, Present, and Future has been co-published simultaneously as *Journal of Teaching in Travel & Tourism*, Volume 5, Numbers 1/2/3 2005.

The Haworth Hospitality Press®
An Imprint of The Haworth Press, Inc.

New York • London • Victoria (AU)
www.HaworthPress.com

Published by

The Haworth Hospitality Press®, 10 Alice Street, Binghamton, NY 13904-1580 USA

The Haworth Hospitality Press® is an imprint of The Haworth Press, Inc., 10 Alice Street, Binghamton, NY 13904-1580 USA.

Global Tourism Higher Education: Past, Present, and Future has been co-published simultaneously as *Journal of Teaching in Travel & Tourism*, Volume 5, Numbers 1/2/3 2005.

The development, preparation, and publication of this work has been undertaken with great care. However, the publisher, employees, editors, and agents of The Haworth Press and all imprints of The Haworth Press, Inc., including The Haworth Medical Press® and Pharmaceutical Products Press®, are not responsible for any errors contained herein or for consequences that may ensue from use of materials or information contained in this work. With regard to case studies, identities and circumstances of individuals discussed herein have been changed to protect confidentiality. Any resemblance to actual persons, living or dead, is entirely coincidental.

The Haworth Press is committed to the dissemination of ideas and information according to the highest standards of intellectual freedom and the free exchange of ideas. Statements made and opinions expressed in this publication do not necessarily reflect the views of the Publisher, Directors, management, or staff of The Haworth Press, Inc., or an endorsement by them.

Cover design by Karen M. Lowe

Library of Congress Cataloging-in-Publication Data

Global tourism higher education : past, present, and future / Cathy H. C. Hsu, editor.
     p. cm.
     "Co-published simultaneously as Journal of Teaching in Travel & Tourism, Volume 5, Numbers 1/2/3 2005."
     Includes bibliographical reference and index.
     ISBN-13: 978-0-7890-3281-2 (hard cover : alk. paper)
     ISBN-10: 0-7890-3281-3 (hard cover : alk. paper)
     ISBN-13: 978-0-7890-3282-9 (soft cover : alk. paper)
     ISBN-10: 0-7890-3282-1 (soft cover : alk. paper)
     1. Tourism–Study and teaching (Higher) I. Hsu, Cathy H. C.

G155.7.G56 2006
338.4'79100711--dc22

2005037774

Indexing, Abstracting & Website/Internet Coverage

This section provides you with a list of major indexing & abstracting services and other tools for bibliographic access. That is to say, each service began covering this periodical during the year noted in the right column. Most Websites which are listed below have indicated that they will either post, disseminate, compile, archive, cite or alert their own Website users with research-based content from this work. (This list is as current as the copyright date of this publication.)

Abstracting, Website/Indexing Coverage . . . . Year When Coverage Began

- *(IBR) International Bibliography of Book Reviews on the Humanities and Social Sciences (Thomson) <http://www.saur.de>* 2006

- *(IBZ) International Bibliography of Periodical Literature on the Humanities and Social Sciences (Thomson) <http://www.saur.de>* 2001

- *Australian Education Index (Australian Council for Educational Research) <http://www.acer.edu.au>* 2001

- *CAB ABSTRACTS c/o CABI Publishing, CAB International. Available in print, diskettes updated weekly, and on INTERNET. Providing full bibliographic listings, author affiliation, augmented keyword searching <http://www.cabi.org/>* 1993

- *Cambridge Scientific Abstracts is a leading publisher of scientific information in print journals, online databases, CD-ROM and via the Internet <http://www.csa.com>* 2004

- *CIRET (Centre International de Recherches et d'Etudes Touristiques). Computerized Tourism & General Bibliography. <http://www.ciret-tourism.com>* 2001

- *Database of Research on International Education <http://www.aei.dest.gov.au/general/research.htm>* 2001

- *EBSCOhost Electronic Journals Service (EJS) <http://ejournals.ebsco.com>* 2002

- *Elsevier Scopus <http://www.info.scopus.com>* 2005

(continued)

- *FRANCIS. INIST/CNRS <http://www.inist.fr>* 2001

- *Google <http://www.google.com>* 2004

- *Google Scholar <http://scholar.google.com>* 2004

- *Haworth Document Delivery Center
  <http://www.HaworthPress.com/journals/dds.asp>.* 2001

- *Hospitality & Tourism Complete* 2006

- *Hospitality & Tourism Index (EBSCO).* 2006

- *Human Population & Natural Resource Management (Cambridge
  Scientific Abstracts) <http://csa.com>* 2006

- *INSPEC is the leading English-language bibliographic information
  service providing access to the world's scientific & technical
  literature in physics, electrical eng., electronics, communications,
  control eng., computers & computing, and information tech.
  <http://www.iee.org.uk/publish/>* 2001

- *Internationale Bibliographie der geistes- und sozial-
  wissenschaftlichen Zeitschriftenliteratur . . . See IBZ
  <http://www.saur.de>.* 2001

- *Leisure, Recreation & Tourism Abstracts (c/o CABI Publishing)
  <http://www.cabi.org>* 2001

- *Links @ Ovid (via CrossRef targeted DOI links)
  <http://www.ovid.com>* 2005

- *Lodging, Restaurant & Tourism Index* 2001

- *Management & Marketing Abstracts <http://www.pira.co.uk/>* 2001

- *Ovid Linksolver (Open URL link resolver via CrossRef targeted
  DOI links) <http://www.linksolver.com>* 2005

- *PASCAL, c/o Institut de l'Information Scientifique et Technique.
  Cross-disciplinary electronic database covering the fields of science,
  technology & medicine. Also available on CD-ROM, and can
  generate customized retrospective searches <http://www.inist.fr>* 2003

- *Referativnyi Zhurnal (Abstracts Journal of the All-Russian
  Institute of Scientific and Technical Information–in Russian)
  <http://www.viniti.ru>* 2001

- *Rural Development Abstracts (c/o CABI Publishing)
  <http://www.cabi.org>* ....**

- *Scopus (See instead Elsevier Scopus) <http://www.info.scopus.com>* ... 2005

- *Tourism Insight <http://www.tourisminsight.com>* 2003

- *TOURISM: an international interdisciplinary journal* 2001

(continued)

- *Travel Research Bookshelf, a current awareness service of the Journal of Travel Research "Abstracts from other Journals Section" published by the Travel & Tourism Association* 2001

- *World Agricultural Economics & Rural Sociology Abstracts (c/o CABI Publishing) <http://www.cabi.org>* ....*

  *Exact start date to come.

Special Bibliographic Notes related to special journal issues (separates) and indexing/abstracting:

- indexing/abstracting services in this list will also cover material in any "separate" that is co-published simultaneously with Haworth's special thematic journal issue or DocuSerial. Indexing/abstracting usually covers material at the article/chapter level.
- monographic co-editions are intended for either non-subscribers or libraries which intend to purchase a second copy for their circulating collections.
- monographic co-editions are reported to all jobbers/wholesalers/approval plans. The source journal is listed as the "series" to assist the prevention of duplicate purchasing in the same manner utilized for books-in-series.
- to facilitate user/access services all indexing/abstracting services are encouraged to utilize the co-indexing entry note indicated at the bottom of the first page of each article/chapter/contribution.
- this is intended to assist a library user of any reference tool (whether print, electronic, online, or CD-ROM) to locate the monographic version if the library has purchased this version but not a subscription to the source journal.
- individual articles/chapters in any Haworth publication are also available through The Haworth Document Delivery Service (HDDS).

Global Tourism Higher Education: Past, Present, and Future

CONTENTS

Preface   xiii

Tourism Education in Canada: Past, Present and Future Directions   1
  Don MacLaurin

Global Tourism Higher Education–The British Isles Experience   27
  Tom Baum

Tourism Education in Austria and Switzerland:
  Past Problems and Future Challenges   39
  Klaus Weiermair
  Thomas Bieger

Tourism and Hospitality Higher Education in Israel   61
  Arie Reichel

Tourism Higher Education in Turkey   89
  Fevzi Okumus
  Ozcan Yagci

Tourism Higher Education in China: Past and Present,
  Opportunities and Challenges   117
  Wen Zhang
  Xixia Fan

The Past, Present, and Future of Hospitality and Tourism Higher
  Education in Hong Kong   137
  Ada Lo

Tourism and Hospitality Higher Education in Taiwan:
    Past, Present, and Future   167
        Jeou-Shyan Horng
        Ming-Huei Lee

Travel and Tourism Education in Thailand   197
        Manat Chaisawat

Past, Present, and Future of Tourism Education:
    The South Korean Case   225
        Mi-Hea Cho
        Soo K. Kang

Australian Tourism Education: The Quest for Status   251
        Philip L. Pearce

Index   269

ABOUT THE EDITOR

Cathy H. C. Hsu, PhD, is Professor and Associate Head in the School of Hotel and Tourism Management at The Hong Kong Polytechnic University. Prior to joining the Hong Kong PolyU in July 2001, she was on Kansas State University (USA) faculty for 3 years and on Iowa State University (USA) faculty for 9 years.

She is the editor and chapter author of the book, *Legalized Casino Gaming in the US: The Economic and Social Impact*, published in 1999, and of the book, *Casino Industry in Asia Pacific: Development, Operations, and Impact*, published in March 2006, both by The Haworth Hospitality Press. She is the lead author of the *Marketing Hospitality* textbook, published in June 2001 by John Wiley and Sons. Her research foci have been the economic and social impacts of casino gaming, tourism destination marketing, tourist behaviors, and hospitality/tourism education. She has over 100 refereed journal and proceedings publications. She has served as a consultant to various tourism organizations, such as the World Tourism Organization, Garden Hotels in Guangzhou, Kansas Travel and Tourism Development Division, and Lawrence Convention and Visitors Bureau.

Professor Hsu is the past Chairman of the Board and past President of the International Society of Travel and Tourism Educators, and is the Editor-in-Chief of the *Journal of Teaching in Travel & Tourism*. She also serves on 7 journal editorial boards. She received the Best Article of the Year award from the *Journal of Hospitality and Tourism Research* in 2000. She is listed in *Who's Who Among Asian Americans*.

Preface

There has been a tremendous growth in hospitality and tourism education on a global basis in the past 30 years. This is a reflection of many factors, including the blossoming of the travel and tourism industry stimulated by the improvements to economic conditions in the decades after the Second World War, changed attitudes towards leisure activities, and liberalized government policies on outbound travel for some historically state-controlled societies. As the industry matures and becomes more sophisticated and specialized, the need for professionally trained managers and front line employees becomes more urgent. The traditional apprenticeship and vocational programs can no longer fulfill the needs of the industry, and higher educational institutions, in recognition of this, began to offer programs with curricula based on science and management principles.

The idea of compiling a collection of papers on the historical development, present situations, and future directions of travel and tourism education around the world came from discussions with educators at various conferences. Many felt isolated, unsure of the route taken, at a crossroads, and uneasy about the explosive and seemingly disorganized development of tourism education in their country. The most often pondered questions included: "Are we growing too quickly, are we doing the right thing, do we meet the needs of the industry, do we provide proper education for our students, what can we learn from other countries?"

This compilation of papers on tourism education cannot answer all the questions, but it provides some reference points for educators who are interested in finding out what others have done, what others are do-

[Haworth co-indexing entry note]: "Preface." Hsu, Cathy H. C. Co-published simultaneously in *Journal of Teaching in Travel & Tourism* (The Haworth Press, Inc.) Vol. 5, No. 1/2, 2005, pp. xxvii-xxix; and: *Global Tourism Higher Education: Past, Present, and Future* (ed: Cathy H. C. Hsu) The Haworth Press, Inc., 2005, pp. xiii-xv. Single or multiple copies of this article are available for a fee from The Haworth Document Delivery Service [1-800-HAWORTH, 9:00 a.m. - 5:00 p.m. (EST). E-mail address: docdelivery@haworthpress.com].</

xiii

ing, what are the lessons learned, and what others see as the future directions. Some of the articles in this collection document tourism education in countries that have been through the growing pains, as well as the expansion and consolidation of tourism education, and therefore can be labeled as "mature" tourism education locations. Others reported the history and current status of tourism education in their countries or regions as "developing," where more changes are likely to be seen before a best-fit education system would be achieved. These diverse scenarios can provide readers from different countries at various stages of tourism education development with a good overall worldview.

Many authors encountered problems obtaining historical information when conducting research for this collection, which indicated that many of the developments and events were simply not available in any print form. Several authors made great efforts to interview "pioneers" and "living legends" of tourism education, as well as trying to unearth and piece together information from various sources. This process of documenting the origin, growth, and development of tourism education by itself is a tremendous contribution to the literature. This publication could be a "history book" for hospitality and tourism education covering many countries and regions.

It is important to know where we came from, how we evolved, and learn from the past. It is also important to learn from each other. The publication's authors' list is extremely heterogeneous, yet many common issues were observed across national borders. Thus, educators should not feel that they are "alone" and unique in this long, and sometimes difficult, development process. For example, educators from many countries have experienced the diversity of tourism education in terms of degree level, degree title, and departmental affiliation. This is partly due to the interdisciplinary nature of the field, different organizational structures of various institutions, and unique government educational policies in different jurisdictions. There also appears to be a perceived mismatch between the expectations of the industry and the students, and to a lesser extent the educators, in several of the countries and regions represented in the collection. This illustrates the importance of collaboration between educational institutions and the industry, as well as instilling students with a positive attitude and realistic expectations, which has been practiced with some success in more mature tourism education locations.

Many tourism education programs, especially those in less mature countries, are experiencing a shortage of qualified teaching staff with professional education and industry experience. This signaled opportunities for tourism higher educational institutions with advanced degree programs to provide current hospitality and tourism educators with continuing education opportunities, in two main categories. Firstly, some educators have prior education and/or industry experience in a specific discipline. However, they need a higher degree, whether a master's or doctorate, to maintain or raise their future career prospects. Secondly, some educators have received advanced education, some even with a doctoral degree in an unrelated discipline, but due to the rapid expansion of tourism programs and organizational restructuring, they were assigned to teach hospitality and tourism classes. These individuals would benefit from a "conversion" course, much like the original concept of the master of business administration (MBA) which converted non-business majors into professionals with proficient business skills. Such courses could be degree-granting or for short-term professional development.

The geographical and regional coverage in this collection is by no means comprehensive. Colleagues and readers are encouraged to document tourism education development in other countries and regions, and contribute to the *Journal of Teaching in Travel & Tourism*, so that more information is available on the past, present, and future of worldwide tourism education.

Cathy H. C. Hsu

Tourism Education in Canada: Past, Present and Future Directions

Don MacLaurin

SUMMARY. This paper explores the past, present, and future directions of tourism education in Canada, from its origins in the late 1960s until today. The study reviews the development of tourism education over four decades, with a particular focus on developments in Ontario. The influence of tourism organizations, and the impact of legislation on tourism and hospitality education in developing future industry leaders capable of sustaining and growing Canada's tourism industry are discussed. The paper also reflects on the current status of tourism education in Canada, the lack of government support for tourism research initiatives, and the loss of research talent to overseas universities. The research discovered a paucity of past historical documentation of tourism education in Canada and this paper is perhaps the first concerted effort to chronicle the 40-year cumulative history of formal tourism education in Canada. *[Article copies available for a fee from The Haworth Document Delivery Service: 1-800-HAWORTH. E-mail address: <docdelivery@haworthpress. com> Website: <http://www.HaworthPress.com> © 2005 by The Haworth Press, Inc. All rights reserved.]*

KEYWORDS. Tourism education, tourism industry, Canada, Ontario

Don MacLaurin is Associate Professor, School of Hospitality and Tourism Management, University of Guelph, Guelph, Ontario N1G2W1, Canada (E-mail: dmaclaur@uoguelph.ca).

[Haworth co-indexing entry note]: "Tourism Education in Canada: Past, Present and Future Directions." MacLaurin, Don. Co-published simultaneously in *Journal of Teaching in Travel & Tourism* (The Haworth Press, Inc.) Vol. 5, No. 1/2, 2005, pp. 1-25; and: *Global Tourism Higher Education: Past, Present, and Future* (ed: Cathy H. C. Hsu) The Haworth Press, Inc., 2005, pp. 1-25. Single or multiple copies of this article are available for a fee from The Haworth Document Delivery Service [1-800-HAWORTH, 9:00 a.m. - 5:00 p.m. (EST). E-mail address: docdelivery@haworthpress.com].

INTRODUCTION

Canada is blessed with modern clean cities, friendly people from varied cultural backgrounds, wide open spaces offering lakes, rivers and mountains, and all readily accessible as tourism attractions. Industry and government experts agree that tourism, already Canada's single largest employer, will increase significantly well into the twenty-first century.

However, major challenges still exist, and Canada is currently running a significant and growing travel trade deficit with the rest of the world. Despite one of the best performing economies in the Western world since 1997, with continuous federal government surplus budgets and a healthy overall balance of trade surplus, Canada had a 2003 travel trade deficit exceeding $4 billion (CAD) with the rest of the world ($1.00 US = $.80 CAD). This international travel deficit was the largest in nine years (Canadian Tourism Commission, 2004). The World Tourism Organization (2004) ranked Canada as the ninth most popular tourism destination in the world in 2001, attracting 19.7 million visitors, or 2.8%, of world visitor demand.

Canada's largest tourism customer internationally is the United States (US). However, relations between Canada and the US are currently strained by a number of issues, such as Canada choosing not to directly support the US war effort in Iraq, trade disputes in softwood, wheat, steel and beef. Philosophical shifts have also affected relations, as the US increasingly turns politically right and inward, while Canada continues a more liberal and inclusive political path characterized by the recent legalization of same-sex marriage, planned decriminalization of marijuana, and similar initiatives. The value of the Canadian dollar, relative to the US dollar, increased by a record 21.7% in 2003, and a further 8.4% as of early November 2004 (Weber, 2004). This places Canada in a position where the relative monetary value of a Canadian vacation experience has declined by approximately 30% in the past two years for Canada's largest international visitor market.

This news is not all bad for Canada. Prashad (2004) observed that 115,016 Americans visited the Immigration Canada website the day after the US Federal election. Several new marketing campaigns will focus on the US market to Canada. Canadian marketing firm Capital C will roll out the campaign, "North of the 49th Parallel–Unparalleled!" on Canada Day (July 1) 2005. Another program, called "Outing Canada," promotes Canadian ideas and imagination to be celebrated internationally. High-quality Canadian products will be marketed in stores in Tokyo, London and New York.

The Canadian tourism industry offers a variety of rewarding careers and will create more than 90,000 new jobs over the next two years. With gross sales exceeding US$2.75 trillion, tourism is the world's largest and fastest growing industry, according to the World Travel and Tourism Council (WTTC) (Canadian Tourism Human Resource Council, 2004). The 1.6 million Canadians working in the tourism industry have many faces–people working in travel, accommodation, adventure tourism and outdoor recreation, attractions, transportation, food and beverage service, and events and conferences. These people work in the 159,000 tourism businesses in Canada today (Canadian Tourism Human Resource Council, 2004).

This paper will profile the past, present, and future directions of tourism education in Canada.

METHODS

Sourcing information for this manuscript began in the summer months of 2004. A request for content information and research resources was e-mailed to all Canadian members of the Travel and Tourism Research Association (TTRA) and the Council on Hotel, Restaurant and Institutional Education (CHRIE) requesting their potential contributions to this project. Several prominent Canadian tourism organizations and retired industry veterans were also solicited for their inputs. Surprisingly, the author received many e-mails supporting the worthiness and timeliness of the research request, but few if any leads on past historical documentation of tourism education in Canada. The following databases were also searched: ERIC (education database); ABI/INFORM (business database); Hospitality & Tourism index; World Tourism Organization library; and Google. After months of exhaustive searching, the reality surfaced that this would be the first concerted effort to chronicle the 40-year cumulative history of formal tourism education in Canada.

The 1960s

Formal tourism education programs are now entering their fourth decade of operation in Canada. The seeds for formal tourism education in Canada were first sown in the late 1960s. The latter part of this decade witnessed substantial growth and development of the Canadian college and university system in response to increasing enrolments as a result of the first baby boomers entering their traditional postsecondary age cohort. Approximately one-third of the Canadian population was born in the 20 years following World War II. By 1969, specialized tourism and hospitality programs were operating at several Canadian colleges and universities, while many other institutions had supplementary peripheral tourism courses, such as tourism geography within geography departments (Taylor, 2004).

The Ontario Experience

In 1967, the Provincial Government of Ontario, Canada's most populous province, decided to augment the post high school education and training system with 22 community colleges. These colleges were to be substantially different from the liberal arts colleges located in the United States in that they were not intended to provide credits or a stepping-stone towards the existing Canadian university system. Each college was intended to provide specialized training for its local community at extremely modest prices. All initial, and most continuing capital costs, were provided by the provinces. A typical tuition fee for a 36-week program in a college in 1983 was $610 CAD (Cooper & MacLaurin, 1986).

It soon became obvious that, with the colleges developing similar but not identical programs, certain colleges would outgrow others. Programs and delivery gradually became radically different, due to the availability or otherwise of capital funds and local advisory committees. As a direct result, to preserve credibility in the quality of the programs, several of the major hospitality-related colleges saw the need to develop a common core curriculum, built on a traditional DACUM System, which became known as the INDECORE (Industry Developed Core Curriculum) (Cooper & MacLaurin, 1986).

DACUM stands for 'Developing a Curriculum.' DACUM is a curriculum development process that has been found to be effective, quick and valid. DACUM is also an approach to occupational analysis in terms of duties, tasks, knowledge, skills, traits and attitudes.

The DACUM process is based on the premise that:

- Expert workers are better able to describe or define their occupation than anyone else.
- Any job can be effectively and sufficiently described in terms of tasks that successful workers in that occupation perform.

- All tasks have direct implications for the knowledge and attitudes that workers must have in order to perform the tasks correctly (Harrisburg Area Community College, 2002).

In response to increased specialization and a general maturation of the hospitality industry, new programs based on "spin-offs" of traditional hospitality training areas have been developed (Cooper & MacLaurin, 1986). An example of this increased specialization can be found in a new three-year convention management program offered by the Tourism and Hospitality Administration Centre of Sir Sandford Fleming College in Peterborough, Ontario. Developed in direct response to the manpower requirements of Canada's dynamic convention industry; the program began in 1985. During the preceding five-year period, over one-half billion dollars had been invested in new convention centre construction in major Canadian cities. However, no formal training program existed for training the specialists required for the new "world class" facilities and support businesses (Cooper & MacLaurin, 1986).

In addition to the common subject material of Ontario tourism and hospitality programs, the new program, believed to be one of the first of its type in North America, featured unique specialized courses in the convention field. These courses included trade show operations, successful meeting planning, convention bureau operations, convention services and, hotel sales and marketing, to name a few. All students also participated in a college sponsored one-month site inspection tour of major Canadian convention facilities, plus a one-month supervised work placement with the industry (Cooper & MacLaurin, 1986).

The 1970s

Substantial growth in the number of tourism and hospitality programs, and the number of students enrolled, continued throughout the 1970s. The Ontario Hostelry Institute (OHI) was established in 1977 by hospitality industry leaders concerned about the scarcity of well-trained and educated hospitality professionals.

Private industry leaders, the community colleges, the Ministry of Tourism and Recreation, and the Ministry of Colleges and Universities, who had come together to form the OHI, worked to reverse this situation. Programs to achieve the official mandate of the Institute, "The advancement of the hospitality industry toward excellence," were initiated. With initial funding from the Ontario Ministry of Colleges and Universities, the Institute embarked on its first major project—a successful fundraising campaign which resulted in a new campus for the Centre for Hospitality and Tourism excellence at George Brown College in 1987. Although the OHI does not operate an actual educational campus per se, the Institute also played a role in the establishment or expansion of tourism and hospitality schools at Niagara College, Canadore College, Georgian College and other colleges in Ontario (Ontario Hostelry Institute, 2004).

The new OHI centre for the development of culinary and hospitality excellence at George Brown college in Toronto encompassed three much needed features of hospitality education:

a. A leading hospitality institute for graduates: the most promising students completing hospitality courses in community colleges in Ontario would be able to enrol in an additional one-year program at the Institute. During this period, they will bring their skills in culinary and management techniques up to high international levels. Students graduating from the Institute will be sought after by first-class establishments that have long called for this post-apprenticeship level of training.
b. A professional upgrading centre: those already employed in industry could enrol in specialized courses, which will nurture a higher degree of professionalism. The courses will be scheduled to accommodate those working. Intensive outreach and summer courses would also be available.
c. A school for executives: professionals, both junior and senior, would be able to participate in up-to-date programs on the most recent managerial techniques for increased productivity, higher levels of staff satisfaction, and customer service. Innovative and successful entrepreneurs and specialists from Canada and abroad would be invited to conduct seminars and workshops.

The Institute would employ the latest audio-visual and pedagogic techniques. It would also house a large reference library to provide the best sources of information on hospitality in Canada (Cooper & MacLaurin, 1986).

The development of this Institute and the growth of hospitality skill training was a direct result of participation by government, industry and educators. Federal and Provincial governments committed over $10 million to the project. Industry trade associations and individual industry members and suppliers raised the additional $1.5 million of the total cost. Educators would develop the curriculum and offer the ongoing training once the Institute had been launched. Below is a list of facts of the development in the decade:

a. The Ontario Hostelry Institute commissioned a series of hospitality training manuals to provide students with an inexpensive source of Canadian instructional material that will ensure that the students have been exposed to the required objectives of INDECORE.
b. The OHI developed a series of provincial, national, and international culinary competitions between colleges, called "Taste of Canada," to create high levels of public support and interest in the industry. This image development project has helped create a dramatic increase in the number and quality of applications to the industry-related programs.
c. The OHI created an industry outreach program through a series of visitations to major North American hospitality colleges to present new concepts to college educators from across Ontario.
d. A series of 28 industry-based seminars offered at George Brown College were developed for presentation in community colleges in conjunction with industry trade associations, such as the Ontario Hotel Motel Association and Ontario Restaurant and Foodservice Association. These seminars were available to all Canadian colleges for use by any provincial or national trade association.
e. Concerted career literature and film materials were developed for high school guidance programs across the province promoting the college system and the industry.
f. Upgrading and training programs for hospitality educators.
g. An exhaustive survey on productivity and job satisfaction was refined in 1984 through pilot studies undertaken in outstanding hotels and restaurants.

As is the case in the Canadian experience in Ontario, the Ontario Hostelry Institute is a product of a close alliance between governments, colleges, and industry. The Ministry of Tourism invests a significant portion of the staff salaries; the Ministry of Colleges and Universities provides a grant for salaries and operating costs, including rent of the present office premises. The office was moved to its permanent home when the new OHI complex was completed in 1987. The research activity is directed by OHI, the publication of student textbooks, and revisions to INDECORE are the responsibility of the colleges, while the industry provides leadership and serves on advisory committees to ensure a high level of input into the program development (Cooper & MacLaurin, 1986).

Today, the Institute undertakes various projects whose primary objectives are to serve as catalysts in raising standards of post-secondary hospitality and tourism programs; to serve as an advocate for the industry in matters relating to post-secondary education and training, including apprenticeship; and to promote and recognize professional excellence in Canada's foodservice-hospitality industry. Among on-going programs of the Institute are the prestigious Student Awards and Faculty Professional Development Award. The generous support by the foodservice and hospitality industry to the Institute and its annual fund-raising initiative, the Gold Awards Dinner, have resulted in the continued growth in value and the number of awards. Outstanding members of the hospitality-foodservice industry and student award recipients are recognized at the Gold Awards Dinner (Ontario Hostelry Institute, 2004).

The 1980s

Cooper and MacLaurin (1986) postulated that Canada, as is the case in most of the Western Alliance countries, had both the private sector and governments to make and enforce rules of behavior and regulate the distribution of wealth. The term that best describes the type of society where both the private sector and governments have jurisdiction over the activities of people is pluralism. Under pluralism, most goods are produced and services are provided by individuals or groups, with governments regulating many of these activities. Important political battles are fought over just how much regulation there should be. In these political battles, the private sector and governments often compete for the power to rule certain of these activities, and their competition is the chief feature of this pluralistic society. Tourism education in Canada successfully evolved through the pluralistic development model.

The National Training Act of 1981

The impact of the recession became apparent to Canadian politicians in late 1981 and early 1982. They and their public officials both realized that much of the work accomplished by the job retraining and skill development programs were no longer meeting Canada's priorities for jobs in the 1980s. A change was deemed necessary. The National Training Act was introduced by Lloyd Axworthy, the Federal Minister responsible for the Canadian Employment and Immigration Commission

(CEIC), both as a correction of these "misdirected training initiatives" of the federal and provincial governments, and an attempt to increase the public awareness that these considerable funds came from the federal government (Cooper & MacLaurin, 1986).

A list of occupations of national importance was developed by the CEIC. The listed occupations became the recipients of millions of dollars of special funding. Not surprisingly, the researchers who made up the lists designated high technology occupations and advanced skills for these funds. Tourism and hospitality, although not only representing the largest single source of employment but also representing the area with the greatest potential employment growth, was not initially part of the designated list of critical occupations. A call to arms was initiated by a determined group of industry professionals, government officials, and educators in order to attempt to reverse this serious threat of reduced government funding (Cooper and MacLaurin, 1986).

Alliance Building in the 1980s

Although tourism is Canada's largest single employer (figures released by Tourism Canada as of April 1982 indicated that employment in this industry generated 1.13 million related jobs), there has traditionally been a reluctance to focus on a common proposal to the governments by provincial trade associations. Provincial restaurant associations, for instance, may well call for a "free enterprise" expansion of liquor licences, while the provincial hotel associations may lobby for restricted and controlled growth mainly in conjunction with large accommodation facilities. Similar polarized views exist in almost all narrow interest groups within hospitality and tourism. It is obvious that the large industry-related trade associations do not often have either the enthusiasm or the unity for a direct assault on government policy-making. Within the resulting void, there is a significant opportunity for a strong grouping of key individuals and organizations to influence government and industry, and they are:

a. *Tourism Canada* (a federal government department). Although armed with the prospect of a vastly improving market that in the 1980s had increased annually by 12%, Tourism Canada's Industry Improvement Secretariat found itself unable to obtain substantial new initiative training funds. Responding quickly to the National Training Act, the Industry Improvement Secretariat commissioned first a Delphi Study and Task Force to quantify the true manpower needs of Canada's tourism industry until the year 2000. Secondly, the Secretariat united with industry and other government agencies to form an Implementation Task Force to recommend whether a set of national standards and certification would aid in improving Canada's hospitality industry.

b. *Canadian Employment and Immigration Commission (CEIC).* Within this federal government department, which determines the direction of so much federal government spending (human resource retraining grants, apprenticeship training, capital funding for designated skills, and training institutions for occupations of national importance), there were strong supporters of increased hospitality/tourism training and development. However, those bureaucrats who were designated to study hospitality and tourism industry were faced with some longstanding frustrations associated with the industry, such as its high proportion of part-time employees, low wages, irregular hours, high turnover, and poor career image. In order to retain the designation of high national importance, the industry itself had to provide evidence that it could develop clearly defined levels of professionalism, through certification and other programs. The industry would have to provide its CEIC supporters with an acceptable set of standards and statistical base in order to prove its case for increased training initiatives.

c. *The Canadian Tourism/Hospitality Advisory Committee on Human Resources.* This body was formed as an answer to the frustrations encountered by provincial Ministry of Tourism, Tourism Canada, private enterprises, industry associations, and educators to provide the required information, statistics, and communications to map out a common strategy of industry manpower planning. Bi-annually, this loosely federated committee met to exchange research and training materials and develop strategies that would unite provincial and national efforts toward increased levels of manpower training within the tourism/hospitality industry.

d. *The Canadian Hospitality Institute.* Government officials, regardless of their faith in the industry, would not speak on behalf of that industry unless compelled by industry-based enthusiasm and hard-core facts. Educators were under the same constraint to maintain a similarly low profile, although government agencies and educators often have significant insight into the industry's needs more so than the industry itself. The Canadian Hospitality Institute (CHI) was formed to permit both government and educators in equal association with the industry to influence and support the setting of professional standards and certification. CHI's members agreed to serve on provincial and national advisory committees, and association executives across Canada dedicating their efforts to increased training and human resource development for the tourism industry (Cooper & MacLaurin, 1986).

A National Manpower Training Strategy

With the aid of each of the national alliances, including suggestions from Canada's provincial advisory committees and its national industry trade associations, the 1983 National Manpower Strategy report delineated the manpower requirements that both industry and government agreed were necessary to meet the needs of Canada's largest employment growth industry.[1] The general findings may be summarized as follows:

- the future indicated a significant gap between labour demand and supply in the hospitality industry, with demand far surpassing supply;
- existing training programs were not adequate to meet current demand and were insufficient to meet the pressures of future demand;
- demand in the tourism and hospitality industry was not for labour per se, but for appropriate labour; basic skills were becoming increasingly sophisticated, partially due to technologies providing impetus for increasing training levels in an industry concerned with quality of service;
- tourism was already Canada's single largest employment sector;
- future growth rates in the industry were expected to exceed the levels of other economic sectors and were predicted by a Delphi study to steadily continue for the following three decades.

Some of the specific statistics developed as part of the 1983 strategy report were that:

- of the 571,000 workers employed in Canada's accommodation and foodservice sector of tourism, 88% had never had a training course related to their job and 63% had never experienced on-the-job training;
- although women represented over 60% of those employed in the industry, they experienced less per capita on-the-job training and less per capita formal training than their male counterparts;

- employment in tourism was expected to grow from 571,000 to 2,109,000 by the year 2000;
- nationally, 88.9% of food and beverage experts agreed there would be a shortage of employees in the industry, and 95% of accommodation experts agreed there would be a shortage; 88% agreed that there was too little emphasis on skills training; 70% agreed that there was too little emphasis on management training; 91.6% of the experts agreed that a program emphasizing the combination of institutional and on-the-job training would be best.

As a direct result of this study, which pinpointed the demand for the length and style of training, a second study was commissioned that looked at the supply side of the equation. Included in this report were:

a. a study of the required programs that should be highlighted in the Canadian training institutions of advanced skills training;
b. a study of Canada-wide institutionalized hospitality/tourism programs to gauge their ability to meet Canada's future growth of world tourism;
c. a study on the need for a provincial/national administered national certification program (Cooper & MacLaurin, 1986).

This report was commissioned by the Canadian Council of Tourism Officials (the association of provincial Ministers of Tourism and their federal counterparts).

The previously mentioned INDECORE curriculum had been refined by industry and educators to provide the minimum common subject headings. These headings were more completely defined in a document that was presented to the Ministry of Colleges and Universities for review and implementation as a minimum acceptable INDECORE program for Ontario's community colleges that provided hospitality and tourism training. The INDECORE programs, when accepted by Ontario's Council of Regents, would form the base of a strong Provincial Certification program that would ensure that Ontario students:

- had guaranteed transfer credits;
- had the same minimum level of food preparation, service and management skills;
- were provided with a similar level of instruction, although each college, due to its emphasis on training in some particular aspect of industry needs, would have a varied delivery system;

- utilized Canadian material and Canadian experiences in their courses and programs.

As a philosophy, this was fine, but as a practical case, there were basic problems with the system. In some colleges, tourism and hospitality programs held high status, while in others they were treated as insignificant components of a business, engineering, or applied arts division. In some institutions, as in the case of George Brown College, approximately 60 faculty and staff were dedicated to hospitality training programs by 1985, while in other institutions, two or three generalists were expected to teach the entire INDECORE program–an almost impossible task (Cooper & MacLaurin, 1986).

In September 1987, The Ontario Hostelry Institute opened in Toronto, Ontario. This unique facility was intended to provide advanced levels of culinary and hospitality training to augment existing programs being offered in 19 of Ontario's 22 community colleges. Across Canada by 1985, over 105 colleges, vocational institutes and universities sponsored hospitality/tourism training with varying degrees of success. In the province of Quebec, for instance, a major training facility in Montreal (Institut de Tourisme et d'Hotellerie du Quebec) provided excellent culinary, service, and tourism/hospitality supervisory training in its superb facilities and, through extensive outreach programs, commencing at grade 10.

A 1985 study indicated that the 571,000 Canadian accommodation and foodservice employees would expand by 270% by the year 2000. This would create a severe shortage of trained personnel unless significant investment was made by industry, government, and educators in new training facilities and with continued financial support of ongoing hospitality/tourism and educational programs (Cooper and MacLaurin, 1986).

A strong lobby argued that high technology development and training was the investment direction that must be encouraged for Canada to successfully compete in world markets. Technological changes created substantial economic wealth for the nation, pushing Canada's productivity higher; however, there was a resultant reduced need for employees. The November 1983 issue of *Fortune* Magazine forecast that the food and beverage industry would add nearly three times as many jobs than would exist in the computer industry by 1990 (Cooper & MacLaurin, 1986).

In Ontario in the 1980s, and in many provinces throughout Canada, a student's investment in a college hospitality program approximated to

10% of the true cost of a program, mainly due to government tuition, subsidies, and capital investments into college facilities. Students had opportunities through provincial and federal grants and interest-free loans, apprenticeships, and Canada employment retraining policies to reduce these costs even further (Cooper & MacLaurin, 1986). Through a network of friends, an opportunity in one province is quickly available in another province. Canada, unlike most US states, does not impose cost-prohibitive "out-of-province" tuition rates. This means that Canadian students can attend any institution in any province for the same tuition fees as residents of that province.

The 1990s

The 1990s were a mixed decade for tourism education in Canada. The decade began with a significant North American-wide economic recession, followed by several years of lethargic growth. This decade will also be known as a period of retrenchment for most levels of Canadian government, which subsequently negatively affected funding mechanisms for postsecondary education. The federal government in Canada does not set college and university tuition rates, deferring this responsibility to provincial governments instead. As governments' financial contributions declined, student tuition rates increased dramatically in most Canadian provinces. The private sector also increased funding support for tourism and hospitality education during the decade and assisted with capital funding for new educational infrastructure at several Canadian institutions.

The 1990s were also a decade for consolidation and refinement of tourism education in Canada. A new emphasis was placed on articulation agreements between colleges and universities that would allow learners to seamlessly advance through different levels of educational attainment. An articulation agreement is a formal, systematic, written collaboration between two institutions designed to identify equivalent courses and clarify requirements so students can more easily transfer between the two institutions (Reid, 2004).

For tourism, articulation is often based on the notion of a *block transfer* that allows students who have successfully completed a group of courses at one institution to receive advanced standing at another–without needing to have their previous studies assessed on a course-by-course basis. Completing these agreements can often be a lengthy process that involves the faculty and administration at both organizations. Arrangements/agreements must also be periodically updated to reflect any changes in curriculum or requirements at the institutions involved (Reid, 2004).

Three Types of Articulation

1. *Unilateral:* An institution unilaterally grants exemption from specific courses or grants admission to 2nd and 3rd years of a specific program for students who have completed certain courses/programs at other institutions.
2. *Bilateral:* Negotiation of specific agreements between institutions to recognize certain components as prerequisites for entry into specific degree programs (e.g., degree completion).
3. *Multilateral:* System-wide agreement, such as that in the provinces of British Columbia (B.C.) (collection of bilateral institutional arrangements) and Alberta (Reid, 2004).

Most Canadian colleges with tourism programs have actively sought both program and course-by-course articulation for many years, but with the exception of BC, and to a lesser extent, Alberta, block transfers have become palatable to Canadian universities only in the last 10 years for several reasons:

- Canadian education is provincially rather than federally regulated/legislated, resulting in different approaches to articulation and related issues among and between the various provinces.
- Canadian university and college systems have different roles and mandates. University programs are designed to broadly educate, usually in the liberal arts tradition, with some explicitly linked to specific occupations (e.g., business administration). Colleges are more applied and have a defined mandate to educate for specific careers or segments in the labour market. This fundamental difference in education approaches has created a hierarchy in which universities are sometimes viewed as "superior" (mostly by themselves) to their college counterparts.
- Receiving institutions (in this case, universities) are in a powerful position in the transfer process. Thus, there is a resistance from universities to change the status quo.
- Tourism and hospitality as a discipline has seen slow acceptance in Canadian universities. Most tourism and hospitality programs at Canadian universities in the past decade have been new programs.

- In 1999, 12 universities had tourism/hospitality related degree programs (Table 1).
- There were approximately 67 two-year college diploma programs in 1999 (Reid, 2004).

One of the reasons universities are sometimes reluctant to form "blanket" partnerships with colleges is the varied nature of the titles and content of college diploma programs. Since each college and university throughout Canada independently designs its own programs, a diploma and/or degree in one discipline can often be quite different from one institution to another–in design, emphasis, and requirements. The lack of consistency across curricula, plus the innovative nature of colleges that are mandated to serve regional needs, means that programs vary, both in content and perceived quality. When this is coupled with the complexity and multi-disciplinary nature of tourism and hospitality, the variety of programs and foci are not surprising (Reid, 2004).

The Canadian Tourism Human Resource Council as Part of Post-Secondary Tourism Education in Canada

The Canadian Tourism Human Resource Council (CTHRC), or The Council is one of thirty councils created with funding assistance from the Canadian federal government since the early 1990s. The councils bring together the labour market partners from an industry or group of industries to address that sector's labour market issues.

In the mid-1980s the federal government Department of Tourism formed a group of national industry associations to begin to look at education and training for the tourism industry, following a broad industry consultation which identified this as an area of concern. National statistics had shown the tourism sector as having lower levels of education and training than the Canadian workforce as a whole. The group of national industry associations began with the development of occupa-

TABLE 1. Number of Tourism and Hospitality Programs in Canada

	1999	2004
High School HT Programs (CATT)	8	20
College 2-Year HT Diploma Programs	67	71
4-Year HT Degree Programs	12	17

tional standards to try and articulate the skills and knowledge required for competent performance. The group and the activities grew over the following years until the tourism sector formed a sector council (Swedlove, 2004).

In 1993 the Council was formed as a non-profit organization with a Board of Directors from business, labour, national industry associations, education, and government. An ex-officio, voting seat was reserved for one organization representing the labour market interests of the tourism industry in each of Canada's provinces and territories. These organizations formed the backbone of the Council, representing industry, workers, education, and government from their jurisdiction at the national level, and being the distributor of all Council products and programs in their jurisdiction (Swedlove, 2004).

Since 1993, the Council has developed over 50 occupational standards documents. Workplace and independent study resources, based on the standards, have been produced for 35 front-line and management occupations. A recognition framework has been created providing formal, national recognition at five levels. Recognition is acquired following successful completion of a written exam for essential or core skills, for front-line occupational knowledge, and for supervisory knowledge. Full occupational certification is awarded at both the front-line and supervisory levels upon successful completion of a performance evaluation and with designated pre-requisites and experience (Swedlove, 2004).

These resources and programs are available across Canada under the brand name "emerit" (visit *www.emerit.ca* for further information). The Council is beginning to place these resources on-line and will be working towards offering completely customized skill/knowledge groupings against which learning and testing materials would be provided, allowing a business to provide customized training against national standards with credit towards certification (Swedlove, 2004).

Many programs at the college level in Canada use these resources as part of their programs. Innovative initiatives are underway to combine the use of standards and training in the classroom with work placements and Council testing and performance evaluation, to provide students with professional certification before they graduate. Another initiative is to match learning outcomes of post-secondary college programs to the Council's supervisory skill standards to facilitate "credit for learning" and transfer of this credit between institutions and into the workplace (Swedlove, 2004).

Another Council program, entitled "Ready to Work," focuses on preparing the unemployed for work in the tourism sector. As labour shortages are expected to grow over the next decade, this program will assist in addressing the industry's need for frontline workers. At the same time, the Council will work with groups such as new immigrants, aboriginals, and people with disabilities to provide the support and training necessary for them to become productive employees in the tourism sector. The Ready to Work program will utilize the comprehensive essential skills materials and partner with organizations providing language training and other support services (Swedlove, 2004).

The Council has provided front line, workplace training where none existed. Public sector institutions in Canada provide pre-employment training, mostly at the supervisory and management level. The Council has developed resources that can be used by employers and employees, while at the same time providing resources, based on national industry standards, for use as part of institutional programming (Swedlove, 2004).

The Council also addresses labour market issues other than training and education, such as the sector's poor career image and lack of training culture. It provides a unique forum where business, labour, and education can come together, and identify and address issues with less duplication than might otherwise arise. The Tourism Council is one of the largest and strongest of the sector councils as a result of the strong support of its broad constituency and its solid distribution network (Swedlove, 2004).

Present-Day Tourism Education in Canada

Tourism industry associations in Canada do not always share the same priorities for tourism education. The Tourism Industry Association of Canada (TIAC) periodically surveys its members to identify issues that should receive highest priority for policy initiatives. Human resources issues are repeatedly ranked near the bottom. Perhaps as a reaction to the industry failure to perceive human resources issues as important, few Canadian tourism researchers have identified human resources as a high priority research topic for their own work (Smith, 1999).

With the exception of recognizing the need for improvement in the labour market module of the tourism satellite account, human resources have yet to emerge as a research or industry competitiveness issue within the Canadian Tourism Commission's (CTCs) programs. One should note, of course, that this survey is conducted among TIAC members with respect to what they would like TIAC to do. The low-ranking of human resource issues may rest on the assumption that other associations are addressing human resource issues and that TIAC need not allocate attention or resources to the topic.

The Hotel Association of Canada (HAC) has long-recognized human resources as a priority issue for its members. Other industry organizations and leaders, especially those involved with provincial and territorial tourism education councils (TECs) and the Canadian Tourism Human Resource Council (CTHRC), also persuasively argue for the importance of human resources in determining the overall competitiveness of the Canadian tourism industry. They note, too, that service quality is fundamentally a human resource issue. While the TECs and CTHRC argue for the importance of investing in human resources, they are unable to invest resources in research on human resources because they have to focus available funding on activities, such as the development of training materials, that can be sold to allow them to become self-sufficient.

Only HAC has invested significantly in human resource issues. HAC also has linked its concerns for marketing and product development with human resource development needs. The association, for example, conducts training programs to assist employees to work more closely with clientele from Asia Pacific cultures. Through its Access Canada Program, HAC has developed guidelines and training programs to help accommodation facilities and their employees better serve travelers with physical disabilities (Smith, 1999).

The need for more accurate and comparable data and research to support human resource decisions includes the following:

1. Data pertaining to seasonal employment, including information on why individuals accept seasonal jobs, their occupational status before accepting a seasonal tourism job (e.g., in school, unemployed, employed in another seasonal tourism job), and their occupational status after leaving the seasonal position (e.g., return to school, become unemployed, move to another seasonal tourism job).
2. Data on compensation levels and career-path opportunities.
3. Information on unpaid family labour and volunteers in tourism businesses and organizations.

4. A conceptually and empirically valid model for assessing return on investment from training and other human resource development practices.

Continuous growth and maturation in tourism education in Canada has fostered an increased emphasis on tourism-related research. Tourism faculty at Canadian universities actively participate in applied research initiatives that directly support broader educational initiatives. Research projects often involve direct tourism industry participation and funding. Research activity is not usually expected of tourism faculty in the Canadian college system.

On October 23, 2000, Simon Cooper, President of Ritz-Carlton Hotels International, then-Chair of the Canadian Tourism Commission's (CTC) Research Committee, presented the CTC Board of Directors with several recommendations for changes in the research and information functions of the CTC. These recommendations were subsequently approved in principle at the October 25-26, 2001 Board meeting. One of these was to create the Social Sciences and Humanities Research Council (SSHRC) academic partnership combining SSHRC and CTC research initiatives (Smith, 2002). The Social Sciences and Humanities Research Council is a Canadian federal government initiative funding Canadian University research activities in social sciences and humanities.

The omission of tourism from federal government's research initiatives means that other fields gain substantial research funding while tourism research becomes increasingly marginalized. At the same time, other countries that provide greater tourism research opportunities, such as Australia, New Zealand, and the US, are recruiting Canada's tourism researchers and graduate students. This loss of research talent represents a long-term problem for the industry in terms of a loss of talent and information on which sound business decisions can be based (Smith, 2002). Table 2 lists some of the tourism academics that have left Canada for positions in other nations between 1991-2001 (Smith, 2002).

This loss of research talent is also an issue because universities will be facing a shortfall of tourism professors over the next decade. Already universities are finding it difficult to recruit qualified tourism professors. While tourism is a subject of intrinsic interest to many students and faculty, in the long run, faculty and graduate students naturally focus efforts on those fields that provide funding for research and educational initiatives. Tourism is not one of those fields (Smith, 2002). Unless the current funding situation changes dramatically, faculty and graduate students will choose specializations other than tourism. The result will

TABLE 2. Canadian Faculty and Graduate Students Who Have Taken Research Positions in Other Nations: 1991-2001

Name	From:	Now In:
Faculty		
Russ Brayley	Lakehead University	George Mason University, USA
Jim Burke	Ryerson Polytechnic University	California Polytechnic University, USA
Richard Butler	University of Western Ontario	University of Surrey, UK
Geoffrey Crouch	University of Calgary	LaTrobe University, Australia
Frank Go	Ryerson Polytechnic University	Erasmus University, The Netherlands
Walter Jamieson	University of Calgary	University of Hawaii, USA
Thomas Muller	McMaster University	Griffith University, Australia
Peter Murphy	University of Victoria	LaTrobe University, Australia
Chris Ryan	University of Saskatchewan	Waikato University, New Zealand
Mark Searle	University of Manitoba	Arizona State University West, USA
Gordon Titchener	University of Calgary	Wiriki University, New Zealand
David Weaver	University of Saskatchewan	George Mason University, USA
Betty Weiler	University of Alberta	Monash University, Australia
Ray Weeks	University of Victoria	Griffith University, Australia
Canadian Students (now employed as faculty)		
Dwayne Baker	University of Saskatchewan	Arizona State University, USA
Keith Dewar	University of Waterloo	Massey University, New Zealand
Charlotte Echtner	University of Calgary	James Cook University, Australia
Tazim Jamal	University of Calgary	Texas A&M University, USA
Robert McKercher	Carleton University	Hong Kong Polytechnic University
Lori Pennington-Gray	University of Waterloo	University of Florida, USA
Sarah Richardson	University of Waterloo	California State University at Chico, USA
Pascal Tremblay	Université du Québec à Chicoutimi	Northern Territory University, Australia
Philip Xie	University of Waterloo	Bowling Green State University, USA

Adapted from Smith, 2002.

be a serious under-staffing of Canadian universities as they try to cope with growing undergraduate student demand.

The CTC and its primary research partners–Statistics Canada and the provincial and territorial tourism ministries–tend to focus on issues of immediate concern, such as market research and the collection of data to track industry performance. Funding and managing this work requires sustained, co-ordinated, inter-governmental effort. For example, the core tourism demand and supply-side surveys and analytical tools (Tourism Satellite Account and National Tourism Indicators) can be developed and maintained only within a governmental framework. Commercially oriented research, such as travel motivation studies, advertising tracking, and destination awareness studies are appropriately done through contractual relationships between government agencies and professional consultants (Smith, 2002).

However, many strategic and fundamental research issues are not adequately addressed by the current tourism research infrastructure. These include consumer behaviour, supply-side issues, economic and policy concerns, and business systems and strategic management issues. The role of technology and the potential of e-commerce in tourism continue to garner substantial interest, yet there is very little strategic research on these issues. Had a formal network of university tourism research centres been in existence prior to September 11, 2001, the research talents and resources of these centres could have been brought to bear to assist the CTC, provincial ministries, and industry in the efforts to track the impacts of such a tragic event, to develop strategies to cope with events like this, and to track the ongoing impacts on and responses in the market (Smith, 2002).

More generally, current government and industry-funded tourism research does not support the development and exploration of new concepts and theories that are essential to the sustained progress of any field of enquiry and human endeavour. Beyond the lack of support for strategic and fundamental research, there are also significant limitations to the ability of the CTC to disseminate and translate research to the thousands of small- and medium-sized enterprises and destinations across Canada. These are areas in which universities can make significant contributions (Smith, 2002).

Universities represent a significant potential research partner for the CTC. They contain a largely untapped pool of research and educational talent that can significantly supplement and expand the CTC's information production and dissemination efforts. They have strong regional ties that can be the basis for information transfer to Canada's widely dispersed tourism firms and agencies, especially small- and medium-sized enterprises (SMEs) and destination marketing organizations (DMOs). They can fill a role not filled by public sector researchers, research staff in tourism firms, or private consultants. Other industries have long-recognized the potential benefits of working strategically with universities. The time and need for the tourism industry to do so is now (Smith, 2002).

Universities with tourism-related graduate programs will be encouraged to partner with universities that do not have graduate programs, as well as community colleges with tourism research-related activities, to broaden the impacts of the centre and to help develop a deeper and wider pool of research talent. These partner institutions may be either in the same immediate region as the lead institution, or located elsewhere in the country. A national secretariat will need to be set up to coordinate and oversee the activities and communications of the participating universities/colleges. All participants in the program would participate in an annual conference, reporting on accomplishments and comparing experiences and work plans (Smith, 2002).

The Future of Tourism Education in Canada

Tourism education in Canada will likely continue to exist in a pluralistic operating environment that is composed of semi-autonomous groups through which power and funding is diffused. No one group has overwhelming power over all others but each has a direct or indirect impact on another. In the Canadian hospitality/tourism industry, government and educators' interests are often at odds with other's jurisdiction and speed of action. In spite of these ongoing problems, a strong alliance for progress has been forged to provide Canada's tourism industry with a sustainable source of skilled employees for the years ahead.

The future of tourism education will likely include the increasing use of electronic and other distance learning technologies. Kanuka (2001) noted that universities developing distance MBA programs recognize that it is a measure of a university's future success in how well it meets the needs of a growing adult learning population in partnering with organizations that seek to recruit and retain human capital and create leadership competency as a strategic capability anywhere it is needed. Cox (2003) postulated five key educational benefits of the electronic MBA in tourism and hospitality management: learning provides lessons for leadership; learning builds intelligence;[2] learning mobilizes competency and capability; learning creates competitive advantage; and finally, learning links people and knowledge and strategy.

Tourism educators will be tasked with the responsibility of developing future industry leaders capable of sustaining and growing Canada's tourism industry. This will not be an easy task, given limited financial resources accorded to higher education, and increasingly sophisticated competition from new and emerging global tourism destinations specifically developed as tourism intensive economies.

NOTES

1. Changed following findings to past tense, as it was reporting on events in the 1980s.
2. Not sure what is meant here.

REFERENCES

Canadian Tourism Commission. (2004). *Travel deficit highest in more than nine years* [On-line]. Available: *http://research.canadatourism.com/en/ctc/ctx/ctx-ind_watch/ tourism_stats/displaypage.cfm?folder=7&file=2003.html*

Canadian Tourism Human Resource Council. (2004). *Overview of tourism in Canada* [On-line]. Available: *http://www.cthrc.ca/aboutus.shtml*

Cooper, B. M., & MacLaurin, D. J. (1986). A pluralistic alliance-training within the Canadian hospitality industry. In *Proceedings of the International Training and Personnel Conference for the Hotel and Catering Industry* (pp. 19-31). Middlesex, England: The Hotel and Catering Industry Training Board.

Cox, M. (2003). The E-MBA action learning: Lessons for hospitality leaders. *International Journal of Contemporary Hospitality Management, 15*(6), 352-355.

Harrisburg Area Community College. (2002). *Dacum overview* [On-line]. Available: *http://www.hacc.edu/DACUM/dacum.html*

Kanuka, H. (2001). University perceptions of the use of the Web in distance delivered programs. *The Canadian Journal of Higher Education, 31*(3), University of Manitoba, Winnipeg.

Ontario Hospitality Institute. (2004). *Organizational profile* [On-line]. Available: *http://www.ohischolarships.com/contact_us.html*

Prashad, S. (2004, November 6). Wanted: A 'brand' that defines Canada. *Toronto Star* [On-line]. Available: *http://www.thestar.com/NASApp/cs/ContentServer?pagename= thestar/Layout/Article_Type1&c=Article&cid=1099695010684&call_pageid= 970599119419*

Reid, L. (2004). *Connecting the dots . . . Educational pathways for hospitality & tourism–Are they truly more connected?* Paper presented at Atlantic Canada Tourism Educators Conference, Fredericton New Brunswick.

Smith, S. L. J. (1999). Toward a national tourism research agenda for Canada. *Tourism Management, 20*(3), 297-304.

Smith, S. L. J. (2002). *Discussion paper for an SSHRC-CTC academic partnership.* Unpublished document.

Swedlove, W. (2004). [The Canadian Tourism Human Resource Council as part of post-secondary tourism education in Canada]. Unpublished personal correspondence.

Taylor, G. D. (2004). [A personal role in the development of higher education in tourism]. Unpublished personal correspondence.

Weber, T. (2004, November 8). Loonie cracks $.84. *The Globe and Mail* [On-line]. Available: *http://www.theglobeandmail.com/servlet/story/RTGAM.20041108.wdoll1108/BNStory/Business*

World Tourism Organization. (2004). *World's top 15 tourism destinations, 2001* [On-line]. Available: *http://research.canadatourism.com/en/ctc/ctx/ctx-ind_watch/tourism_stats/displaypage.cfm?folder=5&file=TourismDestination.html*

Global Tourism Higher Education– The British Isles Experience

Tom Baum

SUMMARY. The British Isles includes five educational and tourism environments and jurisdictions which have much in common, particularly in terms of their underpinning tourism products. Their higher educational provision likewise exhibits some common features but also significant diversity. This paper addresses the development of tourism education within the colleges and universities of the British Isles, taken to cover the United Kingdom (England, Scotland, Wales and Northern Ireland) as well as the Republic of Ireland. The paper demonstrates the impact of jurisdictional autonomy on educational programmes, their underlying philosophy and structure. *[Article copies available for a fee from The Haworth Document Delivery Service: 1-800-HAWORTH. E-mail address: <docdelivery@haworthpress.com> Website: <http://www.HaworthPress.com> © 2005 by The Haworth Press, Inc. All rights reserved.]*

KEYWORDS. British Isles, Ireland, vocational education, tourism education, universities, colleges, certification

Tom Baum is Professor, International Tourism and Hospitality Management, The Scottish Hotel School, University of Strathclyde, Glasgow, Curran Building, 94 Cathedral Street, Glasgow G4 0LG, Scotland (E-mail: t.g.baum@strath.ac.uk).

[Haworth co-indexing entry note]: "Global Tourism Higher Education–The British Isles Experience." Baum, Tom. Co-published simultaneously in *Journal of Teaching in Travel & Tourism* (The Haworth Press, Inc.) Vol. 5, No. 1/2, 2005, pp. 27-38; and: *Global Tourism Higher Education: Past, Present, and Future* (ed: Cathy H. C. Hsu) The Haworth Press, Inc., 2005, pp. 27-38. Single or multiple copies of this article are available for a fee from The Haworth Document Delivery Service [1-800-HAWORTH, 9:00 a.m. - 5:00 p.m. (EST). E-mail address: docdelivery@haworthpress.com].

doi:10.1300/J172v05n01_02

INTRODUCTION

This paper addresses the development of tourism education within the colleges and universities of the British Isles, taken to cover the United Kingdom (England, Scotland, Wales and Northern Ireland) as well as the Republic of Ireland. The scope is deliberate in that the five jurisdictions have common elements in both their tourism products and the higher education systems to provide for them. They also, however, exhibit considerable diversity and demonstrate cogently how external environmental factors in both the tourism sector environment and the educational context shape the current delivery of learning and programmes of study within this field.

Tourism education (taken here to include elements of hospitality) when set alongside more traditional and perhaps less "synthetic" disciplines such as law and history, has a relatively recent history within academia. However, the origins of this field of study, in the European context, can be traced back to the late 19th century (EURHODIP, 2003; Gillespie & Baum, 2000, 2001). European Hotel Diploma (EURHODIP) identified the first formally recognised training programmes in education for tourism-related subjects in the late 18th and early 19th centuries with the post-unification apprenticeship schemes in Germany after 1870. Lausanne Hotel School, founded in 1893, is identified as the first specialist school of its kind in Europe and was followed by a number of other colleges in the early years of the 20th Century in countries as diverse as Portugal, France and the United Kingdom. Programmes in different European countries adopted very different educational models according to local practice, with diversity in terms of duration, level, content and structure, particularly in terms of the role played by the tourism industry in programme delivery.

The development history of tourism management education varied according to the character of the sponsoring institution and the educational and tourism industry framework within which it is located. In many countries, tourism education has developed from training at the practitioner level, designed to meet the skills needs of the local hotel and restaurant industries through a process of academic and professional evolution whereby new and higher tiers were added to existing provision in response to both industry and student demand. Thus, both the Dublin College of Catering in Ireland and Westminster College in London started as professional culinary schools in the early years of the 20th century. Both have maintained this tradition but have extended their range of courses in both horizontal and vertical terms, offering a range of allied programmes in tourism and leisure at operational through to management degree levels. Similar patterns can be found in the development of a number of Asian schools, notably Singapore Hotels Association Technical Education Centre (SHATEC) and the National Khaosiung Hospitality College in Taiwan. In a minority of instances, programmes were established with a focus on higher-level management education from their foundation, what might be styled the Cornell model. My own institution, The Scottish Hotel School, was established as a specialist management college in 1944 as the oldest university provider of tourism education in Europe and the first to offer both degree and postgraduate courses in this area.

Tourism education programme diversity is, in many respects, one of the real strengths of provision at an international level. This strength comes from the manner in which programmes are able to respond flexibly to industry needs at a local level or in terms of the specialist sub-sectors that they aspire to support. There has been ongoing debate about the extent to which such diversity is, indeed, a virtue (Baum, 1997). Attempts to achieve harmonisation of training and qualifications in tourism, within countries and at a trans-national level, have been relatively unsuccessful despite support from international organisations such as The European Centre for the Development of Vocational Training (CEDEFOP) and EURHODIP in Europe. Within this diverse environment, therefore, the issue of internationalisation is of particular interest. This paper explores key features of the internationalisation of programmes and curricula in tourism and considers these in the light of experience in the United Kingdom and Ireland.

INTERNATIONALISING TOURISM EDUCATION

Notwithstanding the global nature of the tourism industry, educational provision in this area remains remarkably parochial (Baum, 2000). This can be attributed largely to structural factors within education and training at a national level and the dominating imperative in most countries to conform to wider policies and practice in the vocational development sector. Educational systems at a national level appear to be innately conservative and major changes do not take place without debate and resistance. When change does occur within the system, it is generally on the basis of a universal model that is applied across vocational sectors without necessary adaptation to specific industry requirements. Thus, recent changes to vocational qualifications in the Republic of Ireland have imposed structural modifications on tourism programmes which, it could be argued, run contrary to local industry needs (Connelly, 2000). Such factors generally act against the ability of tourism education providers to take an instrumental role in creating common parameters for programmes across national boundaries, one legitimate interpretation of the concept of internationalised tourism education. The fragmented nature of public policy development in the area of tourism education in most countries (Amoah & Baum, 1997) also mitigates against effective change in this area.

The debate about internationalising tourism education goes beyond structural impediments at a national level. A major consideration relates to the nature of the tourism sector in most countries. Tourism, unlike most other sectors of the economy, brings its workforce at all levels into frequent and sustained contact with its consumer base, the international tourist (Baum, 1993). Thus, an imperative for students at all levels in tourism education is an understanding of the international nature of tourism products and markets. This translates into a need for skills that reflect internationalised and gobalised services–for example, foreign languages, cultural acumen and skills for the preparation of international culinary products. In many cultures, these can represent sophisticated skills considerably beyond the normal description of tourism work as "low skills" (Baum, 1996, 2002). Educational programmes, therefore, need to reflect the need to prepare students for work on a global stage within their home industry. Internationalisation, however, extends beyond the needs of local hotels and restaurants. Tourism is an industry that encourages and facilitates vocational mobility across national and cultural boundaries to an extent that is unusual within the services sector. Expatriatism in tourism has a long history in Europe, North America and Asia and applies to skilled craft areas, such as chefs, as well as to all levels of management (Baum, 1995). Today, opportunities to work at an international level provide one of the main attractions to those recruited onto hospitality programmes and this aspiration needs to be fully recognised within curriculum design and delivery. Finally, there is growing student demand to complete all or part of their studies in tourism aboard, whether at a skills level, as a part of their undergraduate studies, or in order to undertake masters or doctoral programmes. UK and Irish providers have been particularly successful in attracting international students to study in the tourism area, both in-country and as part of off-shore provision across the globe. The internationalisation of tourism education programmes is, in many institutions, driven by the need to meet the pedagogic, professional and personal needs of a global student population.

TOURISM EDUCATION IN THE UK

Tourism education in the UK is extensive and well established within both the vocational/technical college sector and within higher/university education (Cooper et al., 1994). Programmes are offered from initial skills training at apprenticeship level, to diploma and undergraduate degree level, as well as through masters and doctorates. Provision is offered through a combination of full-time, part-time, and distance learning modes, and industry involvement is considerable at all levels. Tourism education also has a growing place within secondary/high schools through the establishment of school-level qualifications in tourism-related subjects to English General Certificate for Secondary Education (GCSE) and Scottish Higher levels.

Tourism education in England, Wales and Northern Ireland is offered on the basis of a five-level framework (EURHODIP, 2003). (In Scotland, a comparable framework exists but has ten levels.) The five levels are:

Level 1 provides students with a range of competencies which involve the application of skills in the execution of a varied range of vocational activities, most of which are routine or predictable.

Level 2 equips students with competencies which involve the application of skills in the execution of a series of significant activities which are complex or non-routine and which require a certain level of responsibility or autonomy. Working with others, as part of a team, for example, is a frequent requirement.

Levels 1 and 2 equate to qualified work status and lead to the award of a Certificate.

Level 3 is a specialist qualification and leads to the award of a Diploma. Level 3 offers students competencies which involve the application of skills in the execution of a wide range of varied professional duties, executed in a wide-ranging series of different contexts, most of which are complex and non-routine. A considerable amount of responsibility and autonomy is required, as well as frequently involving team management and supervision of other workers.

Level 4 provides training for the advanced specialist and leads to the award of a Degree. Level 4 brings students competencies which involve the application of skills in the execution of complex, technical or professional activities, performed in a wide-ranging field of different contexts and involving a substantial level of personal responsibility and autonomy. Responsibility for the work of others and the allocation of resources are often involved.

Level 5 is designed for the education of senior executives through postgraduate courses for MBA and equivalent qualifications. Level 5 provides students with competencies which involve the application of a series of fundamental principles in a variety of extensive and often unpredictable contexts. A very substantial level of personal autonomy and often significant responsibility for the work performed by others and the allocation of substantial resources are often characteristic of work at this level. There will also be personal responsibility for the analysis, diagnosis, design and execution of planning and assessment.

The UK tourism education system has, at its core, the notion that individual levels are attained on the basis of the achievement of competence in specified areas for that level and not necessarily on the completion of specific programmes or periods of training. Some approaches build their credit value and structure of assessment on the completion of prescribed hours of training within a recognised training environment (generally a college). The UK system does not generally stipulate how or where a student should gain training and experience in order to meet the competency requirements for each level or parts thereof. Therefore, a student or tourism worker may demonstrate competence in a specified area at any level on the basis of training that may have taken place in a college, within a formal industry-based programme (a company scheme) or as a result of professional practice in the workplace over a number of years. Thus certification for skills at the five levels of National Vocational Qualification (NVQ) (or Scottish Vocational Qualifications, SVQ, in Scotland) may be gained in the workplace or in college or through a combination of the two, depending upon individual and organisational circumstances.

The UK tourism education system is designed to be flexible and progressive, providing opportunities for students and industry employees to progress through the five levels at the initial training stage as well as within subsequent continuous professional development (CPD). Colleges and universities, therefore, also tend to provide courses at a range of differing levels in order to meet diverse student needs at entry but also to provide a progression ladder for those within the system who aspire to enhance their qualifications at various stages in their career. Institutions, such as the Birmingham College of Hospitality, Tourism and Creative Studies, offer programmes at all five levels, and some students do progress through the full range of provision.

The Higher Education Funding Council for England (HEFCE, 2001) gives formal recognition to the value of higher-level qualifications in tourism in a report which states that:

- Qualifications have a strong impact on the career development of managers in the corporate industry. There are a number of points in the management hierarchy that are difficult to pass without a degree level qualification, currently in the area of senior management.
- As the industry continues to develop and managerial roles and companies become more complex, the nature of the unit management role will increasingly require the skills and knowledge that graduates bring.
- While in-house programmes will continue to offer internal development, qualifications will be increasingly important in career progression, especially in larger companies.

HEFCE notes that the tourism industry favours specialist graduates over those from other disciplines. They are preferred for a number of reasons, including their understanding of the way that the industry works, the fact that they were more likely to "stay the course" and in general for their passion for and commitment to the industry.

Tourism education in the UK is subject to widespread evaluation and reflection through pedagogical research (see, for example, Baum & Nickson, 1998). The national Learning and Teaching Support Network (LTSN) for Hospitality, Leisure, Sports and Tourism (recently reconstituted as *The Higher Education Academy Network–Hospitality, Leisure, Sport & Tourism*) provides a link between the work of many educators in tourism and allied disciplines. As such, LTSN supports pedagogic research as well as provides the opportunity to showcase best practice in the area. As an example, LTSN recently supported an evaluation research project which looked at the international curriculum delivered off-shore by The Scottish Hotel School in Iran and Hong Kong.

TOURISM EDUCATION IN THE REPUBLIC OF IRELAND

The educational culture of tourism education in the Irish Republic has similarities to that in the UK but also exhibits clear differences. The majority of formal vocational programmes are offered within a national system of Institutes of Technology (IT) and this provision ranges from initial craft or skills programmes through to management diplomas, degrees and masters courses. Outside of the IT system is the quasi-private Shannon College of Hotel Management, which is operated by the state-owned airport operator, Aer Rianta. Shannon has strong international brand recognition and has attracted a significant number of international students since its foundation some 50 years ago. The major university provider of tourism education is the University of Limerick, which is also the location of the National Centre for Tourism Studies. In addition to IT and university programmes, a number of secondary schools offer programmes in tourism, leading to recognised certification at Intermediate and Leaving Certificate level.

What is of particular interest in the Irish Republic's tourism education system is the overarching role played by the public agency Failte Ireland (formerly CERT) for tourism education and training. Founded in 1962, this agency has played a central and, arguably, pivotal role in the development of Irish tourism. The success and growth of the sector since 1987 is in part attributable to the quality of the workforce at all levels available within the industry, and public investment in skills enhancement has been a key element in achieving this. The country's investment in integrated human resource development over an extended period (Connelly, 2000; Dineen & Deegan, 1996; Walsh, 1993) has been closely linked to its wider economic growth, particularly investment through European Regional and Social Development funding. This European support has now substantially been replaced by national government funding with relatively little change in the value of investment.

The key role of Failte Ireland is, on behalf of government, to co-ordinate inputs into human resource development within the tourism sector at all levels. At a policy level, Failte Ireland advises government on investment decisions with respect to human resource development in tourism and provides a key link between wider tourism policy objectives and the contribution that human resource development makes in their achievement. The Failte Ireland role also involves, in operational terms, extensive research into the tourism labour market in Ireland; skills and training needs assessments; development of national education programmes at all levels from craft skills to management and executive development; funding of student training in a network of colleges (ITs) across the country; delivery of training programmes in support of social inclusion objectives for the long-term unemployed; and the delivery of training needs assessments and on-site training within tourism enterprises.

This proactive coordination and operational role which the Irish government delegates to Failte Ireland is probably unique in the experience of international tourism education and training. It is designed to ensure that all initiatives in the field of tourism education and training are consistent with wider tourism policy and that such initiatives are responsive to changing tourism priorities, labour market developments, and developments in terms of market opportunities.

INTERNATIONALISATION OF TOURISM EDUCATION IN THE UK AND IRELAND

Early influences on tourism education in the UK and Ireland were strongly international as many of the fledgling schools employed eminent directors with experience of the international, generally European industry. Therefore, there has been long-standing recognition of the need to place the teaching of tourism in an international and, increasingly, a global context. This influence, in turn, led graduates of UK tourism programmes to seek work experience and employment elsewhere in Europe, in North America and further afield with major international companies.

Tourism schools sought to internationalise their curricula in order to ensure that the programmes on offer reflected the needs of graduates working within an international tourist market at home and for international companies abroad. This challenge was and continues to be addressed by means of a variety of curriculum-related means:

- Inclusion of a range of foreign language modules as core and elective subjects (French, German, Japanese and other languages);
- A focus on key business subjects in the international context (e.g., international marketing, international human resources management) within the curriculum;
- Recognising the importance of comparative studies in areas of tourism (e.g., law, human resources management);

- Addressing the international tourism industry context, especially the globalisation policies of major companies and the role of major international organisations in the development of the tourism sector; and
- Considering issues relating to multi-cultural management within the domestic industry and internationally.

The internationalisation of the curriculum is complemented by many schools through collaborative arrangements with international partner schools. Such arrangements can involve student exchanges for some or all of a class group, as well as innovative degree programmes that involve study at colleges and universities in a number of different countries, leading to joint awards and qualifications.

Another driver of internationalisation of tourism education in the UK is the long-standing tradition of attracting and catering for the needs of students from a wide variety of countries and cultures. Universities in the UK were among the first to offer degree and master's programmes which were designed to reflect the needs of international students. Irish universities have only more recently entered this international market, in part because national demographics have, until recently, meant that there was little by way of spare capacity for other than local students. The Strathclyde and Surrey master's courses date from 1972 and they have consistently recruited about 60% of each cohort from outside of the UK. This diverse student body imposes clear demands on teachers and on institutions in terms of:

- The context and content of teaching and learning–cases and examples are drawn from a wide range of international situations;
- The delivery of teaching and learning opportunities–pedagogic methods are employed that do not disadvantage international students and provide support for new teaching and learning experiences;
- The assessment of teaching and learning outcomes–making assessment fair for all students and recognising that students come to the programme with diverse prior experiences of assessment;
- The support of teaching and learning–ensuring that international students have access to a range of support services and learning opportunities, whether these are related to English or study skills; and

- Career opportunities for international students–ensuring that recruiters visit the school and are able to offer real opportunities to students from a wide variety of cultural and national backgrounds.

Providing an international learning environment in tourism is not just about a one-way flow of support and benefits. A tourism programme, which represents a range of nationalities and cultures, provides learning opportunities for all students (home and international) through the sharing of experiences and perceptions. It also gives teachers the opportunity to build upon the varied backgrounds of students in the class and to learn from cases, examples, coursework, and dissertations/theses that they write about hospitality in their own country.

Tourism education in the UK is also internationalised in other respects. Many colleges and universities deliver their programmes offshore in partnership with local colleges while others offer quality assurance for programmes offered by local partners.

CONCLUSIONS

This paper has sought to provide an overview of the development of tourism education and the main features of internationalisation of tourism education within UK and Ireland. The response of different colleges and universities in the UK and Ireland to the challenges of internationalisation are varied but the features identified here represent best practice examples from the system in the UK and Ireland (Sigala & Baum, 2003). There is little doubt that the tourism education in the British Isles represents real diversity in terms of internationalisation, meeting the needs of stakeholders (e.g., the hospitality industry, students) within both the home and overseas markets.

REFERENCES

Amoah, V., & Baum, T. (1997). Tourism education: Policy versus practice. *International Journal of Contemporary Hospitality Management, 9*(1), 5-12.

Baum, T. (1993). *Human resource issues in international tourism.* Oxford: Butterworth-Heinemann.

Baum, T. (1995). *Human resource management in the European tourism and hospitality industry.* London: Chapman and Hall.

Baum, T. (1996). Unskilled work and the hospitality industry: Myth or reality? *International Journal of Hospitality Management, 15*(3), 207-209.

Baum, T. (1997). Tourism education at the crossroads? *Insights, 11*(12), A34.

Baum, T. (2000). Education for tourism in a global economy. In S. Wahab, & C. Cooper (Eds.), *Tourism in the age of globalisation* (pp. 198-212). London: Routledge.

Baum, T. (2002). Skills and training for the hospitality sector: A review of issues. *Journal of Vocational Education and Training, 54*(3), 343-363.

Baum, T., & Nickson, D. (1998). Teaching human resources in hospitality and tourism: A critique. *International Journal of Contemporary Hospitality Management, 10*(2), 75-79.

Connelly, M. (2000). The republic of Ireland. In M. Lefever, S. Hoffman, & C. Johnson, C. (Eds.), *International human resource management in the global hospitality industry* (p. 85). East Lansing: Educational Institute of the AHMA.

Cooper, C., Shepard, R., & Westlake, J. (1994). *Tourism and hospitality education.* Guildford: The University of Surrey.

Dineen, D., & Deegan, J. (1996). *Tourism policy and performance: The Irish experience.* London: Thomson Learning.

European Hotel Diploma (EURHODIP). (2003). *Euroformation. White paper.* Brussels: Author.

Gillespie, C. H., & Baum, T. (2000). Innovation and creativity in professional higher education: The development of a CD-Rom to support teaching and learning in food and beverage management. *The Scottish Journal of Adult and Continuing Education, 6*(2), 147-167.

Gillespie, C. H., & Baum, T. (2001). Developing a CD-ROM as a teaching and learning tool in food and beverage management: A case study in hospitality education. *Journal of Teaching in Travel and Tourism, 2*(1), 41-61.

Higher Education Funding Council for England (HEFCE). (2001). *Getting ahead: Graduate careers in hospitality management.* Bristol: Council for Hospitality Management Education/Author.

Sigala, M., & Baum, T. (2003). Trends and issues in tourism and hospitality education: Visioning the future. *Tourism and Hospitality Research: The Surrey Quarterly, 4*(4), 367-376.

Walsh, M. E. (1993). The Republic of Ireland. In T. Baum (Ed.), *Human resource issues in international tourism* (pp. 201-216). Oxford: Butterworth-Heinemann.

Tourism Education
in Austria and Switzerland:
Past Problems and Future Challenges

Klaus Weiermair
Thomas Bieger

SUMMARY. Both Austria and Switzerland are small countries with a long tradition hosting tourists. Irrespective of high levels of economic development, the two countries also have high levels of tourism intensity when measured either in terms of number of tourists per native population or in terms of tourism receipts per population (e.g., per gross national product). Consequently, both countries also display a long tradition and evolution in their development of systems of tourism education and training albeit under differing market conditions and pressures. Both countries provide similar products like in the field of cultural tourism and alpine tourism. The tourism structure is also comparable. Both countries are dominated by family owned small and medium size businesses. However, their political structures are very different. This paper shows how each country under the three forces of labour market pres-

Klaus Weiermair is Head, Center for Tourism and Service Economics, University of Innsbruck, Universitätsstr. 15, 4. Stock Ost, A-6020 Innsbruck, Austria (E-mail: Klaus.Weiermair@uibk.ac.at).

Thomas Bieger is Dean, Department of Management/Business Administration and Head, Institute for Public Services and Tourism, University of St. Gallen, Dufourstrasse 50, CH-9000 St. Gallen, Switzerland (E-mail: Thomas.Bieger@unisg.ch).

[Haworth co-indexing entry note]: "Tourism Education in Austria and Switzerland: Past Problems and Future Challenges." Weiermair, Klaus, and Thomas Bieger. Co-published simultaneously in *Journal of Teaching in Travel & Tourism* (The Haworth Press, Inc.) Vol. 5, No. 1/2, 2005, pp. 39-60; and: *Global Tourism Higher Education: Past, Present, and Future* (ed: Cathy H. C. Hsu) The Haworth Press, Inc., 2005, pp. 39-60. Single or multiple copies of this article are available for a fee from The Haworth Document Delivery Service [1-800-HAWORTH, 9:00 a.m. - 5:00 p.m. (EST). E-mail address: docdelivery@ haworthpress.com].

sures and industry requirements, on the one hand and tourism education policy initiatives on the other has evolved two slightly different tourism education systems. Furthermore, an attempt was made to provide, based on the discussion in the first part of the paper, a more general explanation with respect to the response of tourism schooling/training supplies to varying conditions in tourism product markets, tourism employment and labour market systems, public choice decisions and general economic conditions. Finally, the paper discusses the paradigmatic shift (i.e., structural change) of tourism factor and product markets from the "Old to New Tourism" and discusses its implications for new types of tourism schooling and training in these two countries. *[Article copies available for a fee from The Haworth Document Delivery Service: 1-800-HAWORTH. E-mail address: <docdelivery@haworthpress.com> Website: <http://www.HaworthPress.com> © 2005 by The Haworth Press, Inc. All rights reserved.]*

KEYWORDS. Tourism education, Austria, Switzerland

INTRODUCTION

Tourism is one of the world's most labour intensive industries. The quality of the tourism product is therefore not only dependent on the quality of the natural resources tourists ask for, but on the quality of the people working in the tourism industry. Today, quality is more than ever a guarantee for successful tourism development. Good management in service organisations and tourism enterprises certainly qualify as strategic success factors of destinations and regions, foremost a consideration for the dynamics of markets in terms of changing consumer behaviour and skills in choosing, maintaining and developing effective teams of human resources is required (Heskett, 1988). Assuming that it is often entrepreneurs who concern themselves with business logistics and environmental scanning, the conclusion is that staff and entrepreneurs must constitute the most critical factors of success and/or competitiveness in tourism in general, and in alpine tourism in particular. In many parts of the alpine tourism industry, such as in Austria and Switzerland, a long tradition exists in human resource development in the tourism sector.

Qualifications and qualified manpower, which are offered to the hospitality industry, largely depend on the process of human capital formation. In small and medium enterprises (SME) dominated industries, this qualified workforce and the respective training systems can be considered as a kind of public good. Therefore, political influences are decisive.

STRUCTURAL CHANGES IN THE TOURISM INDUSTRY

Tourism has developed into and has, until recently, been considered a "fragmented industry." A fragmented industry typically consists of the supply side of many small- or medium-sized enterprises producing and selling very competitive or slightly differentiated products or services, which face, on the demand side, small regional markets with buyers displaying strong local and locational preferences. Fragmentation has been far stronger and more prevalent in vacation tourism as compared to business tourism and has also played less of a role in underdeveloped or newly developing economies where tourism arrived late and with the helping hand of multinational and/or trans-national enterprises (Clegg, 1987).

In the mid-1980s to the mid-1990s, new competitive forces radically changed the structure and functioning of the tourism industry towards a "new tourism," subject to new forms of governance. Before these new competitive forces will be described, the competitive forces of the old tourism are explained. In the main, there are two forces which shape the patterns of growth and development in any industry:

a. the quantity and quality of entrepreneurs forming new tourism businesses and/or sustaining and developing existing ones, and
b. the existence and/or development of competitive forces shaping the competitiveness of entire regions and/or industries as can be analyzed with Porter's (1993) diamond.

Entrepreneurs and entrepreneurship have always played an inordinate role in the alpine tourism industry. Among all apprenticable occupations and/or apprenticeship schooling programs, those specializing in accommodation and food related businesses have the largest percentage of graduates who went into forming their own businesses and/or taking them over from their parents (Tschurtschenthaler, 1998).

In the wave of the post World War II build up of mass tourism covering the period 1955 to 1975/80, many resource owners in the primary sectors of the economy, such as agriculture, converted their resources into tourism properties and became owners/managers of small hotels, restaurants or other tourism related businesses. Among them only a small proportion were true entrepreneurs in the Schumpeterian sense (e.g., individual entrepreneurship, focus lies on the development of new products or services) who single-handedly transformed little fishing villages or sleepy alpine farming communities into mega-destinations or resorts. Next to these tourism pioneers, the remaining great majority of tourism entrepreneurs entered the tourism sector in the 1960s and 1970s at a time when a sellers' market existed in many European regions. This enabled them to enter the market with absolute and relative low entry barriers in terms of physical, financial or human capital; technology; and management know-how. Also the ease of entry into the industry was not matched with a symmetrical ease of exit for reasons of high net opportunity cost of market exit for tourism entrepreneurs (Weiermair & Fuchs, 1997). Thus, many entrepreneurs in tourism enjoyed local monopolies and could afford to pursue satisfying instead of maximizing behaviour yielding what might be termed a "life style entrepreneur" (Weiermair, 1998). The conditioning and functioning of entrepreneurship fitted very well the remaining competitive environment for tourism at the time. It could best be analyzed and described using Porter's diamond of competitiveness (Figure 1).

The four corners, or determinants, of the above diamond model are shown to simultaneously codetermine competitiveness and thereby dynamically reinforce competitive processes. Thus, the dominant form of mass tourism consisted largely of conservative inexperienced tourists who generally wanted traditional holiday products at affordable (low) prices. As long as holiday products provided the right location (e.g., mountain or sea side) at low perceived risk, in terms of financial and information uncertainty or food habits, customers easily turned into loyal repeat visitors that vacationing their entire life at the same destination and/or in the same accommodation. This led to little pressure towards tourism entrepreneurs from the demand side to innovate their products/services or marketing of traditional holidays. As long as traditional tourism services were offered at the right location and at the right time, a competitive equilibrium prevailed. The latter was helped by the low cost and availability of traditional production conditions in terms of nature and tourism infrastructure, low cost and sufficiently qualified labour (usually a mix between unqualified seasonal guest workers from neighbourhood countries and vocationally trained indigenous workers), the availability of financial capital (usually provided through conventional financing in the form of mortgage finance), and the existence of small scale

FIGURE 1. Competitive Factors of the "Old Tourism" (Based on Porter, 1993)

tourism enterprises. Only very few other sectors could be considered or treated as related industries, namely agriculture and food processing.

Starting in the mid-1970s and early 1980s, the competitive conditions conducive to the traditional form of tourism and hospitality have radically changed (Poon, 1993). A number of these dramatic changes occurred in the 1970s which moved the tourism industry much closer to the characteristics of the new economy. On the demand side, the undifferentiated conservative and economizing mass tourist gave way to a much more travelled, experienced and quality conscious individualist: mass tourism seemed to have been replaced by the individualized mass (Poon, 1993; Weiermair & Peters, in press).

This new customer thereby exercised pressure upon the tourism industry and enterprises to develop new products, services and experiences. Thus, global companies very quickly began penetrating formerly fragmented and local tourism markets. This process involved and benefited from a new set of factors of production and an enlarged and better integrated clusters of tourism-related businesses and industries. These new competitive conditions re-enforce each other in the same competitive diamond to create the "new tourism" as can be seen in Figure 2.

FIGURE 2. Competitive Factors of the "New Tourism" (Based on Porter, 1993)

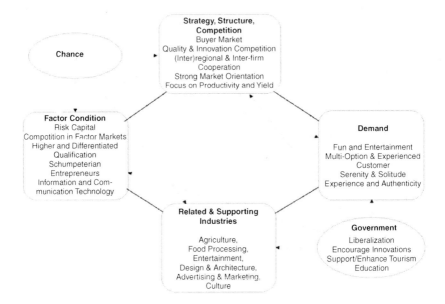

The new competitive conditions can be interpreted as follows: Novel information and communication technologies changed the competitive conditions through, often specifically designed technology for the tourism industry, such as the CRS (computer reservation systems) or DIS (destination information systems), and tourism websites. Labour in tourism became much more human capital intensive and was generally considered by enlightened management and tourism entrepreneurs as an asset rather than a cost item (Tschurtschenthaler, 1998). As a consequence, there has been a fundamental change in the schooling and education system for the tourism labour force (Weiermair & Fuchs, 1997). Location and climate still remain important factors of production for tourism products/services, but share their importance now with other man-made factors, such as design and entertainment (Pine & Gilmore, 1999).

Therefore, in alpine tourism, training systems for home demand developed relatively late. Whereas big international companies run their own training systems and programs, very often in the form of company universities, SMEs have to rely on publicly available training systems. These systems can be offered by the government, industry associations, employee associations, or trade unions. These publicly accessible training systems, therefore, are subject to powerful interest groups.

Tourism education is sector specific. According to labour economics, one can conclude that the closer an education program is related to the needs of the employment system, the more internal gains can be expected for the employer and the smaller the resulting positive externalities. There are even negative externalities; for example, when people with narrow qualifications are laid off in times of structural change. Therefore public education has to be considered as a part of an industry specific policy. According to public choice theory (Buchanan, 1999), all public spending is subject to the influence of lobbying organizations and power groups. In the case of tourism education, we have to mention regional politicians who try to found schools in their region, industry associations who try to get as much specialized schools as possible to create benefits for their members and thus create exit barriers for employees, and trade unions that view schools as means to qualify employees (i.e., their members) for better jobs (and salaries) but to create barriers to exit from the industry.

Therefore the following hypotheses can be derived:

H_1: High influence of industry associations tends to result in specialized schooling

H_2: High influence of general politics tends to result in decentralized schooling

H_3: High influence of trade unions tends to emphasize on schooling for less qualified staff

H_4: International education (e.g., tourism education as export goods) is mainly based on private entrepreneurship

Austria and Switzerland despite their similarities in culture, tourism products and company structure show in this regard important differences:

- In Austria, industrial and employee associations are much more powerful than in Switzerland, where the working of a more direct democracy caused the associations to be less important.
- In Switzerland, due to its neutral and liberal past, international and, especially, intercontinental tourism has a long tradition.

Therefore based on the above mentioned hypotheses and differences in structure, it can be expected:

- That, thanks to its long tradition in international tourism, international study programs, especially in the accommodation and hospitality sector, developed earlier in Switzerland than in Austria.
- That, due to the influence of branch and employee associations in Austria, more specialized and lower skill training programs have been developed.
- That due to the strong general political support and subsidies, a more decentralised system should have emerged in Switzerland.

TOURISM EDUCATION–
THE CASE OF AUSTRIA

Austria's tourism and leisure industry plays a vital role in the Austrian economy. In 2002, the total foreign currency earnings from tourism amounted to approximately 14.13 million € (+ 5.5 percent compared with 2001). Thus, tourism accounts for 18.6 percent of Austria's total export earnings and employs some 500,000 people.

Since 1992 Austrian tourism has been declining in terms of arrivals and bed nights. Tourism to Austria from the USA, Italy, Spain and the UK was negatively affected by weakening currencies in the early 1990s. Austria has also been adversely affected by growing competition from Eastern Europe and a revival of tourism in some of the republics of former Yugoslavia.

Austria boasts two main tourist seasons with different customer profiles. The summer season extends from May to October and the winter ski season runs from December to April. Tyrol is the leading tourism region, followed by the province of Salzburg. City tourism (Vienna, Graz) has grown in the last decade, bringing in a wider variety of international visitors.

Traditionally grown, the main market for Austria is Germany. Between 1990 and 1996 the UK fell from third to fifth place in terms of overnights, pulling back to fourth in 1997.

By international standards Austria holds an excellent position in the tourism industry. The advancement of quality in the Austrian tourism industry is, of course, only possible with a highly qualified workforce.

The Austrian system of tourism education and training is made up of the following components:

- Traditional Apprenticeship education and training (dual system).
- Full time vocational (secondary) tourism schools.
- Post secondary non-university degree programmes.
  - Polytechnic tourism education.
  - University study programmes.
- Tourism education at the university level.

Apprenticeship Training

Company-based vocational education and training is based on the principle of the dual system. It combines educational and employment systems and is called "dual" because vocational training is carried out at two parallel levels: by the employer and by vocational schools. On the job training within the company and theoretical school-based instruction at vocational compulsory schools complement each other. Apprentices receive their practical training mainly at work, while being taught the theoretical aspects of their occupation as well as general-interest subjects in vocational schools.

Vocational Tourism Schools

The educational goal of secondary level schooling for the hotel industry and the catering occupations is to provide students with branch-specific, basic knowledge and skills enabling them immediately to exercise a profession in the field of the hospitality and catering, with special emphasis on hotel operations. For this reason, focus is placed on practice-oriented instruction as well as on trying out learning contents within the framework of accompanying practical seminars. Training usually ends with a final examination. It is also possible to change over from an intermediate school for the hotel industry and the catering occupations to a higher technical and vocational school (Berufsbildende Höhere Schule) with the same training focus–or vice versa. A simultaneous moving up to a higher grade at the end of the year is possible only after successful completion in all subjects which were taught at the respective school type. Under certain preconditions, examinations will also be held to reach this goal.

These vocational schools, normally two-year post secondary course in tourism provides similar knowledge and skills as provided in vocational schooling programmes. It is supplied for students who have successfully completed high school and wish to pursue industry specific education related to hospitality and tourism. Practical work experience in companies and institutions of the tourist industry lasting twelve weeks during main summer holidays before the third semester is compulsory. A five-year training in high schools for tourism is still part of this specialised secondary educational system, which is intended to provide students with the theoretical and practical knowledge and skills necessary for starting a career in tourism and hospitality. Upon successful completion, students have "Reifeprüfung" (qualifying examples) entitling them to study at a university. An essential part of the educational goal of vocational school type is to obtain a high qualification for advancing into leading positions in hotel, restaurant or travel enterprises as well as in institutions of tourism administration.

Post Secondary Non-University Tourism Programmes

Polytechnic Tourism Education

In 1994/95, Austria opened a new full time educational programme path for a variety of fields: study programme at polytechnic colleges (i.e., non-university institutions of higher education). Because of the shorter duration of studies and their job-oriented learning content, they represent a supplement and an alternative complement and/or substitute to studies at university. Apart from the Federal Government of Austria, regional provinces, public organisation, institutes such as chamber of commerce, and/or private firms can be the operating authority of these polytechnic universities (Fachhochschule).

Every polytechnic study programme is completed with a diploma (non-university degree). Successful completion of a polytechnic study programme entitles graduates to hold the academic degree of "Magister"/Master (Mag.) FH or "Diplomingenieur"/Graduate Engineer (Dipl.-Ing.) FH, with an additional specification characterising their respective field of work. The education at polytechnics is more practice-oriented. Graduates from a polytechnic university are entitled to continue their education at the university leading to the degree of a PhD at university, with the duration of the study prolonged by at least four semesters. In the field of tourism and leisure, four such polytechnic colleges exist in Krems, Innsbruck, Salzburg, and Vienna. The duration of the study is between 7 and 8 semesters. At the present time, all tourism polytechnic universities have received the autonomy from the Austrian government to establish master level programmes making them comparable to education at the university level.

University Study Programmes (Diploma Courses)

The aim of the university study programmes for tourism as extension programmes provided by universities is to convey and deepen the students' knowledge with the most modern, state-of-the-art management tools for activities in the hotel industry, in tourism associations (e.g., non governmental organisations) as well as in tourism related branches of economic activity. Apart from conveying skills purely connected to business administration and management, tourism specific knowledge and skills are required and are communicated to the participants of these programmes. In Austria, there are several such diploma programmes: one by the University in Klagenfurt, one by the Vienna Economic University and one is provided by the Center for Tourism and Service Economics at the University of Innsbruck.

Specialised Tourism Education at the University Level

Two universities in Austria provide specialized programmes in tourism (i.e., the Vienna Economic University and the University of Innsbruck). During the last portion of graduate studies, students have the option to specialise in tourism within designated institutes and to qualify themselves in the field of tourism.

As shown in Table 1, there has been a strong and increasing demand for postsecondary higher tourism education, on the one hand, at the level of polytechnic colleges and, on the other hand, at university levels. Tourism related higher education recorded an increase of 36% in the years from 1997 to 2003. In the same period, the demand for secondary-level education in tourism decreased by 6%. This development emphasises the general trend towards higher education and the disappearance of mid-level education.

Facts About the Austrian Tourism Industry

This section presents some facts about the Austrian tourism industry regarding education and employment. In the Austrian tourism industry, strong trends exist towards higher education and apprenticeship training. Throughout the past 5 years, we can observe an increase of 15% for apprentices and an increase of 36% for graduates of postsecondary tourism education, such as universities and colleges. On the other hand, the number of graduates from secondary tourism schools declined in the same period by 6%.

TABLE 1. Development in Tourism Education from 1997 to 2003 (Source: WKÖ, 2004)

	1997	1998	1999	2000	2001	2002	2003	+/– %
Apprenticeship training in tourism	11.589	12.145	13.031	13.515	13.233	12.974	13.330	+ 15%
Vocational (secondary) tourism schools	2.549	2.642	2.804	2.802	2.659	2.446	2.396	– 6%
Postsecondary tourism education	5.247	5.921	6.623	7.002	7.313	7.373	7.137	+ 36%

Using these figures, the trend towards higher education, especially at university level can be identified. Besides an increase of tourism graduates, as mentioned before, tourism is one of the most labour intensives industries, which can be supported by the development of the numbers of employees in the tourism industry as shown in Table 2.

In the years from 1997 to 2003, an increase of 7.5% of employees in the Austrian tourism industry was recorded, which reflects the importance of this industry for the Austrian labour market. By the same token, Austria's unemployment rate has remained at a very moderate level of 4.3%, the fourth lowest unemployment rate in the European Union (the average of 15 EU countries was 7.6%).

Figure 3 shows the development of the overnight stays in Austria (summer and winter seasons) and thereby highlights the Austrian development of the tourism industry. According to the period from 1998 to 2003, two different developments can be identified. First, winter tourism in Austria showed a continued increase in overnight stays. The growth rate over this period is about 11.4%. Second, summer tourism had a large decrease in the years after 1998 reaching the lowest level in 2001. Since then, summer tourism has recovered slowly. In total, summer overnight stays per year showed an increase of 5% from 1998 to 2003.

Table 3 shows the distribution of tourists across different hotel star categories for the period 1999 to 2003. The 5- and 4-star hotels especially recorded an enormous increase of over 16 percent in overnight stays. In contrast to the 5- and 4-star segment, the other categories showed rather disappointing results: The 3-star hotel category was in a position to hold their level from 1999, showing only a small increase of overnight stays of less than 3 percent. A decrease of overnight stays or

TABLE 2. Employees in Tourism from 1997 to 2003 (Source: WKÖ, 2004)

	1997	1998	1999	2000	2001	2002	2003	+ %
Employees in tourism	161.817	163.322	167.028	168.806	170.400	173.643	173.942	7,5 %

FIGURE 3. Overnight Stays in Austria from 1998 to 2003 (Source: BMWA, 2004)

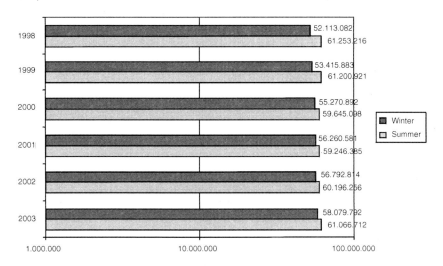

loss of customers was registered by the 2- and 1-star hotels. In the years from 1999 to 2003, they lost nearly 15 percent of their clientele.

This development–the increase of 5/4-star categories and the stagnancy and/or decline of the 3-star and 2/1-star categories–stresses the general development for more or higher (service) quality on the part of the customer. This trend is reflected not only in the increase of the demand to 5/4-star hotels but also in the increase of higher qualified employees, as shown in Table 1, where an increase of 36 percent of postsecondary tourism education could be identified in the time from 1997 to 2003. Thus, developments in the markets for tourism products and tourism education seem to converge suggesting that the education types and education policies by the government have moved in the right direction.

TABLE 3. Overnight Stays per Category (Source: WKÖ, 2004)

	1999	2000	2001	2002	2003	%
Cat. 5/4 St.	29.667.664	31.533.579	32.513.666	33.628.559	34.494.451	+ 16,3
Cat. 3 St.	26.300.641	26.494.930	26.916.762	27.153.923	27.074.967	+ 2,9
Cat. 2/1 St.	14.396.045	13.620.342	13.123.095	12.740.992	12.298.265	− 14,6
Total	70.364.350	71.648.851	72.553.523	73.523.474	73.867.683	+ 5,0

TOURISM EDUCATION–
THE CASE OF SWITZERLAND

The History of Tourism in Switzerland

Tourism has a long tradition as an economic branch in Switzerland. The first steps were done in the 19th century. The emergence of industrialisation and the improvements in mobility and accommodations boosted the development of tourism. The number of guest beds was tripled to 211,000 from 1880 to 1912 wherefore this time is also called "Belle Époque" (Bieger, 2004; Swiss Tourism Federation, 1999). The lion's share of this capacity was provided by the hotel industry. Since at that time Switzerland was a neutral and peaceful country with excellent tourism infrastructures like the concept of the palace hotel or the first mountain railways of Europe (for example 1871 on Mount Rigi), it became very popular among the noble and wealthy people of Europe. At that time and also after World War II, when Switzerland was the only country in central Europe not affected by war, it was one of the most important tourism countries of the world, measured in arrivals as well as in overnight stays (Bieger, 2004). The quantity of beds provided by the hotel industry has just moderately increased up to 258,700 since that time; however, the total number of beds has increased enormously up to approximately 1,053,000 (Federal Statistical Office, 2004). The rise is attributed to a shift from the hotel sector to beds in supplementary accommodations (like apartments or group accommodation), which has taken place during the last 40 years. Governmental intervention and support did increase in the period of the world economic crisis prior to World War II but even more with the competitiveness problems of the tourism sector in a very developed and expensive country at the end of the last century (Keller, 2001).

From the beginning until now tourism has been an important factor in and one of the main export branches of the Swiss economy. In 1998, tourism was directly responsible for 3.4% of Switzerland's gross domestic product, placing it into the sixth position among branches of the Swiss economy, previous to the telecommunication and insurance sector (Federal Statistical Office, 2004). In the ranking of export revenue by industry, tourism is placed as third (*ibid.*) with a total of export revenue of 12.6 billions. The important emotional role tourism plays for some peripheral regions in Switzerland, such as Grisons, Bernese Oberland and Central Switzerland, or its image factor in the marketing of places should also be considered.

Types of Tourism in Switzerland

Related to the origin of tourists, Swiss guests account for 36 million overnight stays, which represented the lion's share, followed by Germans with 11.5 million in 2003. With 24 million, the European tourists are dominant in the group of foreign tourists, which counts 37 million in total. In the seasonal view there is only a slight difference between winter (46%) and summer season (54%) (Federal Statistical Office, 2004). Many Swiss destination and hotel managers claim that the average duration of all stays in Switzerland is declining, which is a statistically proven perception (Bieger & Laesser, 2002). A reason could be the decrease of foreign visitors combined with fewer overnight stays of Swiss tourists and new travel patterns with more and shorter vacations.

Labour Market Situation

The tourism sector plays an important role on the labour market. The direct tourism employment in Switzerland reached 165,500 full-time equivalent. Including the indirect employment effect, one person in twelve is involved directly or indirectly in the tourism sector. The main employers are the accommodation (34%), the food and beverage (19%) and the passenger transport industries (Federal Statistical Office, 2004).

Recently, the tourism labour market is in a tense situation and it is difficult to attract new workforce to the sector. The branch struggles with image problems and tough work conditions, such as the work hours. On the one hand it is difficult to get a qualified workforce for common jobs; on the other hand, there are not enough jobs for the highly qualified graduates of the higher vocational colleges. The working conditions are considered to be unattractive and the average wage is low compared to other branches (Icg, 2002). Very often tourism jobs serve as training possibilities. After having acquired enough qualification in the field of social competencies, employees leave the sector, which leads to a high cross industry mobility (Bieger, Laesser, & Boksberger, 2004). A consequence of this image is the attraction of unqualified workforce which has a negative impact on the service quality.

On the market for highly qualified employees, the situation is contrary. There, the relation of graduates to job vacancies is 4:1. Since 2002, the supply of high and middle cadre positions is declining. The problem is impaired by the desiderative flexibility of the applicants to accept a job in a peripheral region (Stampfli, 2004). All together, the current situation is characteristic for a branch during a structural change.

Supply Side of the Swiss Tourism Market

The supply side of the Swiss tourism economy can be characterised as very heterogeneous. Especially in alpine regions, the main tourism regions in Switzerland, small- and medium-sized enterprises dominate (Bieger, 1997). As mentioned above, the quantity of beds has not changed considerably during the last 40 years (Swiss Tourism Federation, 1999). The expansion of guest beds was mainly caused by supplementary accommodations, such as vacation apartments, camping sides and group accommodation, and for a small part by youth hostels. Vacation apartments account for the lion's share (42%) (Federal Statistical Office, 2004). Despite these changes, the hotel industry is still the major player in Switzerland's tourism industry. Despite the fact that the number of overnight stays is equal in both types of accommodations, the hotel industry generates a much higher added value.

The hotel industry is dominated by small- and medium-sized hotels and in 61% of all hotels the average overnight stay ranges between CHF 50 and 150 (Federal Statistical Office, 2004). The heterogeneous structure has been one of the major sources for the problems which the industry is struggling with. It is expected that structural changes will force the restructuring of the hotel industry and strengthen the consolidation at the level of business units (Bieger, Laesser, & Caspar, 2002). Other tourism sectors, like the cable car sector, are equally dominated by SMEs.

Educational System of Tourism in Switzerland

In Switzerland, like in Austria, the apprenticeship system has a strong and traditional position. Tourism education in Switzerland started with the very famous hotel schools in Lausanne or Glion in the aftermath of World War II. These schools very soon targeted international markets.

At the time of the first structural crisis in tourism and the emergence of new tourism, contrary to other countries, Switzerland did not have a comprehensive tourism training system including higher educational institutions outside the classical hotel industry. Within the 1990s, this gap has been filled by the opening of higher college type schools as development in the field of formal education (Greuter, 2000). These schools in the main focused on general tourism management and have been strongly subsidised by the federal and state government. The tourism education will be restructured during the next years. The new federal law containing vocational training (Neues Berufsbildungsgesetz, nBBG) became operative as from 1 January 2004. A reorganisation became necessary because of the complex structure caused by an uncoordinated development of different educational institutions and the fast changes of the economy which demands new and different competencies (Müller, 2002). The new structure of tourism education introduces apprenticeships in tourism/hotel/gastronomy, travel agencies and public transportation and increases the transparency.

Since tourism is a cross sectional branch, tourism education can be described in a horizontal and vertical model. Within the horizontal model, tourism education can be divided into four parts: the hotel and restaurant industry, tourism organizations, experience sectors and transport and mobility, as shown in Figure 4. The model in Figure 5 shows the different tourism relevant areas of the educational system which have to be consid-

FIGURE 4. Horizontal Model of Tourism Education (Source: Müller, 2002)

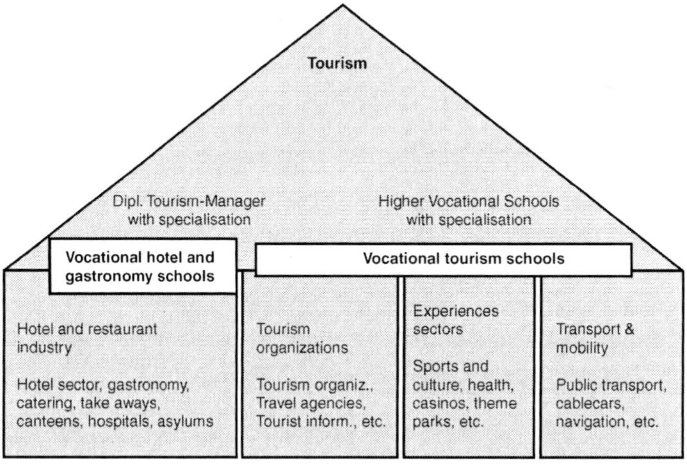

FIGURE 5. Vertical Model (Renner-Bach)

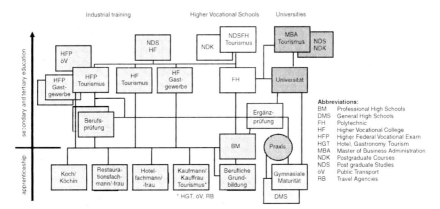

ered. The vertical dimension points out different ways to obtain tourism education in Switzerland and equally shows that programs are now available at all levels of education.

Typically, there are different ways to obtain higher education in Switzerland. The most important ones are: the higher vocational diploma "dipl. Toursimusexperte," the vocational college schools of tourism, the polytechnic schools with a major in tourism and the universities with a mayor or minor in tourism. The lion share of graduates comes from vocational colleges of tourism. Around 600 graduates leave these schools each year.

Analysis of the Development of the Education System

The evolution of the tourism education system can be characterized by the following changes:

- From private to governmental: The first schools in the 1950s and 1960s have been founded as private schools of industry associations and private companies. Eventually, more government intervention in terms of educational and structural policy came to the fore by creating new degrees and diplomas as well as governmental schools.
- From tourism education as an export service to supplying the home market: While the first hotel schools, as they still exist in

Lausanne and Glion today, as expanded to international markets and exported Swiss hotel management know how internationally, governmental schools mainly served the national market. The by far biggest numbers of tourism diplomas granted (i.e., the diplomas of higher vocational colleges), cannot even be accredited internationally nor do they fit into a bachelor/master system of education.

- From specialised hotel schools to a wide variety of programs for all tourism sectors: With the emergence of new sub-branches of tourism, new programs for general tourism, event management, and cable cars have been developed.

These developments are in line with a priori theoretical reasoning:

- As a result of growing governmental influence, regulations and subsidisation, there are now less incentives to focus on international markets.
- With the weakening of the sector and associated economic problems and the increasing influence of the government, tourism schools have been implicitly used as means of regional development (cp. map of places of tourism schools) and therefore as an instrument to collect votes in the widest sense (cp. public choice theory). Tourism schools therefore can be found in all peripheral areas of Switzerland, the upper Engadin, the Valais or the Ticino.
- The emergence of schools with a sub-critical size and strong lobbying leads to a situation which yields much institutional inertia.

COMPARISON OF SWITZERLAND–AUSTRIA

The biggest differences between the Swiss and Austrian educational system can be described as follows: In Austria, the social partners, particularly trade unions, still exert a strong influence on the structure and content of vocational education in tourism, particularly at the level of dual type apprenticeship training. Because of the highly fragmented tourism industry in Austria, with its absence of large hotel or travel intermediary, chains there has shown less innovation, experimentation intensions and privatisation than in Switzerland. Also the Swiss tourism education system started much earlier with internationalization and globalisation. In contrast to the Austrian type, which is driven to a large extent by the social partners, in Switzerland governments and the private sector have been the driving forces (in terms of regulations). Both systems, however, share in common:

- A strong regional focus and/or concentration in terms of decentralised provision of tourism education and training at the regional level.
- Education carried out in relatively small units.
- Distinct from the U.S. and other western models of tourism schooling. Austria and Swiss tourism education/training systems continue to be narrowly specialising towards industry requirements rather than to provide more general type or generic education, such as management knowledge related to all branches of economic activity or at least the service sector. This can be explained by the strong influence of sectoral interests compared to general educational interests.

FUTURE CHALLENGES AND DEVELOPMENTS

With the advance of new information technologies, globalisation of the industry and more quality conscientious tourists, the tourism education/training system in both countries has seen an uncontrolled mushrooming of education/training initiatives and developments, leading to governmental intervention and regulation. This still begs though the question of restructuring and cooperation between different educational suppliers (Renner-Bach, 2003). An indication of this challenge can be gathered from the ratio between job vacancies and graduates in different skill and job categories.

A possible situation, for example, in Switzerland could be the limitation of tourism specialized vocational schools and a harmonisation of the hotel industry certificates (Müller, 2002). To increase the level and to gain efficiency, it is necessary to create bigger units in tourism education and to assure the quality in teaching content. By taking such measures, the international recognition of Swiss or Austrian tourism education would also increase. Another problem area is the lacking horizontal mobility of tourism graduates into other service based jobs in the economy. Education reforms under way in both countries and movements towards higher, more general types of learning will hopefully address this question. Whether this in the end will work in tourism depends on the industry's working conditions and its image among employees.

Movement towards higher quality and more complex tourism products will no doubt reinforce the upgrading endeavours of the education system; however, this process is a tedious one in many tourist destinations populated by SME enterprises where the future could be characterized by a mind change of all tourism stakeholders. In general, with the emergence of the new tourism and the respective requirements, such as more individualised products and higher productivity,

- Broader and more general public programs combined with internal company training will appear.
- More international mobility especially on higher educational levels will be strengthened.
- New structures of the school in the form of newly defined public-private partnerships as well as bigger units will appear.

REFERENCES

Bieger, T. (1997). *Tourismusausbildungsland Schweiz* [Tourism education country Switzerland]. Neue Zürcher Zeitung.

Bieger, T. (2004). *Tourismuslehre–Ein Grundriss* [Tourism studies–A layout]. Bern: Haupt.

Bieger, T., & Laesser, C. (2002). *Travel Market Switzerland 2001*. St. Gallen: IDT.

Bieger, T., Laesser, C., & Boksberger, P. (2004). *Fluctuation and retention factors of tourism professionals–An analysis of the cross-industry mobility in Switzerland.* Unpublished, Universität St. Gallen.

BMWA. (2004). *Datenblatt Tourismus* [Tourism Statistics]. Wien: Author.

Buchanan, J. M. (1999). *Public finance and public choice: Two contrasting visions of the state, Mass.* Cambridge: MIT Press.

Clegg, J. (1987). *Multinational enterprises and world competition.* London: Macmillan.

Federal Statistical Office. (2004). *Swiss Tourism in Figures.* Bern: Author.

Greuter, F. (2000). *Bausteine der schweizerischen Tourismuspolitik–Grundlagen, Beschreibung und Empfehlungen fur die Praxis* [Building blocks of the Swiss tourism policy–Principles, description and recommendations for the practice]. Unpublished doctoral dissertation, Universitat St. Gallen, Bern.

Heskett, J. (1988). *Management von Dienstleistungsunternehmen* [Management of service enterprises]. Wiesbaden: Gabler.

Icg. (2002). *Ein Berufsstand in Bewegung/"Qualitäts- und Bildungsoffensive" im Gastgewerbe* [A profession in move/"Quality and Education Offensive" in hospitality]. Neue Zürcher Zeitung.

Keller, P. (2001). *Tourism growth and global competition.* (Report 51st Congress 2001, Malta.) St. Gallen: Editions AIEST.

Müller, H. (2002). *Grundlagen zu einem touristischen Berufsbildungskonzept* [Principles of a tourism education concept]. Jahrbuch der Schweizerischen Tourismuswirtschaft 2001/2002 (pp. 93-113). St. Gallen: Universität St. Gallen.

Pine, J. B., & Gilmore, J. H. (1999). *The experience economy.* Boston: Harvard Business School Press.

Poon, A. (1993). *Tourism, strategy and competitive strategies.* Wallingford: C.A.B. International.

Porter, M. E. (1993). *Nationale Wettbewerbsvorteile: Erfolgreich konkurrieren auf dem Weltmarkt* [National Industrial Competitive Advantage]. Wien: Ueberreuter Special Edition.

Renner-Bach, J. (2003). *Bildung hat Konjunktur–auch im Tourismus* [Education is booming–also in tourism]. Bergamo: Montagna, 4.

Stampfli, D. (2004). *Absolventen sollten flexibler sein* [Graduates should be more flexible]. Hotel + Tourismus Revue, 27, 3.

Swiss Tourism Federation. (1999). *Tourismus in der Schweiz* [Tourism in Switzerland]. Bern: Schweizer Tourismus-Verband.

Tschurtschenthaler, P. (1998). *Humankapitalentwicklung als tourismuspolitisches Instrument zur Bewältigung der Tourismuskrise* [Human Resource Development as instrument to accomplish the crisis in tourism]. In Weiermair, K., Fuchs, M. (eds.) *Rettourism III Strategiekonferenz: Zukunftsstrategien für eine optimale Humankapitalentwicklung/-verwertung in der Tourismuswirtschaft* (pp. 16-39). Innsbruck, ITD Eigenverlag.

Weiermair, K. (1998). *Personalmanagement im Tourismus* [Human Resource Management in Tourism]. Limburgerhof: FBV-Medien-Verl.-GmbH.

Weiermair, K., & Fuchs, M. (1997). (Eds.), *RETTOURISM II Strategiekonferenz: Zukunftsstrategien für eine optimale Humankapitalentwicklung/-verwertung in der Tourismuswirtschaft,* Proceedings of the conference in Innsbruck University Press.

Weiermair, K., & Peters, M. (in press). Tourist attractions and attracted tourists: How to satisfy today's fickle tourist clientele? *Journal of Tourism Studies.*

WKÖ. (2004). *Tourismus in Zahlen* [Tourism in figures]. Wien: Author.

Tourism and Hospitality Higher Education in Israel

Arie Reichel

SUMMARY. This paper presents the past and present of higher education in tourism and hospitality management in Israel.

The paper discusses the growth of higher education in hospitality and tourism through local initiatives and by franchising and extensions from foreign institutions. The nature of the higher education system in Israel and the accreditation processes of local academic programs is discussed. The case of Ben-Gurion University is introduced to illustrate the development of an academic program in hospitality and tourism management.

The paper also compares the current state of the available academic programs to the year of 2000, at the eve of the Palestinian uprising. The paper analyses the complex relations between the Israeli hospitality industry and the higher education programs, as well as the challenges of future graduate programs and industry-academe relationships. *[Article copies available for a fee from The Haworth Document Delivery Service: 1-800-HAWORTH. E-mail address: <docdelivery@haworthpress.com> Website: <http://www.HaworthPress.com> © 2005 by The Haworth Press, Inc. All rights reserved.]*

KEYWORDS. Hospitality training, tourism training, higher education, Israel

---

Arie Reichel is Dean, School of Management and Profesor, Department of Business Administration and the Department of Hotel and Tourism Management, Ben-Gurion University of the Negev, Israel (E-mail: arier@som.bgu.ac.il).

[Haworth co-indexing entry note]: "Tourism and Hospitality Higher Education in Israel." Reichel, Arie. Co-published simultaneously in *Journal of Teaching in Travel & Tourism* (The Haworth Press, Inc.) Vol. 5, No. 1/2, 2005, pp. 61-88; and: *Global Tourism Higher Education: Past, Present, and Future* (ed: Cathy H. C. Hsu) The Haworth Press, Inc., 2005, pp. 61-88. Single or multiple copies of this article are available for a fee from The Haworth Document Delivery Service [1-800-HAWORTH, 9:00 a.m. - 5:00 p.m. (EST). E-mail address: docdelivery@haworthpress.com].

INTRODUCTION

The State of Israel extends over an area of 22,000 square kilometers (approximately 8,500 square miles), with a population of 6.5 million people. The population is highly diverse, with 80 percent Jews and 20 percent Arabs. Most of the Jewish inhabitants immigrated from numerous countries around the globe. Since its independence in 1948, Israel has been in varying states of conflict and war with its Arab neighbors. The last two decades have been marked by gradual peace processes, commencing with the peace treaty between Israel and Egypt signed in 1978. The country maintains a large military, which constitutes a significant economic and social burden. During its early years, the State of Israel relied heavily on agriculture. However, major technological improvements and investments have increasingly shifted the economy toward service industries and advanced technology. These processes have been accompanied by major liberalization and privatization, exposing the local economy to global competition. Clearly, the tourism and hospitality segment of the Israeli economy is an integral part of the changes in the economic and social structure.

The purpose of this paper is to present the past and present of higher education in tourism and hospitality management in Israel. It should be noted that these two sectors of the economy are highly interwoven, and it is only natural in Israel to design academic programs that integrate the two. As will be demonstrated, the development of academic programs in hospitality and tourism has been gradual and highly connected to geopolitical, social and economic trends.

HISTORIC PERSPECTIVE

Through 1994, managers or employees with university academic degrees in tourism and hospitality were scarce. The percentage of hospitality and tourism university graduates among them was negligible, as no such programs existed in Israel. Since priority was given to promotion from within, the career paths in hospitality were very clear: from bellhop to general manager. Being promoted to managerial level depended on starting at the lowest level job and working up the organizational hierarchy. Similarly, most tourism organizations employed people who had, at best, completed a basic travel agent course or learned on the job. Furthermore, the tourism and hospitality industry was not attractive to college graduates, since it provided no incentives for educated people. This, in turn, established a poor image of the industry and its employees. At the same time, traditional service occupations were considered inferior compared to the "learned" Jewish image. Specifically, the highly esteemed "learned" or scholarly role in the Jewish Diaspora tradition was in sharp contrast to menial or service jobs that supposedly did not require brain power.

For decades the paths were set: employees in hospitality were supplied either by relatively low-level professional schools or "off the street" without training and education. During their years with the organization, they would be trained both on the job and in various professional-technical courses, such as cooking. Those who aspired to managerial positions had to overcome a major obstacle: a government license. Becoming a hotel general manager required taking and passing a government test that included written and oral sections. The committee that prepared the test and examined the candidates comprised mainly senior managers who reflected the experience, values and attitudes of the tradition of the industry. To be qualified to take the governmental examination, candidates had to complete a two-year diploma course, but not an academic degree program. Subjects included in the course were related to operational hotel issues, including reception, purchasing, food and beverage management, and basic accounting and finance. The diploma courses were offered by several organizations that relied on the approval of the Ministry of Tourism. The most dominant organization was the Division of Continuing Education and External Studies at the prestigious Technion–Israel Institute of Technology. The Technion has been positioned as the most prestigious engineering training and research institution in Israel, with very selective admission criteria. The Division of Continuing Education and External Studies often employed instructors from the industry, although they lacked an academic background. Given the prestige of the parent organization, the Technion, the program managed to attract instructors despite the very low remuneration. Similarly, the reputation of the Technion and the location of the extension in the heart of Tel Aviv, Israel's major city, helped attract numerous applicants.

The mix of industry-based instructors and governmental as well as industry-based licensing could be advantageous in emphasizing relevant applicable issues. In reality, it created a relatively traditional, insulated, self-perpetuating manager training system that developed its own culture, body of knowledge, hierarchy and procedures, and was protected by the government. Some of the critics toward the prevailing system maintained that instead of concentrating on modern up-to-date marketing and profitably issues, the courses as well as the content of the formal examination focused on outdated topics such as linen materials and table-setting methods. Apparently, what suited the traditional European hospitality industry was no longer valued in the Americanized, "globalized" trend of the hospitality industry toward the end of the 20th century.

In addition to the Technion, the Division of Continuing Education and Extension Studies of Haifa University also offered a hospitality management track, as did several small regional colleges: Eilat College, Ruppin College, and Jordan Valley College. These colleges, extending from the south of Israel up to Galilee, attracted mainly local applicants versus the national appeal of the Technion Division of Continuing Education and External Studies. The various programs offered by the schools, such as reception, housekeeping, and integrative hospitality courses, were closely supervised by the Israel Ministry of Tourism and the Ministry of Labor. Furthermore, there were small schools in Jerusalem (Hadassa Professional College) and Arad near the Dead Sea that offered professional courses in hospitality. The latter attempted to attract and train new immigrants for employment in the hospitality sector.

Hospitality education for lower-level organizational positions is offered primarily at two governmental-industry controlled organizations: the Tadmor and Dvir schools. Tadmor was founded in 1961 as a governmental corporation with partial ownership of the Israel Hotel Association. The government involvement stemmed from two major motivations:

a. Concerns by the Israel Ministry of Tourism to supply the hospitality industry with qualified professionals; and
b. Interests of the Israel Ministry of Labor to train low-level professionals for the hospitality industry, in order to find a solution for unemployment, particularly among young people who had been recently discharged from military service.

For over four decades, Tadmor was the main source of trained hospitality employees. The lengthy internship required of the students enabled hotels to have free low-level employees, whose income was provided by the Ministry of Labor. The involvement of the hospitality industry was further manifested in its ability to have input on the content of courses and also to encourage the opening of specific courses based on industry-driven demands. Again, this training system, similar to the executive training system, was self-perpetuating, convenient for all parties involved, and insulated from modern, global developments. The location of

Tadmor (in the middle of an exclusive neighborhood) and its proximity to luxurious hotels in the center of Israel added a significant asset to its appeal and supported its dominant, almost monopolistic, position. Graduates of Tadmor received professional ranks or licenses (such as that of "chef") from the Israel Ministry of Labor. These licenses were recognized by the hospitality sector, but considered less important in the restaurant segment. The second, smaller school, Dvir, is situated in the city of Haifa on Mt. Carmel. Operated by the Dan hotel chain, it primarily supplies low entry-level employees to the Dan chain and other hotels.

This intensive governmental involvement was also evident in the case of travel and tourism education in Israel. The government owned and operated the Central School of Tourism, which offered a variety of courses geared toward tourism professionals. Courses trained tour guides, guides for escorting tourists abroad, travel agents, and travel agency experts. The most demanding programs offered by the School were for tour guides and travel agency experts. Tour guide studies spanned almost 2 years and entailed a thorough knowledge of the history and geography of Israel. Similarly, the travel agency expert course entailed a year and a half of geography and business courses, in addition to all the relevant information on airlines and inbound and outbound tourism. Demand for the School and its programs was assured via an extensive governmental licensing requirement. Even the lowest level agent or tour escort needed a license from the Ministry of Tourism. Clearly, tour guides required a license that had to be renewed on a regular basis (through additional training), and no travel agency could open and operate without the presence of an "expert" on the premises. Several other schools, including the Division of Continuing Education and Extension Studies at the University of Haifa and the regional colleges, attempted to enter this segment of education, but with mixed results.

In the late 1980s, the Israeli government encouraged regional colleges in the northern part of Israel to open specially designed courses for the growing bed and breakfast industry. The trend toward developing the bed and breakfast industry in Israel was not a spontaneous, natural progression, but rather an intentional, well-planned process. The declining agricultural industry in Israel endangered the viability of numerous small towns and villages, mainly in the Galilee area. National priorities, in terms of population distribution and the development of peripheral areas, dictated a search for alternative means of economic survival. Given the economic structure of small farms and the natural beauty of this region, it seemed logical to suggest a transition to bed and breakfast, or "rural tourism" (Fleischer & Pizam, 1997). It became apparent that the farmers-turned-entrepreneurs required special training in finance, marketing, and preparing business plans (Lerner & Haber, 2001). Instruction was provided either through personal consultants or through special courses offered by regional colleges in northern Israel, such as the Jordan Valley College. The entrepreneurs paid a nominal fee, while the government shouldered most of the expenses. Entrepreneurs were encouraged to take these courses in order to develop better managerial skills that qualified them for additional governmental subsidies. Again, the role of the government in tourism training was evident.

It should be noted, however, that although the Israeli government played a dominant role in hospitality and tourism training and education, market forces had their impact as well. For example, an organized and relatively homogenized hospitality segment followed government regulations closely and hired employees according to license and rank. Yet, given the fragmented nature of the hospitality and tourism industry in Israel and the proliferation of micro and small ventures, it was possible to employ non-professionals who were trained on the job. Restaurants and fast food operations were noted for ignoring license requirements and tended to train employees on the job. In addition, several large travel agency operators started their own training systems, mainly for lower end positions. At the same time, the tourism industry attracted numerous people who were interested either in a career change or in supplementary income and were ready to pay various schools and colleges for this opportunity. While no statistics are available, it is estimated that thousands of people took tourism certificate courses, though eventually less than ten percent remained in the field.

THE "MILLENNIUM REVOLUTION": DEREGULATION TRENDS

In the run up to the new millennium, the tourism and hospitality industry in Israel underwent several revolutions. First, as part of the efforts to meet the requirements of free international trade agreements, the State of Israel embarked on an intensive process of privatization and deregulation. Consequently, the Ministries of Tourism and Labor had to cancel most license requirements. The only hospitality and tourism industry role left with licensing requirements was that of a tour guide. All other tourism roles or occupations no longer needed formalized training and licensing. This meant that it became the sole responsibility of the owner to decide who fits the job. The "new order" was in line with traditional criticism of hotel owners against the hotel manager accreditation process, that can be summarized in a common complaint: "I am skilled and experienced enough to run a financial empire, yet I am not allowed to run a hotel in the chain I own." Furthermore, travel agents and travel agency experts were no longer licensed. The free trade agreements actually freed the hospitality and tourism industry of legal training responsibilities and ensured "freedom of occupation."

Second, the privatization and deregulation processes were accompanied by another trend: industry leaders stated support for training academically qualified staff for the tourism and hospitality industry. Until the end of the 20th century, the percentage of degree holders among executives and leaders of the hospitality and tourism industry was extremely small. While no statistics are available, the common notion is that most of the executives were graduates of diploma courses from Tadmor or the other tourism programs that offered professional courses. A cursory examination of the columns of new appointments in industry trade journals would list very few people with academic credentials. A very small minority of executives were graduates of institutions that were considered very prestigious, but granted no academic degrees, for example, the Lausanne Hotel School. Industry leaders began recognizing the importance of higher education and started promoting training programs for university graduates. Such "conversion" programs appealed to social sciences and liberal arts university graduates who were expected to join the industry in managerial positions. Most of these programs were tailored to the specific needs of the hospitality industry and were supported by the Ministry of Tourism and Ministry of Labor. Both ministries saw these programs as a means of finding new avenues for university graduates and for upgrading the quality of the industry. Unfortunately, while the programs were meticulously planned and conceived, the retention rate of graduates was extremely low. After three years of operation and approximately 200 trainees, only 5 percent remained in the hospitality industry. It is interesting to note that this failure did not stop industry leaders from their efforts to promote the academic qualification process.

The desire to upgrade the image of the tourism industry, and mainly of the hospitality segment, was shown in the lesser-known efforts of some hoteliers to establish a special non-governmental organization called the Organization for Promoting the Academization Process in the Hospitality and Tourism Industry in Israel in 1989. Headed by the German-born general manager of the Tel Aviv Sheraton hotel, this non-governmental organization was looking for an Israeli university ready for initiatives to develop academic programs in hospitality and tourism. As will be shown later in this paper, this organization made several attempts to contact universities before it sunk into oblivion.

The penetration of international hotel chains, restaurants, and tourist organizations into the Israeli market had a positive effect in terms of the expectations to provide higher education for the tourism and hospitality sector. Attracted by the ease of entry, easy franchising conditions, and the high hopes for the peace process, numerous organizations established branches in Israel (Preble, Reichel, & Hoffman, 2000). Representatives of these organizations formed a climate of appreciation for a sophisticated cadre of young managers with specialized higher education in tourism and hospitality. The forgotten early hopes of the general manager of the Sheraton hotel were aired again by a new generation of foreign and foreign-educated managers who came to Israel with the trend towards globalization.

Another trend worth noting that took place in Israel and had bearing on tourism and hospitality education was the democratization of higher education in Israel. Through the beginning of the 1990s, the system of higher education in Israel was highly centralized and state controlled. There were six comprehensive universities, an open university and the Weizmann Institute, devoted exclusively to research and graduate studies, mainly in life sciences. Clearly, the small number of universities dictated very high admission standards. The waves of immigration from the former Soviet Union added close to one million people, boosting the population of the State of Israel to over six million. The pressures exerted by native Israeli and new immigrants, coupled with an emerging post-modernist orientation of egalitarian higher education, paved the way for a major breakthrough in the concept of higher education in Israel. No longer the domain of a select few with very high credentials, the system of higher education opened its gates to groups that never previously had the opportunity to be exposed to its benefits. The revolution in the higher education system took shape across four main dimensions:

   a. Increasing the Capacity of Existing Universities–Each university had a "ceiling" for the number of students. In theory, universities can exceed the ceiling; however, they will not be subsidized more than the official ceiling. The state system in Israel subsidizes each student according to the nature of the degree (e.g., liberal arts vs. engineering). The tuition itself covers no more than 50 percent of the estimated expenses for each student. Increasing the number of students at each university means that the state has to allocate more resources than intended. Setting ceilings enables the Ministry of Finance and the Ministry of Education to control university budgets. Even if universities exceed their ceiling, the regulating committee, the Council for Higher Education, still limits the subsidy to the ceiling. Moreover, the budget for physical facilities, such as classrooms, reflects the ceiling as well. Thus, universities will have to raise their own funds to subsidize extra students and build additional facilities, as they are not allowed to raise tuition. This trap deters universities from exceeding the ceiling. The mounting demand during the 1990s convinced the government to raise the ceiling, particularly for the younger, "peripheral" universities.

b. *Developing a System of Regional Colleges*–The burgeoning demand, coupled with the democratization process and the ideology of access to higher education, triggered one of the most significant revolutions in the Israeli education system: the regional or "budgeted" colleges. The latter name reflects the fact that these colleges are subsidized by the government as opposed to private colleges that depend on tuition. The regional colleges were designed to siphon as much demand as possible from the established universities. This model called for the universities to focus mainly on graduate level education. Moreover, the planners of the Israel Council for Higher Education had a clear vision of the desired structure of higher education in Israel. Specifically, the mission behind the establishment of the colleges was to provide access to students from peripheral areas, and to ease the economic burden of undergraduate education for the universities. Note that most undergraduate programs in Israel require 3 years of studies (vs. the four-year American system). Situated, in most cases, in peripheral areas away from major cities, these colleges offered higher education to populations that could never before meet the minimal entry standards of the major universities. At first, all degree programs offered were authorized and supervised by the established universities. Gradually, the colleges were expected to build their own academic programs, granting their own degrees and maintaining their own academic staff. By the summer of 2004, most of the colleges were halfway to independence. Apparently, what seemed to be a highly desirable process has proven to be especially threatening as demand started to decline. It seems that the "independent" degrees are less desirable than the university "branded" ones awarded before their "independence." Additionally, the labor market at present shows signs of recognizing the differences between university and college degrees, in most cases giving preference to the former degrees. Finally, the universities seem to be reluctant to give up their undergraduate populations, as they cannot reach the ceiling with graduate students alone. The colleges, on their part, are oscillating between offering "copies" of the previously granted degrees or designing their own original and innovative degrees. Some of them exert considerable pressure on the Council for Higher Education to extend their affiliation with the universities in order to smooth the transition to total independence.

c. *Opening Private Institutions of Higher Education*–The increase in Israel's population during the 1990s, and the accompanied pressure to provide more opportunities for higher education, resulted in an unprecedented trend for establishing private institutions of higher education. All private institutions were actually not-for-profit organizations whose founders managed to receive considerable management remunerations that easily justified their investment. The first institution to be established, long before the tidal wave of the 1990s, was The College of Management, whose undergraduate degree programs were the first ever to gain accreditation as a non-university, independent institution. The College attempted to develop a degree in tourism management, but failed to attract appropriate faculty and resigned itself to offering several certificate programs, such as travel agent certification. Several new private colleges established their own accredited degree programs, while some depended on foreign institutions, as will be outlined below.

d. *Penetration of Foreign Institutions Into the Israeli Market*–The development of higher education in tourism and hospitality in Israel cannot be fully understood without close examination of the influx of foreign-based university and college extensions into the Israeli higher education scene. The growing demand for higher education was sensed by astute businesspeople, who saw considerable opportunities in developing local extensions of foreign institutions of various qualities and reputation. Israel's high degree of involvement in free international trade agreements paved the way for the penetration of numerous academic extensions, mainly from the United States and Britain. Institutions such as Bournemouth, Derby, Manchester, Bradford Coventry and Heriot-Watt represented the British "invasion." Nova Southwest, New England

College, Boston University, Clark University, New York Polytechnic, as well as institutions like Champlain College, represented the American contingent. In addition, Unissa of South Africa and The University of Latvia opened extensions as well. While the Council for Higher Education imposed extremely strict measures of quality for accreditation, it somehow did not have the legal power and authority to stop the ever-growing wave of foreign invasion. During the mid-nineties, agile businesspeople would board a plane and return with a franchising agreement, which in most cases virtually allowed the local franchisee total control over the quality of the programs. In very few cases did the parent organizations impose very strict quality assurance measures, which were often considered an unavoidable nuisance. One of the most sought after subjects to be offered was tourism and hospitality management.

In light of the above trends, a university or college degree in Israel has almost become a commodity. Numerous positions, both in the public and private sectors, that only required high school diplomas up through the mid-1990s have now begun to require a degree from an academic institution. In many cases, the quality and duration of studies are not of concern. Numerous organizations failed to distinguish between high-quality programs and ones of dubious quality. Clearly, these developments had a direct effect on the hospitality and tourism industry in Israel. To understand the extent of these changes, a review of the history of the efforts to develop tourism and hospitality academic programs is presented below.

EARLY EFFORTS TO DEVELOP ACADEMIC PROGRAMS IN TOURISM AND HOSPITALITY

From a historical perspective, the efforts to develop academic programs in hospitality and tourism management began as early as 1973. Until that time, Haifa University offered a certificate program for hotel managers through its Division of Continuing Education and Extension Studies. This division offered non-academic courses aimed at community development, (i.e., offering courses to the general public). In essence, most of them aspired to serve as cash cows for the organization. The academic leaders of University of Haifa had the vision to open the first program of its kind, with the support of the Israel Ministry of Tourism. The Yom Kippur war that erupted in October of 1973 resulted in a sharp decline in the number of incoming tourists to Israel (Mansfeld, 1999). In a clearly shortsighted perspective, the University decided that there was no point in investing in a declining market and terminated all preparations for the program.

This failure put the academic process back into a deep freeze, until new attempts in about 1986 from the most southern academic institution in Israel, Eilat College (now defunct and re-established in 2002 as the Eilat Campus of Ben-Gurion University of the Negev). The management of Eilat College envisioned an academic program in tourism. Established as one of the regional colleges, Eilat College was affiliated with Ben-Gurion University (BGU). Most students spent two years on campus and had to transfer to BGU in Beer-Sheva (the Biblical city of Beersheba) for the third year of study. Lacking sufficient local demand, Eilat College suffered from "diseconomies of scale." Classes were very small, and no bright future could be predicted. However, the major advantage of Eilat College had to do with the City of Eilat as the major resort in Israel. Situated on the Red Sea, surrounded by magnificent mountains of the Syrian-African Rift, at the cross borders of four nations (Israel, Jordan, Saudi Arabia, and Egypt), Eilat has always been a special tourist site. Hundreds of thousands of foreign and domestic tourists flocked into this isolated city that offered accommodation, from budget to the luxurious. Moreover, the significance of the tourism industry was acknowledged by the government, and it encouraged young Israelis to work for at least 180 days in order to qualify for a special financial bonus. Termed by the industry as Commando 180 (Reichel & Amit, 2000), hundreds of such young people who streamed into Eilat were viewed as a potential high quality workforce for the hospitality industry. It seemed logical from the viewpoint of the leaders of Eilat College that a unique academic program in tourism and hospitality that would attract these young people would be a panacea to their demand problem. Unfortunately, the College had to rely on the efforts of its parent university, BGU, to submit a proposal to the Council for Higher Education. BGU at that time had other priorities and so did the Council for Higher Education. Similar to the failed effort of University of Haifa, the idea had to be shelved until a more appropriate time.

It seemed that the right opportunity appeared in 1988 for the Organization for the Academization of the Hospitality and Tourism Industry in Israel (OAHTI). At that time, the concept of an academic program in tourism and hospitality was included in the set of options to be considered by the Rector (provost) of BGU, who was looking for unique new academic programs. The latent but persistent pressure of Eilat College on BGU, as well as the news of OAHTI, prompted a set of meetings between the University and OATHI leaders. The commitment of OAHTI to meet most of the financial requirements for the new programs was a motivating force for BGU to invest in preparing a detailed plan for the program ready for submission. Note that this program had to be submitted to the Council for Higher Education for accreditation and for financing of some of the elements not covered by OAHTI. The successful ongoing contacts between BGU and OAHTI revived the hopes of Israeli academics in the field that a full-fledged academic department would be established. Moreover, it was assumed by the academics and by BGU that OAHTI was an authentic representative of the tourism and hospitality sector. Cooperation with the industry was viewed as crucial for the success of the program. Thus, almost a perfect model of an academic department based on both government (the Council) and industry support was ready for implementation.

Just when all seemed to be ready for a final approval by both parties (BGU and the Organization), the representative of the Israel Ministry of Tourism, a member of OAHTI, declared that it was against the bylaws of the Organization to sign an exclusive agreement with one university. An opportunity had to be given to other universities who might be interested in establishing an academic department. Consequently, an invitation was sent to all the established Israeli universities to apply for the sponsorship of the organization. Ironically, the university that for years had rejected the idea of a tourism and hospitality program, Tel Aviv University, won the bid. The official explanation cited the proximity of Tel Aviv University to Israel's major tourism and hotel attractions. Loyal to its traditional "anti" tourism and hospitality approach, Tel Aviv University never took advantage of its mandate. Another attempt to establish an academic program collapsed. Soon thereafter OAHTI folded.

The academic wave, marked by growing demand for higher education, the raising of the ceilings for the traditional universities, and the economic prosperity of the early 1990s that was associated with the peace process and the growth in incoming tourists, renewed the interest of BGU in reviving the preparations for the program. This time it was decided by the BGU rector (Provost) to update the program previously submitted to OAHTI and to officially submit it to the Council for Higher Education. In the summer of 1994, BGU received a green light from the Council to advertise the program in order to facilitate registration. Over 600 candidates applied for the program, indicating a latent demand that had not been previously fulfilled. At the same time, the Hebrew University of Jerusalem was awarded permission to start a program at its school of Agriculture and Food Sciences campus in the city of Rehovot, south of Tel Aviv. The program intended to take advantage of its expertise in the food sciences area.

Over the next five years, there was a virtual tidal wave of new hospitality and tourism management programs–as if all the frustrating efforts of the previous years were forgotten in light of the trends that affected Israeli higher education in general and the tourism and hospitality industry in particular. A new era had emerged.

WHAT DOES IT TAKE TO OPEN AN ACADEMIC PROGRAM: THE CASE OF BGU

The department of Hotel and Tourism Management at Ben-Gurion University was a pioneer in the sense that it had to be planned from scratch, without relying on the expertise of other units. This is in contrast, for example, to the department at Hebrew University, which from the outset relied heavily on faculty members from food sciences and actually enabled faculty from declining departments to serve students via the interdepartmental program.

After the decision to invest in a program in hospitality and tourism, the Rector of BGU appointed a special coordinator whose responsibility was to review prestigious and high quality programs abroad. Given the Western orientation of BGU, most programs explored were either American or British. The coordinator appointed a multidisciplinary group that assisted him in designing the program. The author of this paper, who gained experience in tourism and hospitality academic education in the United States, represented the Department of Industrial Engineering and Management. It was agreed by the coordinator and the group to adopt the concept suggested by Prof. Abraham Pizam of the University of Central Florida to design an interdisciplinary program that integrated both tourism and hospitality. This integration reflected the structure of the industry in Israel, and enabled students to see the overlap between the various aspects included in each area.

Given the concept of the program, there was a need to design specific syllabi, as requested by the Council for Higher Education. The syllabi preparation required numerous decisions, as there were no academic syllabi in Israel to adopt and emulate. Much of the work involved reviewing available American and British syllabi and adapting them to the unique conditions of the higher education system in Israel. Note, however, that the basic disciplinary courses, such as economics or math; were readily available. The major challenge involved the design of syllabi for courses that had never before been offered in Israel. Each syllabus had to include the topics to be covered as well as the required textbooks and additional readings. Clearly, almost no readings at all were available in Hebrew. To some observers this was not a real deficiency, given the fact that the subject of the studies requires an international language. In addition to the structure of the program and the detailed syllabi, the proposal included a list of proposed instructors, a detailed budget, and a business plan.

After the Senate of the University approved the program, it had to be approved by the University accountants. In April 1994, it was submitted to the Council for Higher Education for approval. The Council policy required the appointment of an ad-hoc academic committee that examined the proposal from an academic perspective. After several months, the University received a report suggesting several changes in the program. For example, the program consisted of three and a half years of study and suggested granting a B.Sc. degree. Apparently, that model was a deviation from most undergraduate programs in Israel, designated for three years only. Moreover, the Council insisted that the B.Sc. was reserved for natural sciences which implied high expenses that include laboratories and equipment. Consequently, the degree was amended to a B.A., granted after three years of study.

The next step involved recruitment of faculty members. Until 1994, the few scholars who conducted research in the area of hospitality and tourism management were well-established members of departments such as geography or sociology. Moreover, their orientation naturally fitted the discipline that was dominant in their department, and not necessarily the management orientation that marked the new program. Two main options were viable: professional re-orientation, and development of new Ph.D. students. Clearly, the latter option required considerable time and resources.

In the first year, the program relied on a mix of local BGU faculty who taught the basic management courses, several guest lecturers from the United States in courses that had no appropriate faculty in Israel (e.g., food and beverage management) and an experimental utilization of adjunct faculty from the industry. The following years marked the recruitment of full-time faculty members, who made the commitment to hospitality, tourism research and teaching, and who were ready to spend time receiving advice from noted experts from abroad. Finally, BGU financially supported Ph.D. students who pursued their studies at top American universities, with the commitment to return to Israel and join the Department. As a result of relying simultaneously on various sources for faculty recruitment and development, by the eighth year following its establishment, the Department had no shortage of highly qualified faculty for all courses.

The timing of the program start coincided with a positive trend in the number of tourist arrivals in Israel. In addition, the general geopolitical climate was encouraging and the belief in a possible "new peaceful Middle East" was pervasive. There also seemed to be a latent demand for academic hospitality and tourism programs that erupted in an unpredicted interest by almost 600 students. Most of the applicants were highly talented and could be easily admitted to the most sought after programs at the University, including the School of Medicine. The high demand required a meticulous admission process that included personal interviews by faculty and industry representatives (Reichel & Milman, 1996). The high caliber candidates reiterated the need for very high quality faculty.

Since no tourism and hospitality academics were readily available, the administrator of the program attracted faculty who were willing to adapt their research and teaching to tourism and hospitality management. For example, a sociologist specializing in the behavior of the "strangers" made the transition to sociology of tourism. A food engineer made the transition to food and beverage management. The mission of the Department was to become a national center of excellence in research and training of tourism and hospitality future managers. Consequently, research produced by faculty members had to be published in the best possible journals, and tenure and promotion procedures were compatible with the strict standards of the University. While the future seemed very bright from the university's perspective, and the development of the program in terms of courses, faculty members and quality students was more than satisfactory, there were some early signs of doubts about the industry's willingness and ability to embrace the revolution in tourism and hospitality education.

ACADEMIC PROGRAMS IN TOURISM AND HOSPITALITY IN THE YEAR 2000

At the end of the year 2000, the following hospitality and tourism management programs of various qualities and orientations were in operation in Israel (listed from the south to the north):

a. The Department of Hotel and Tourism Management at Ben-Gurion University of the Negev in Beer-Sheva.
b. The Program of Hotel and Food Resource Management at the Hebrew University of Jerusalem in Rehovot.
c. Ramat Gan College, located in the City of Ramat Gan in the metropolitan region of Tel-Aviv, offers a program granting graduate degrees from Bournemouth University (U.K.).
d. Tel Aviv extension of Nova Southwestern (of Florida) that offers degrees from Champlain College (Vermont, U.S.A.). Several peripheral extensions of the Tel Aviv center were opened as well.
e. The Israel extension of the University of Derby (U.K.) located in Ramat Gan.
f. The Israel extension of Farleigh Dickinson University of New Jersey, U.S.A. located in Tel-Aviv.
g. A special feeder program at Tadmor School for Johnson and Wales University of Rhode Island, U.S.A.
h. A hospitality track at the Interdisciplinary Center Herzliya (IDC) that also serves as a feeder for the University of Nevada, Las Vegas.
i. A tourism concentration at University of Haifa in the Department of Geography.

Most of the above programs offered three-year undergraduate programs. Annual tuition at the state-funded universities is approximately U.S.$2,500. For the private programs, tuition ranges from $4,000 to $4,500. The programs at Hebrew University of Jerusalem and Ben-Gurion University were originally designed to focus on hospitality and tourism. Each one reflected the unique conditions of the university where it is located. Furthermore, each tried to take advantage of the unique competitive advantage associated with its institution. Both programs were accredited by the Council for Higher Education, assuring high standards and appropriate budget. The program at BGU was initially established (1994) as an extension of the Department of Industrial Engineering and Management (mainly due to the affiliation of the first chairperson). The link with the prestigious Faculty of Engineering Sciences helped position the department in terms of quality and emphasis on management issues. With the establishment of the School of Management at BGU (1995), the Department found a natural "home" and also managed to reap some of the benefits associated with being the "pioneer" unit of the School.

From its outset, the Department of Hotel and Food Resource Management at Hebrew University relied heavily on faculty representing various aspects of food sciences. Most of the courses were taught by faculty who emphasized the properties of food, attempting to carve a niche of food and beverage management for hospitality. The program was supported by the Israeli Dan Hotel chain that also donated the Federman (family) Hospitality Endowed Chair, named after one of the founders of the chain. The high prestige of Hebrew University was a clear competitive advantage. It should be noted that the above two programs accredited by the Israel Council for Higher Education had to rely on full-time faculty members holding Ph.D.s, who were expected to conduct research and publish according to the higher education standards.

The program at University of Haifa concentrated on geography, but offered a specific track of tourism studies. The impact of the track is noted mainly in graduate degrees, where students write Master's theses and doctoral dissertations on tourism. Some of the graduating students joined the faculty of tourism programs in Israel. The university also opened the Center for the Study of Tourism and Pilgrimage, the only center of its kind in Israel. In the middle of the academic development and privatization processes that swept tourism and hospitality education in the late 1990s, University of Haifa acquired the former government-owned School of Tourism. Located in a central area in Tel Aviv, the School offered certificate programs in tourism.

The extension of Bournemouth University in Israel was located at a then-obscure private Ramat-Gan College that managed to flourish in later years due to its innovative strategy: agreements to award degrees from various universities by franchising contracts and similar models of cooperation. The extension offered a graduate degree in tourism and hospitality management. At the beginning, the hosts were very strict in following the rules, regulations, and quality standards of the parent institution. Several full-fledged faculty members from the U.K. were sent to teach in order to complement the local part-time instructors, most without doctoral degrees.

The extensions of Nova Southwestern and Champlain College were established as a business venture and located in an office building near the central bus station of Tel Aviv. While it was an accessible location, it was in sharp contrast to the sprawling and attractive environment of BGU or Hebrew University. The programs were noted for their flexibility in admission standards and class schedules, thus attracting numerous employees from the hospitality and tourism industry. No full-time faculty members were listed in formal publications. The relationship with the parent institutions could not be validated for the purpose of writing this paper. Hundreds of students took classes there, and several peripheral extensions were advertised in the newspapers.

Probably the most successful private foreign extension was from the University of Derby, which managed to attract students through its emphasis on "applied" studies. The Israeli campus accounts for 20 percent of the total 25,000 students of The University of Derby worldwide. Among the programs offered are business administration, behavioral sciences, and tourism studies. An interview with Mr. Avi Bitan, the majority owner and general manager of the extension (in the weekend magazine of the daily *Yedioth Aharonoth*, "An applied university education," 2004), summarized his philosophy:

> . . . I do not accept the philosophy that we are considered "guilty" and have to prove our innocence. If in seven years we have managed to produce more graduates than the Open University that has existed for more than 20 years, there must be a reason. I did not force students at gunpoint to apply, register and pay more than NIS 60,000 for their degree. . . . They come here because of a real need. Most of the students are not interested in a research institution–with all due respect to research–but in a teaching institution with good lecturers and an applied approach that will help them through life. They do not care if their bad instructor is an excellent researcher–which happens quite frequently at the universities . . . An academic institution should not select students according to psychometric tests. You accept with basic credentials such as Matriculation Certificate and do the selection during the course work. . . . (p. 42)

The extension of Farleigh Dickenson concentrated on hospitality education and, after several years of operation, seemed to cease its operations. Efforts to track down its current status failed. Two additional programs developed cooperation models that benefited the parties involved. First, the Interdisciplinary Center Herzliya (IDC), north of Tel Aviv, developed a track in hospitality and tourism. The track consists of five courses as part of all undergraduate degrees in business administration. Most of the instructors are primarily employed in the tourism industry and are expected to bring to their students hands-on experience. The main attraction of this track stems from the agreement with the University of Nevada, Las Vegas (UNLV). According to the agreement, graduates can be admitted to UNLV and complete an additional degree in hospitality management. Given the three-year duration of undergraduate degree studies in Israel, students can earn two undergraduate degrees in four years. This attractive option also enables the students to gain a year of work experience in the hospitality industry in the U.S.

Another bi-institutional agreement was signed between the industry and government-supported Tadmor School and Johnson and Wales University. Students at the two-year certificate program of integrative hospitality management would complete their degree in the United States. In this model, Tadmor serves as a feeder and can advertise the option to complete academic degrees.

As can be seen from the above description, the almost fifty-year void was very quickly filled with numerous options for students, enabling a choice between various degrees, levels and academic standards. The preparations for the millennium celebrations and the expectations for millions of tourists raised the interest in such programs, and there seemed to be enough demand for all these programs. During that period, the leaders of the traditional university programs raised some doubts about the need for so many programs and the possible negative implications to the reputation and quality of higher education in tourism and hospitality management. The concerns of the state-funded programs were shared by numerous researchers from other fields, who felt that the market failed to distinguish between serious high-quality degrees and lightweight programs. Yet, the legal loophole that enabled the penetration of dozens of foreign universities into Israel prevented any serious acts against this phenomenon.

THE NEW SHIFTS OF THE 2000s

The proliferation of hospitality and tourism programs was blocked due to several developments that took place from September of 2000 through 2003:

1. In September of 2000, in the middle of one of the most successful seasons for the tourism and hospitality industry in Israel, the Palestinian uprising, known as the Intifada, broke out. The hostilities between the Palestinians and the Israelis reached unprecedented heights, bringing the tourism industry to a standstill (see Table 1). Although the summer of 2004 was presented in the mass media as a possible change in the trend, it is not yet clear when the industry will return to the high figures of the summer of 2000. Since the

year 2000, over 40 percent of the tourism and hospitality work-force was laid off. According to the estimates of the Organization of Incoming Tour Operators, more than 90 percent of tour guides were left unemployed. The severe crisis resulted in a sharp decline in the number of applicants to academic and non-academic tourism and hospitality programs.

2. The lifting of the license requirement for hospitality management and most of tourism-related occupations, coupled with the Intifada, resulted in an almost total elimination of non-academic hospitality education. Even the industry-supported Center of Hospitality Education was forced to close due to lack of funds. Several attempts by both academic and non-academic institutions to take advantage of the vacuum and offer certificate programs did not succeed. Sporadic travel agency courses were offered, and the School of Tourism at the University of Haifa drastically curtailed its operations. Clearly, the deep crisis did not enable financially troubled hospitality and tourism organizations to spend on training. Moreover, the high unemployment rate discouraged potential employees from investing in industry-related courses, as their future seemed to be bleak.

3. In addition to the industry crisis that severely curtailed the demand for tourism and hospitality programs, the revised Act of High Education, February 1998 (The Council for Higher Education in Israel, 2004), finally dealt with the almost uninterrupted penetration of foreign colleges and universities into Israel, including in the field of tourism and hospitality. The long awaited Act dictated explicit quality control measures. Liberal franchising agreements that enabled businesspeople to open extensions with minimal contacts with the franchisor were banned. The Israeli extension had to be an integral part of the parent institution. Furthermore, a certain percentage of faculty members had to have tenured positions at the parent organization and teach at the extension as well. Similarly, in addition to local adjunct faculty, full-time local faculty was required. The new demands were too restrictive for most programs.

Given the crisis, the abolishing of licensing requirement in most occupations, and the Higher Education Act, as of the summer of 2004 the following institutions' programs survived:

- Ben-Gurion University of the Negev: Beer-Sheva and Eilat.
- Hebrew University of Jerusalem in Rehovot (Hotel and Food Resource Management).

- The University of Derby.
- The Interdisciplinary Center (IDC).
- The Tadmor program.
- University of Haifa (tourism program).

The Department of Hospitality and Tourism Management at BGU suffered a major decline in the number of applicants. Prior to the crisis

TABLE 1. Entry of Visitors, Total Number of Tourists, and Tourists via Air Segment

1985-2003 and Forecast for 2004						
Year	Visitor Entries*		Total Tourist Entries		Via Air Tourist Segment	
	(Thousands)	Rate of Change vs. Previous Year	(Thousands)	Rate of Change vs. Previous Year	(Thousands)	Rate of Change vs. Previous Year
1985	1,436.4		1,264.4		1,079.3	
1986	1,195.9	−17%	1,101.5	−13%	929.6	−14%
1987	1,518	27%	1,379	25%	1,151	24%
1988	1,299	−14%	1,170	−15%	979	−15%
1989	1,425	10%	1,257	8%	1,033	6%
1990	1,342	−6%	1,132	−10%	933	−10%
1991	1,118	−17%	951	−16%	806	−14%
1992	1,805	61%	1,510	59%	1,257	56%
1993	1,946	8%	1,656	10%	1,379	10%
1994	2,169	11%	1,839	11%	1,501	9%
1995	2,531	17%	2,216	20%	1,678	12%
1996	2,360	−7%	2,100	−5%	1,612	−4%
1997	2,296	−3%	2,010	−4%	1,561	−3%
1998	2,200	−4%	1,942	−3%	1,553	−1%
1999	2,557	16%	2,312	19%	1,827	18%
2000	2,672	4%	2,417	5%	1,955	7%
2001	1,219	−54%	1,196	−51%	1,060	−46%
2002	862	−29%	862	−28%	779	−27%
2003	1,063	23%	1,063	23%	972	25%
(forecast) 2004	1,400	32%	1,400	32%	1,250	29%

*Visitor entries = tourist entries + entries on cruise ships

some 500-600 applied each year; during the crisis years demand declined by up to 50 percent. Each of the first three institutions has approximately 150 students. The Haifa program includes 20 graduate students. The IDC trains roughly 20 students in the tourism and hospitality track. It was not possible to determine how many Tadmor graduates continue their studies in the United States.

Despite the crisis and the apparent declining demand, the Israel Council for Higher Education made bold steps by financing and supporting additional programs: one at Eilat and one at the Jordan Valley College. The struggling Eilat College was closed, and a new campus was established with the avid support of the Council: BGU-Eilat, a satellite campus to the main campus of Beer-Sheva. One of the seven undergraduate programs to be offered was Hospitality and Tourism Management. Apparently, the early hopes of the leaders of Eilat College materialized, however, under a newly formed entity. A closer examination would indicate that the dream was only partially fulfilled. After two years of operation, only 26 students are majoring in this track. An analysis conducted by campus academic administration revealed that the two main target populations for the programs, quality youth of "Commando 180" and local Eilat youth, were not particularly interested. The former were mainly concerned to save money for the almost socially requisite act of post-military service: backpacking in India or South America. Very few of these young people saw academic studies as a viable option for the near future. Eilat was seen mainly as an opportunity for work of at least 180 days, receiving the bonus of persistence on a "priority employment" job, and then taking off. Local young people, in contrast, were looking forward to leaving the city and starting a new life in major centers, such as Tel Aviv. Furthermore, they were not necessarily interested in joining the main economy of their city. Consequently, the campus had to try to "import" students from other parts of Israel. However, the option of studying in Eilat was very much like studying abroad: expensive flights and cost of living. The Council offered BGU a "safety net" of six years to reach the break-even point.

The most recent addition to the list of institutions is the Jordan Valley College. Located at the southeast corner of the Sea of Galilee, this regional college is in the middle of the process of reaching independent status, away from the auspices of the parent institution, Bar-Ilan University. Similar to the approach of the defunct Eilat College, the leaders of Jordan Valley College are sure that a program in hospitality and tourism will be a panacea for demand problems. Consequently, they designated it as the first in a series of new independent programs. A proposal for a B.A. in Tourism and Hospitality Studies was submitted to the Council for Higher Education, with details on the content of the program, future faculty members, and budget requirements. Some of the future faculty graduated from tourism and hospitality programs at Israeli universities. The Jordan Valley program received permission for registration in June 2004. Final approval of the degree will be considered only toward the end of the first three years of operation.

INDUSTRY-ACADEMIA RELATIONS

One of the most disturbing issues concerning academic education in tourism and hospitality in Israel involves industry-academia relations. Four domains of industry-academia relations are discussed here: (1) input into the content of academic courses; (2) practical training (internship); (3) placement; and (4) organized cooperation.

Input into Courses

As early as the pioneering efforts of BGU in designing courses that demonstrated the right balance between global accumulation of academic knowledge and the unique needs of the local industry, industry experts and leaders were asked to comment on the developing programs and on specific syllabi. Even the Council for Higher Education included industry experts on some of its ad hoc accreditation committees. The cooperation was most visible when industry leaders came to give guest lectures in many courses. For example, the general manager of the Israel Travel Agents Association gave several lectures at BGU, Rehovot, and other schools about recent trends in the travel industry. Organizations that specialize in IT in tourism frequently give lectures in information technology courses, and hospitality experts contribute their share. In some cases, industry experts even taught complete courses in their areas of specialization, such as human resources management or forms of alliances and franchising in the hospitality segment.

Practical Training

The need for industry experience is a central concept in numerous tourism and hospitality management programs. For example, the planners of the BGU program realized that, in order to gain and maintain academic legitimacy, applied workshops could not offer academic credit.

The solution was to concentrate on academic courses on campus and require the students to spend 1,200 hours in supervised practical training or internships. The length and content of training was designed according to the 1,200-hour internship required for the Hotel Manager Certificate. Consequently, even students who specialize in tourism (as opposed to hospitality) were required to fulfill 1,200 hours in related ventures, as did those specializing in food and beverage management.

The program at Rehovot originally did not require internship. However, graduates as well as students of the program insisted that their position in market would be inferior without an internship. Consequently, the department added 600 hours of optional internship. No other academic programs advertise practical training requirements, except for the newly founded program at Jordan Valley College that requires approximately 500 hours.

Placement

One of the indicators of success of professional academic programs is the ability to place graduates in the industry. The relatively new academic development process has yet to demonstrate significant success. While no statistics are available, there are anecdotal reports that the hospitality industry is the slowest sector to recruit graduates of hospitality and tourism programs. Apparently, the academic development trend shook up the hospitality sector, and it has yet to fully adapt. For example, many student interns complain of a poor attitude from managers who do not have formal academic training. Moreover, while university graduates expect to get appropriate wages that reflect their status and investment, it seems that most hotels refuse to adjust wages. Some of the leaders of the hospitality industry have openly declared preference for graduates of technical or certificate programs due to their additional industry experience in comparison with university graduates. Additionally, it seems that many decision-makers, particularly in the hospitality segment, are bewildered and unable to distinguish between the different degree programs, as no attempts have been made to rank the various academic programs in terms of quality and orientation. Some of the university and college professors tend to explain the problematic attitude toward graduates as refusal to pay more to college graduates and as an apparent fear of the young and bright. The result is often mutual disappointment. However, some graduates are fully committed to the hospitality segment and are ready to conform to the traditional career paths, given the promise that advancement will be much quicker than it has been in the past. Unfortunately, some realized that this path requires years of meager income and had to look for other career options. Furthermore, the Intifada crisis caused some of the devoted young managers to leave their positions due to the LIFO (last in first out) principle.

In contrast, the travel sector turned out to be more welcoming to university graduates. The emerging need for highly computer-skilled travel advisors coincided with the influx of academic program graduates. In addition, the growing number of fast food chains increased the need for talented and educated managers. Young men and women joined local chains, such as Arcafe, or international chains, such as Pizza Hut. Clearly, the welcoming reception of university-educated employees in the travel and fast food industries compensated for the reserved attitude of the other segments of the hospitality industry.

Cooperation

Despite the mixed feeling of industry-academia relationships, there seems to be a climate of cooperation between the industry, academia, and the Israel Ministry of Tourism. Representatives of the tourism and hospitality industry often agree to participate along with academics in Ministry-sponsored committees and conferences. This type of cooperation is also demonstrated in academic conferences, or in the aforementioned guest lectures in various classes. Representatives of academic circles are invited to Knesset (parliament) committees to testify on various tourism issues. Moreover, academics are always invited to the annual meetings of the various organizations in the tourism industry. Industry representatives often volunteer to interview candidates as part of the admission process at BGU. Furthermore, several donations, as well as scholarships for outstanding students, were given to universities from industry leaders.

As of the summer of 2004, the future direction of tourism and hospitality management programs is unclear.

FUTURE CHALLENGES

As noted earlier, the relatively short history of tourism and hospitality higher education in Israel is characterized by numerous failed attempts. Yet, the states-supported institutions seem to overcome major hurdles and offer solid training and research. Clearly, the first phase of the introduction of tourism and hospitality higher education to traditional universities has ended successfully. The question remains whether the Council for Higher Education will support the development of graduate programs. Graduate programs will enable tourism researchers who are members of the Geography or The Study of the Land of Israel departments to be associated with graduate students who are specifically focused on tourism and hospitality whether in their own departments or in specially designed adjacent graduate studies units. This is in contrast to the current situation, where graduate work in tourism and hospitality is often conducted not as part of an official track but as one option among numerous other theses options. Moreover, graduate programs will train instructors for regional or private colleges.

A major challenge for the future concerns the industry-academe relationship. Without a conscious effort to absorb university graduates in the tourism and hospitality industry, tourism and hospitality programs will supply highly trained graduates to other service industries, such as banking, insurance, and telecommunications. The rationale for the existence of these programs will be rightly questioned. Clearly, both industry and academe will lose.

In spite of the four-year crisis of the tourism and hospitality segment in Israel, academic leaders and industry representatives should join force and ensure that present accomplishments will further survive and prosper.

REFERENCES

Fleischer, A., & Pizam, A. (1997). Rural tourism in Israel. *Tourism Management, 18*(6), 367-372.

Lerner, M., & Haber, S. (2001). Entrepreneurship in tourism: Performance factors of small tourism ventures: The interface of tourism entrepreneurship and the environment. *Journal of Business Venturing, 16*(1), 77-100.

Mansfeld, Y. (1999). Cycles of war, terror and peace: Determinants and management of crisis and recovery of the Israeli tourism industry. *Journal of Travel Research, 38*(1), 30-36.

Preble, J. F., Reichel, A. & Hoffman, R. C. (2000). Strategic alliances for competitive advantage: Evidence from Israel's hospitality and tourism industry. *International Journal of Hospitality Management, 19*(3), 327-341.

Reichel, A., & Milman, A. (1996). Selection of hospitality student candidates: Personal interviews vs. objective measures. *Hospitality and Tourism Educator, 8*(2-3), 76-79.

Reichel, A., & Amit, S. (2000). Human resource management in the Israeli hospitality industry. In S. M. Hoffman, C. Johnson, & N. M. Lefever (Eds.), *International hospitality human resource management*. Lansing, Michigan: American Hotel & Motel Association Publishing.

The Council for Higher Education in Israel. (2004). [On-line]. Available: *http://www. che.org.il/*

Yedioth Aharonoth (2004, August 27). An applied university education, p. 42.

Tourism Higher Education in Turkey

Fevzi Okumus
Ozcan Yagci

SUMMARY. This paper discusses and evaluates tourism higher education in Turkey. Turkish universities have been offering associate, bachelor, and postgraduate degree programs in tourism since the early 1990s. However, there have been major problems and challenges in this endeavor, including the lack of qualified academic staff, improperly designed curriculums, limited practical training opportunities for students, and difficulties in keeping qualified graduates in the industry. So far, it is hard to claim that Turkey has developed contemporary tourism higher education policies and plans. If Turkey is to gain more from tourism in the long term, it is essential for the country to improve the standards of tourism higher education. However, to achieve this, some radical cultural and structural reforms are needed, not

Fevzi Okumus is Associate Professor, School of Tourism and Hospitality Management, Mugla University, Mugla, Turkey (E-mail: okumusf@yahoo.com).

Ozcan Yagci is Assistant Professor, Vocational High School, Baskent University, Ankara, Turkey (E-mail: oyagci@baskent.edu.tr).

During the writing up stage of this paper, the first author worked as a Research Fellow at The Hong Kong Polytechnic University. He would very much like to thank this institution for providing him with excellent research facilities and support. The authors would also very much like to thank Professor Salih Kusluvan, from the School of Tourism and Hospitality Management, Erciyes University, Nevsehir, Turkey, for his constructive comments on the earlier versions of this paper. However, any interpretation or omissions are the sole responsibility of the authors.

[Haworth co-indexing entry note]: "Tourism Higher Education in Turkey." Okumus, Fevzi, and Ozcan Yagci. Co-published simultaneously in *Journal of Teaching in Travel & Tourism* (The Haworth Press, Inc.) Vol. 5, No. 1/2, 2005, pp. 89-116; and: *Global Tourism Higher Education: Past, Present, and Future* (ed: Cathy H. C. Hsu) The Haworth Press, Inc., 2005, pp. 89-116. Single or multiple copies of this article are available for a fee from The Haworth Document Delivery Service [1-800-HAWORTH, 9:00 a.m. - 5:00 p.m. (EST). E-mail address: docdelivery@haworthpress.com].

only in tourism higher education, but also in the country's overall higher education system. *[Article copies available for a fee from The Haworth Document Delivery Service: 1-800-HAWORTH. E-mail address: <docdelivery@haworthpress. com> Website: <http://www.HaworthPress.com> © 2005 by The Haworth Press, Inc. All rights reserved.]*

KEYWORDS. Tourism, education, training, Turkey

INTRODUCTION

There have been a substantial number of studies on the development of higher education in the tourism and hospitality field (Amoah & Baum, 1997; Barrows & Bosselman, 1999; Christou, 1999; Cooper, Scales, & Westlake, 1992; Dale & Robinson, 2001; King, 1994; Knowles, Teixeira, & Egan, 2003; Sigala & Baum, 2003). However, as stated by Echtner (1995), King (1994), and Theuns and Rasheed (1991), very few studies provide information and critical discussions on tourism and hospitality higher education in developing countries. As tourism plays an important role in the socio-cultural and economic life of many developing countries (Harrison, 2001; World Tourism Organization, 2002), tourism education at all levels plays a key role in securing and maintaining sustainable tourism development. For example, as a developing country, Turkey has become one of the leading tourism destinations over the last two decades. However, studies on tourism development in Turkey often refer to lack of qualified manpower and poor service quality as one of the tourism industry's main problems (Okumus & Kilic, 2004; Tosun, 2001). It is therefore recommended that, in order for Turkey to improve its competitive advantage, the country needs to invest in tourism education.

There have been very few studies in the international tourism literature on tourism higher education in Turkey (e.g., Brotherton, Woolfenden, & Himmetoglu, 1994; Korzay, 1987). Given the paucity of knowledge in this area, the purpose of this paper is to discuss and evaluate tourism higher education in Turkey. Some background information is first provided on the development of tourism in Turkey. The historical development of tourism higher education in the country is then evaluated. Next, the current status, structure, and trends in tourism education are discussed. The paper also discusses future developments in tourism higher education. Finally, it provides a number of conclusions and recommendations. It is believed that the findings and emerging issues discussed in the paper will be useful and relevant to other developing countries.

TOURISM DEVELOPMENT IN TURKEY

As illustrated in Table 1, Turkey has experienced rapid growth in tourism since the early 1980s. In 1982, a special law (number 2,634) was enacted to encourage the development of tourism, with the aim of ensuring that the necessary arrangements were in place to regulate and develop a dynamic structure for the tourism sector. Between 1985 and 1990, investors received US$422 million worth of cash incentives and US$1.1 billion medium- and long-term bank credits. They also used their own resources, valued at US$1.5 billion, and most of these resources were invested in the hotel industry (Turkish Tourism Investors Association, 1992).

There are 2,124 hotels with operating licenses and 1,138 with investment licenses, corresponding to 396,148 and 222,876 beds, respectively (Association of Travel Agencies, 2004). Many of the hotels with an in-

TABLE 1. Key Statistics on Turkish Tourism in Selected Years Since 1980

Years	Investment Licensed Bed Capacity	Licensed Bed Capacity	Hotels Registered by Municipalities	Inbound Tourism (,000)	Tourism Receipts (,000,000 US$)	Share of Tourism Receipts in GNP (%)
2003	242,603	420,697	399,369	14,030	9,677	5.5
2002	222,876	396,148	408,005	13,247	8,481	6.6
2001	230,248	364,779	335,825	11,569	8,090	6.9
2000	243,794	325,168	344,736	10,412	7,636	3.8
1999	245,543	319,313	n.a.	7,464	5,203	2.8
1998	249,125	314,215	n.a.	9,752	7,808	3.8
1997	236,632	313,298	n.a.	9,689	8,088	4.2
1996	202,631	301,524	n.a.	8,614	5,962	3.2
1995	202,483	286,463	n.a.	7,726	4,957	2.9
1990	325,515	173,227	n.a.	5,389	3,225	2.1
1985	71,521	85,995	n.a.	2,614	1,482	2.8
1980	26,288	56,044	n.a.	1,288	326	0.6

Source: Adapted from the Ministry of Tourism (2005), Association of Travel Agencies in Turkey (2004), and State Institute of Statistics (2004).

vestment license are under construction or have just started operating. In addition, there are 7,637 hotels registered by the municipalities, corresponding to 399,369 beds (Ministry of Tourism, 2005). In 2003, the annual occupancy rate for licensed hotels was around 47% and about 14 million tourists visited Turkey, particularly from Germany, Britain, Russia, and Holland. It is estimated that about 15 million Turkish people also participate in domestic tourism. The tourism industry contributed around US$9.7 billion to Turkey's GNP in 2003, and it is estimated that over 2 million people are employed in the industry (Association of Travel Agencies, 2004).

The growth of the tourism industry has not been supported with sound strategies and strategic plans (Okumus & Kilic, 2004; Tosun & Timothy, 2001). Tourism in Turkey has been facing serious problems for many years, including seasonality, low hotel occupancy rates, a high dependency on tour operators, transportation difficulties, inadequate infrastructure, poor service quality, a lack of qualified staff, a lack of sound marketing programs, a high percentage of lower-income tourists, and the effects of national and global crises (Okumus & Kilic, 2004; Tosun, 2001). All of these problems are significant, but the high dependence on tour operators, the effects of crises on the industry, poor service quality, and a lack of qualified staff are particularly problematic. Over the years, there have been some attempts to overcome poor service quality and the lack of qualified staff by developing sound strategies in tourism education, particularly at the tertiary level. The following discussion will examine the historical development of tourism higher education in Turkey. Before examining the various issues in depth, however, it is imperative to provide a brief overview of higher education in Turkey.

A BRIEF OVERVIEW OF HIGHER EDUCATION IN TURKEY

Since the foundation of the Republic of Turkey in 1923, the country's higher education system has undergone rapid growth. For example, for the last 80 years, the number of universities increased from 1 to 77. The development and structure of Turkish higher education reflects a combination of European and North American university traditions. However, the latter has been more influential in the last two decades. There are currently 24 private (foundation) universities, 51 state universities, and two state advanced technology institutes (YOK, 2004a). Each university consists of:

1. Graduate Schools,
2. Faculties,
3. Four-Year High Schools, and
4. Two-Year Vocational High Schools.

Graduate schools (called social science or science institutions) offer doctoral and master's degrees. Faculties and four-year high schools offer degree programs, and two-year vocational high schools offer associate degrees. Anadolu University also offers two- and four-year programs through distance education. A semester-based system is followed, with each semester consisting of 14 weeks of teaching and one or two weeks for final exams. Some universities offer summer schools that include seven weeks of intensive teaching and one or two weeks for exams.

The supreme authority for the regulation of higher education is the Council of Higher Education (YÖK), which comprises a fully autonomous national board of trustees. There are three other upper administrative bodies in the field of higher education: the Interuniversity Council (UAK), the Turkish University Rectors' Committee (TURC), and the Higher Education Supervisory Board. The Turkish higher education system has a centralized structure. All universities (both state and private, or in a true sense, foundation universities) are subject to the same laws and regulations/rules. The universities are founded by law; and their affiliated faculties, institutes, and four-year vocational/professional high schools are founded by a decision of the Parliament; while the two-year vocational high schools and the departments affiliated to the universities are established by YÖK. The opening of a program at any level needs to be approved by YÖK. Since the foundation of YÖK in 1981, there has been much debate over the reform of higher education in Turkey. However, despite widespread agreement on the issue across the country and repeated promises from all political parties and new governments, attempts at reform have so far failed, since the reform of the higher education system is regarded as a very sensitive political issue.

In the 2002-2003 academic year, about 1.8 million students were registered in bachelor and associate degree programs. About 662,000 of them were enrolled in Anadolu University's distance education programs and about 280,000 of them were enrolled in second education (i.e., night education) programs at different universities. In addition to the above figures, it is estimated that about 100,000 students are enrolled in postgraduate programs (YOK, 2004a). There is fierce competition to study at the university level in Turkey. Every year, over 1.5 million students compete to obtain a place at the tertiary level, but only

200,000 of them are admitted. The first 10% of the places offered are at the top universities in the most preferred fields, such as electronics engineering, computing, and medicine. Since the early 1990s, in order to meet the very high demand for higher education, universities have started enrolling students in associate and bachelor degree programs into second education classes, also called night education, as students attend such classes between 5 p.m. and 11 p.m.

DEVELOPMENT OF TOURISM HIGHER EDUCATION IN TURKEY

At the higher education level, the first formal program on tourism was offered in 1965 when the Commerce Teachers School in Ankara was renamed the "Commerce and Tourism Teachers School." The main aim of the school was to provide teachers for secondary-level commerce and tourism schools. In 1982, when the Gazi University was founded, this school was renamed the Commerce and Tourism Education Faculty. Starting from the late 1960s and early 1970s other universities, such as Ege, Bogazici, Uludag, and Hacettepe, began offering associate degree programs in tourism at their vocational high schools. Except for the program at Hacettepe University, these programs were later upgraded to four-year degree programs, and each university created a School of Tourism and Hotel Management. Cukurova University and Erciyes University also began offering degree programs in tourism in the early 1980s.

At the postgraduate level, the first master's program in tourism was offered in 1969 at Istanbul University's Institute of Economics, Geography, and Tourism; and the first doctoral programs were offered at Bogazici and Ege Universities in 1975-1976 (Boylu, 2002). In 1982, further to forming Dokuz Eylul University, tourism programs in Ege University were transferred to this new university. Starting from the early 1980s, Gazi and Dokuz Eylul Universities have played key roles in postgraduate tourism education. In particular, Emeritus Professor Dr. Hasan Olali from Dokuz Eylul University and his doctoral students greatly contributed to Turkish tourism higher education and the national tourism literature, although their writings were generally conceptual work on tourism economics, planning, and marketing.

Starting from the early 1980s, the tourism industry has rapidly developed in Turkey. A shortage of qualified staff for lower, middle, and senior positions in tourism organizations emerged. This led to a further increase in demand for degree programs in the field. Coinciding with this trend, 25 state and 21 private universities were founded between 1992 and 2004 to further expand higher education. Most of these new universities, as well as the existing ones, started offering programs ranging from associate to bachelor and postgraduate degree programs in tourism and hospitality management. Along with some positive and promising outcomes, the opening of so many programs has resulted in a number of problems and challenges. The following section will examine the current structure, characteristics, and trends in tourism higher education in Turkey.

THE CURRENT STRUCTURE, CHARACTERISTICS, AND TRENDS

There are three different types of programs for tourism higher education in Turkey: pre-degree (associate), bachelor, and postgraduate programs. Table 2 provides some statistical data on the number of students studying tourism higher education in Turkey. Although important similarities exist among them in terms of problems and challenges, there are also differences in how they are managed and structured. Therefore, it is worthwhile to separately examine their structure, characteristics, and problems.

Associate Degree Programs

Two-year associate degree programs aim to provide graduates for lower and middle management level positions in tourism and hospital-

TABLE 2. Students in Tourism Higher Education for the Academic Year 2003-2004

Program	New Admissions			Total Number of Students			2002-2003 Graduates		
	Total	Female	Male	Total	Female	Male	Total	Female	Male
Pre-degree	6,245	2,718	3,527	19,140	7,584	11,556	5,217	1,975	3,242
Degree	1,949	682	1,267	3,908	1,478	2,430	968	403	565
Master's	124	53	71	270	121	149	47	22	25
Doctorate	20	8	12	54	23	31	9	2	7

Derived from: ÖSYM (2004b), *The 2003-2004 Academic Year Higher Education Statistics*, Ankara: ÖSYM Publications, No: 2004-3.

ity organizations. They are placed under two-year vocational high schools at universities. As presented in Table 3, in the 2003-2004 academic year, there are 132 associate degree programs related to tourism, travel, hospitality, and catering areas being offered by 53 universities. In addition, 42 of the above programs offer night education, from 5 p.m. to 11 p.m. As can be seen from Table 3, some programs specialize in certain areas, such as transportation administration and tour guiding, but most of the associate degree programs have a broad and general focus on tourism and hotel management. Some universities offer not only different types of associate degree programs such as tourism and travel management or tourism and hotel management, but also programs at different vocational high schools at their various campuses. A pre-degree (On-Lisans Diplomasi) is awarded after the successful completion of a two-year period of study that normally lasts four semesters. Through its Student Selection and Placement Center (ÖSYM), the Council of Higher Education organizes annual exams and, based on the results, around 10% of the students completing their associate degrees at vocational high schools are allowed to continue their studies at the four-year degree level.

Despite some positive outcomes, there have been some serious problems and difficulties in running these associate degree programs at universities in Turkey (Aymankuy, 2002; Boylu, 2002; Ergin & Yagci, 2003; Kizilirmak, 2000; Okumus, 2003; State Planning Organization,

TABLE 3. Types and Numbers of Pre-Degree Programs Offered at Universities

Type and Title of the Program	Number
Tourism and Hotel Management	94
Tourism and Travel Management	13
Tour Guiding	15
Catering	3
Air Transportation Administration	1
Supportive Services in Transportation	6
Total	132

Derived from ÖSYM (2004), 2004 Ögrenci Seçme ve Yerleştirme Sistemi Yükskögretim Programlari ve Kontenjanlari Klavuzu, ÖSYM, Ankara.

2001; YÖK, 2004b). These problems and difficulties are closely inter-related and can be grouped under several areas as below:

1. locations of the vocational high schools;
2. lack of qualified teaching staff;
3. their management structure;
4. lack of, or insufficiency of, the training, equipment, and facilities;
5. curriculum-related problems;
6. characteristics and qualifications of new students;
7. problems related to industrial placements; and
8. the difficulty of keeping graduates in the industry.

Each of the above problems is briefly discussed below.

Location

Most of the associate degree programs were opened since the early 1990s without any feasibility studies or strategic planning in terms of questioning the appropriateness of the location of the schools and the availability of human and financial resources (Aymankuy, 2002; Ministry of Tourism, 2002). A very high number of the vocational high schools that offer these programs are based in remote towns in rural areas of the country. Therefore, students studying tourism and hospitality actually graduate without encountering many tourism and hospitality organizations and domestic and international tourists. In short, because of their location, the instructors and the students often face difficulties in establishing contacts and long-term working relationships with tourism organizations (Okumus, 2003).

Lack of Qualified Teaching Staff

The lack of qualified teaching staff has been a particularly serious problem at vocational high schools. Some of the first graduates of four-year tourism and hotel schools and graduates of master's programs in the tourism field have filled some of these teaching positions. However, it is also widely known that many of the teaching staff at these tourism-related programs have neither formal education in tourism nor working experience in the industry (Ergin & Yagci, 2003). The question of why and how they were recruited remains to be answered. The lack of qualified staff in these programs has had a negative impact on the teaching of practical and hands-on subjects (Ministry of Tourism, 2002).

Management Structure

In addition to offering tourism-related programs, most vocational high schools deliver other two-year associate degree programs in accounting, computing, electronics and others. As there have been very few tourism academics with PhD degrees at the assistant professor level or above in the country, the heads of these vocational high schools, and also the director of each tourism program, often come from other disciplines. In other words, most of the associate programs in tourism-related areas are run and managed by those who are not really experts in tourism. They often see tourism as an easy field and are unaware of the need for special teaching and training in tourism and hospitality. This has often created major problems in the design of curricula, understanding of tourism students, and building relationships with the industry (Okumus, 2003).

Insufficient Facilities and Equipment

When many universities decided to offer associate degree programs in tourism and hospitality, the requirements for training facilities and equipment were often ignored or underestimated (Aymankuy, 2002; Ergin & Yagci, 2003). The main teaching method at these two-year pre-degree programs is still pure lectures. It is often the case that subjects on the front office, housekeeping, food production, and food and beverage management are taught without any, or with very limited, practical hands-on training, due to a lack of equipment and facilities (Okumus, 2003). Some efforts have been made to remedy the situation. As reported by Brotherton et al. (1994), between 1985 and 1997, a project financially supported by the World Bank was carried out to improve learning and teaching facilities at 31 vocational high schools in Turkey. In 2002, the State Planning Office initiated another project that supported another 26 vocational high schools (YÖK, 2004b). Overall, such projects have partially improved the teaching and learning facilities and equipment in some programs. However, the majority of these programs still face difficulties in providing good training facilities and equipment (Aymankuy, 2002; Ergin & Yagci, 2003).

Curricula

Prior to 2001, criticisms had been raised about the curricula used in associate degree programs. For example, there were radical differences in the curricula of tourism and hospitality programs, and it was often argued that they failed to develop students' skills, knowledge, and attitudes required by the industry. In order to overcome this, the National Ministry of Education and the Council of Higher Education (YÖK) initiated and implemented a joint project in 2001 to standardize the curriculum in all two-year associate degree programs at vocational high schools across the country. As presented in Table 4, according to this new curriculum (for both tourism and travel management and tourism and hotel management programs) students needed to study over 30 subjects and obtain more than 100 credits. After the first two semesters, they were also required to have industrial placements of between 45 and 60 working days in tourism organizations.

However, after three years of implementation (in the 2003-2004 academic year), the new curriculum for tourism-related programs still receives criticisms as it falls short in helping students gain and develop the required skills, attitudes, and knowledge. The new curriculum also fails to recognize regional differences, ignores some important subjects, and puts too much focus on some simple areas (Ergin & Yagci, 2003). In addition, although these programs aim to train students for lower and middle managerial positions, some of the subjects included in the new curriculum–such as tourism economics, special interest tourism, and hospitality accounting–may not be very essential to achieving this aim.

Characteristics of Newly Enrolled Students

Students who enroll in associate degree programs in tourism can be categorized into two groups. The distinct differences between these two groups have led to challenges and problems in teaching and training. The first group come from the three-year secondary vocational hotel and tourism schools. After 11 years of compulsory primary education, students can study tourism and hotel operations for three years in these schools. During this time, they not only develop a good knowledge of the industry but also work in tourism organizations as interns. On the other hand, during their three-year secondary education and training, they do not study main subjects in-depth, such as mathematics, biology, chemistry, and literature; therefore, their chances of getting a place in the national university qualifying exam for other programs are very

TABLE 4. A Sample of the Curriculum Followed in Associate Degree Programs in Tourism and Hotel Management

Course Name	Course Category	Credit
Semester 1		
Turkish Language–I	Compulsory	2
Principles of Ataturk and the History of the Turkish Revolution I	Compulsory	2
English Language–I	Compulsory	4
Computer–I	Compulsory	3
Tourism Economics	Compulsory	2
Principals of Nutrition and Menu Planning	Compulsory	3
Usage and Control of Cleaning Materials	Compulsory	3
Front Office Operations	Compulsory	2
Communication	Compulsory	2
Commercial Mathematics	Compulsory	2
Food Technology	Compulsory	2
Physical Education, Music or Art	Elective	-
Semester 2		
Turkish Language–II	Compulsory	2
Principles of Ataturk and the History of the Turkish Revolution–II	Compulsory	2
English Language–II	Compulsory	4
Computer–II	Compulsory	3
General Accounting	Compulsory	2
Hotel Management	Compulsory	2
Kitchen Services Management	Compulsory	3
Front Office Management	Compulsory	3
Food and Beverage Services Management	Compulsory	3
Cleaning Services Management	Compulsory	3
Physical Education, Music or Art II	Elective	-
Semester 3		
Tourism Marketing	Compulsory	3
Congress and Fair Management	Compulsory	3
Cost Analysis in the Tourism Business	Compulsory	3
Tourism Law	Compulsory	2
Travel Agencies	Compulsory	2
Food and Personnel Hygiene	Compulsory	2
Tourism English–I	Compulsory	3
Front Office-Housekeeping Automation–I	Elective	3
Special Interest Tourism	Elective	2
Protocol Rules	Elective	2

Course Name	Course Category	Credit
Semester 4		
Field: Front Office-House Keeping Department		
Rooms Division Management	Compulsory	3
Housekeeping Management	Compulsory	3
Front Office-Housekeeping Automation–I	Compulsory	3
Furniture and Room Design	Compulsory	3
Tourism English–II	Compulsory	3
Entrepreneurship	Elective	2
Ethics in the Tourism Businesses	Elective	2
Human Resources Management	Elective	2
Accommodation Business Accounting	Elective	2
Field: Food-Beverage and Kitchen Department		
Food and Beverage Cost Control	Compulsory	3
Food and Beverage Management	Compulsory	3
Industrial Food Production	Compulsory	3
Food and Beverage Automation–I	Compulsory	3
Tourism English–II	Compulsory	3
Entrepreneurship	Elective	2
Ethics in the Tourism Businesses	Elective	2
Human Resources Management	Elective	2
Accommodation Establishments Accounting	Elective	2

Students need to complete a minimum of 102 credits.
Source: http://www.myo.eunev.edu.tr/bilgipaketi/index_uk.php?dosya=paket/uk/bolumler.htm

low. When they begin their associate degrees in tourism, on top of their practical skills and knowledge, they want to develop further skills and knowledge in managing tourism and hospitality organizations. However, these students often complain that teaching and learning practices at the associate degree level are a repetition of what they learned at the secondary vocational hotel and tourism schools.

The second group of students who come to the associate degree programs in tourism are those from regular three-year secondary schools. As stated by Kizilirmak (2000), it is known that tourism programs are not among students' top choices, but some of them could not get a place in other fields because of their grades. Their overall scores for secondary education are below average and they are less committed and ambitious than many other students. Before enrolling into the associate degree programs in tourism, they do not often have a clear knowledge about the tourism industry and their career prospects in the long term. Compared to the first group, they not only need to develop their skills and knowledge in managing tourism organizations, but also need to develop some hands-on skills in functional areas. When they start studying tourism and also get their first taste of working in the industry, they are often disappointed and become less keen on working in the industry (Okumus, 2003).

Industrial Placements

Students studying tourism in associate degree programs are required to spend 45 to 60 working days in tourism organizations as part of their formal training. This needs to be undertaken after the first two semesters. The students can find their industrial placement organizations by themselves or, alternatively, vocational high schools can help them find appropriate tourism organizations. However, several problems concerning this issue have been reported (Ergin & Yagci, 2003; Okumus, 2003). First, as stated earlier, many vocational high schools are based in areas far from the main tourism destinations, and often face difficulties in building relationships with appropriate tourism organizations for their students' industrial placements.

Second, the tourism peak season in Turkey starts in early May and ends in September. Therefore, tourism organizations prefer to employ staff during this period. However, the academic year at universities normally begins in mid-September and ends in late June. Universities have tried to overcome this problem by allowing some intensive teaching and training in their tourism programs, and shortening the winter break. However, such arrangements are difficult and tend to create further administrative and bureaucratic challenges for both students and the teaching and administrative staff. Another problem with industrial placements is that the tourism organizations that recruit students often regard them as cheap labor and expect them to work long hours. Students are not prepared for this, which disappoints both parties. Finally, due to resource limitations, it is often difficult for the instructors to visit the students during their internships in tourism organizations.

Difficulty of Keeping Graduates in the Industry

Although the Turkish tourism industry has developed rapidly and employs approximately 2 million people nationwide, research studies indicate that students who graduate from tourism programs at universities often leave the industry for a number of reasons (Yagci, 2001). As stated above, most of the students choose tourism programs without having any clear understanding of the working conditions and career paths in the industry. Again, when they start their internships or begin working as full-time employees, tourism organizations do not always treat them well or pay good salaries. In other words, poor working conditions do not help to keep graduates in the industry. However, such working conditions in the industry are not unique to Turkey's tourism industry. It is often stated as a common problem in the tourism industry worldwide (Kusluvan, 2003).

A further reason for not being able to keep tourism graduates in the industry is that, for the last ten years, there have been several severe economic, political, and ecological crises in and around Turkey. Whenever there was a crisis and a decline in inbound tourism, tourism firms often reacted with cost-cutting measures, which usually meant reducing the number of staff. The industry representatives also often claim that graduates from tourism programs lack essential practical skills, language skills, and a positive attitude (Ministry of Tourism, 1994). Because of the above reasons, it is estimated that more than half of the graduates from tourism programs do not work in the industry after they graduate from associate degree tourism programs.

Four-Year Degree Programs

According to the Student Selection and Placement Center (ÖSYM), 25 universities (16 state and 9 private) offer four-year degree programs in tourism-related areas (ÖSYM, 2004a). Baskent University offers two separate degree programs in tourism: one in its Faculty of Economics and Business Administration and the other in its Applied Sciences High School. Thus, there are a total of 26 four-year degree programs. In addition to Baskent University, Dokuz Eylul and Sakarya universities offer four-year degree programs in their economics and business administration faculties. Gazi University offers a four-year degree program in its Commerce and Tourism Education Faculty. The remaining programs are offered at independent tourism and hospitality high schools. According to ÖSYM (2004a), six of the above institutions offer night education, between 5 p.m. and 11 p.m.

The overall aim of these four-year degree programs has been to provide graduates for the middle and senior management level positions in tourism organizations. A degree (Lisans Diplomasi) is awarded after the successful completion of a four-year period of study that normally lasts eight semesters. Although there are variations among the programs, students need to study over 50 subjects and obtain over 150 credits to graduate. Compared to tourism and hotel schools in the U.S., U.K. and Australia (Hobson, 1999), the students have to study more subjects and earn more credits. Although there may be differences between schools over the duration of a student's industrial placement, it is normally between 60 to 90 working days.

According to ÖSYM (2004b), around 4,000 students were enrolled in these four-year tourism degree programs in the academic year 2003-2004. In terms of the location of these faculties and high schools, with a few exceptions, most are based either in main destinations, such as Antalya, Mugla, Aydin, and Nevsehir, or in big cities like Istanbul, Ankara, and Izmir. Their location helps them develop and maintain good connections and working relationships with tourism organizations in their region and in neighboring regions. The most established tourism programs are at Adnan Menderes, Akdeniz, Balikesir, Bilkent, Dokuz Eylul, Erciyes, Gazi, and Mersin universities. Most of the remaining programs opened over the last ten years and are still in the development stage. Although it is difficult to generalize, these four-year degree programs have also been facing some major difficulties and challenges (Ministry of Tourism, 2002; Timur, 1992). In many ways, their problems are similar to the problems of associate degree programs at vocational high schools, though their difficuties are perhaps less severe compared to associate degree programs (Okumus, 2003).

Similar to associate degree programs, the lack of qualified teaching staff has been a major problem for four-year degree programs in tourism. In the early days, due to a lack of qualified academics in the field, some academics from other disciplines, particularly from economics, management, geography, education, and linguistics moved into the tourism field and occupied key positions. Cooper et al. (1992) also reported similar findings from the academic background of tourism and hospitality educators in the UK. This trend has a great impact on the curricula of both degree and postgraduate programs in tourism. Nevertheless, over the years, graduates of undergraduate and postgraduate programs in tourism have gradually filled some of these academic positions. Compared to associate degree programs in vocational high schools, four-year degree programs have better quality teaching staff.

In terms of management structure, most of these four-year degree programs are offered by independent tourism and hospitality high schools. In the early days, the heads of these schools were academics from other fields. Although this is still the case for many schools, in recent years there has been a gradual transition in the management of such schools from academics outside the field to home-grown tourism academics who completed their undergraduate and postgraduate degrees in tourism and hospitality. It is believed that this transition will continue and its positive impact on the curriculum and other areas will be seen in the future.

When designing a four-year degree program in tourism in the early days, the curriculum of degree programs in economics and management at faculties of economics and business administration were often benchmarked by adding some tourism-related subjects. Korzay (1986) also made similar comments in her earlier work on tourism education in Turkey. For the last two decades, when designing a curriculum for new degree programs, the existing curricula of four-year tourism and hotel schools have often been benchmarked and modified. However, it is still argued by industry members and academics that the curricula followed in these programs fall far short of providing their graduates with the required skills, attitudes, and knowledge (Ministry of Tourism, 2002; Okumus, 2003).

There have been on-going debates and discussions among academics as well as between academics and industry members on how the curriculum of degree programs in tourism can be improved. In recent years, some tourism and hospitality schools have revised their curriculum and started offering specialized degrees. For example, among the 26 programs mentioned earlier (OSYM, 2004a), 13 are four-year degree programs in tourism and hospitality management, while the other half are specialized degree programs in travel (agency) management, hotel management, or tour guiding. However, even if they offer specialized degrees, it is still too early to claim that such specialization has been achieved.

In terms of training facilities and equipment, there are major differences between the programs. Some universities, such as Bilkent University, have good facilities, while some new universities (such as Abant Izzet Baysal, Mugla, and Mustafa Kemal) still do not have sufficient teaching facilities.

At some universities, such as Bilkent, Bogazici and Yeditepe, the medium of instruction is English; while at others it is Turkish, although students are expected to learn one foreign language (mainly English) well and study another language. On the other hand, in some universities, such as Mugla and Mustafa Kemal, the medium is both Turkish and English as some subjects are taught in Turkish and some tourism and hospitality management subjects are taught in English. However, finding academics that can teach in English has been a major challenge. At universities where the medium of instruction is English, students are required to provide a language certificate or pass a university-based language qualification exam. For those students whose level of English is not satisfactory, there are one-year English preparation classes at universities. Despite the importance of language for students in tourism, many students have graduated from universities with poor foreign language skills.

Similar to the associate degree programs in tourism, students who enroll in four-year tourism programs can be categorized into two groups. Those in the first group either come from secondary level three-year vocational tourism and hotel schools, or two-year associate degree programs in tourism. Those in the second group have graduated from regular three-year high schools. Differences between these two groups create difficulties in teaching and learning. It is also known that many graduates of four-year degree programs in tourism leave the industry after their graduation. Their reasons are similar to those of associate degree graduates from tourism programs. The complaint raised by both the graduates and industry members are that such graduates are not distinctly different in practical skills, knowledge, and attitude from graduates of associate degree programs and the secondary level three-year vocational hotel and tourism schools (Kusluvan & Kusluvan, 2000). Some industry members prefer employing graduates from the latter two institutions, or even untrained people. They claim that graduates from tourism schools not only lack the required skills and knowledge in service delivery, foreign languages, and communication skills with customers, but also are not keen to work long hours, and only prefer working in higher positions (Okumus, 2003; State Planning Organization, 2001).

Postgraduate Programs

The Council of Higher Education (YÖK) has established certain rules and regulations for opening and running master's and doctoral programs. For example, university graduates need to obtain a minimum grade in the Postgraduate Education Examination (LES) if they want to study at the postgraduate level. It is also essential for them to have a minimum grade in the Inter-Universities Language Exam (UDS) to prove that apart from Turkish, they are also proficient in a foreign language, mainly English. Universities that offer master's and doctoral programs advertise their quotas for each program annually, usually in August or September. Interested university graduates can apply to enter these programs on the basis of their LES and UDS exam results, as well as their degree grades for master's programs and master's grades for doctoral programs. Further to their application, they may further need to take a university-based written and/or oral qualifying exam.

For the 2003-2004 academic year, 17 universities offered master's programs in tourism-related areas. The aim of these programs was to provide graduates for middle and senior management positions in public and private tourism organizations. There are two types of master's programs: those requiring a dissertation and those not requiring a dissertation. The first program requires a minimum of seven subjects, a seminar, and a dissertation, for a minimum of 21 credits. Generally, the seminar and the dissertation are non-credit bearing and are graded on a pass/fail basis. The aim of these programs is to develop both senior managers for tourism organizations and academics for tourism programs. A master's degree (Yuksek Lisans Diplomasi) is awarded after the successful completion of a two-year period of study. The second type of master's program consists of a minimum of 10 subjects and a non-credit bearing semester project, with a minimum of 30 credits. The semester project is graded on a pass/fail basis. The duration of this type of program is normally one-and-a-half years.

For the 2003-2004 academic year, five universities offered doctoral programs in tourism. These programs consist of a minimum of seven subjects for a minimum of 21 credits, a qualifying exam, a dissertation proposal, and a dissertation. The doctoral programs are normally three to four years in duration. An external examiner from another university is invited to judge the qualifying exam and also the defense of the doctoral dissertation (YOK, 2004a).

Based on history and academic staff, the most well established master's and doctoral programs in tourism are at Dokuz Eylul and Gazi universities, set up in the late 1980s. Most of the remaining master's and doctoral programs have only been set up in the past few years. Looking at the curricula of these programs, as well as the academic staff in each program, a number of issues emerge. First, in some postgraduate programs, only a few of the teaching staff are at the level of assistant professor or above. As only those academics with a doctoral degree can teach in these programs, this means that the majority of the subjects are taught by a few members of the academic staff. In addition, it is known that some of these academics are not very active in conducting research and publishing. Some of the universities that offer master or doctoral programs do not have an undergraduate program in tourism. Mainly academics from areas, such as business, finance, marketing, and economics, teach tourism-related subjects. Finally, compared to U.S., U.K., and other Western countries, master's and doctoral dissertations in Turkey tend to focus on macro areas of tourism, such as tourism planning, tourism economics, and tourism marketing, although in recent years the focus has gradually moved to tourism organizations and their management practices.

DISCUSSION ON FUTURE DEVELOPMENT

Tourism plays an important part in the economic and socio-cultural life of Turkey. According to WTO (2003), Turkey will be among the top 10 tourism destinations worldwide by 2020. It is estimated that Turkey will receive 60 million inbound tourists and generate over US$30 billion annually from tourism. It is also estimated that the bed capacity will double from 1 million to 2 million by 2020. Given this promising future, at least another two million people will be employed in the tourism industry in Turkey. In order to improve the service quality and competitive edge of the country, and maintain the sustainable development of tourism, it is essential to develop a strategic tourism education plan that will be part of the country's long-term tourism planning and national education strategies. Based on the above explanations and discussion, several interrelated key themes emerged in relation to the future development of tourism higher education in the country. These are briefly discussed below.

Revision of Curricula

Despite some positive improvements in recent years, there is still major dissatisfaction with the curricula of associate, bachelor, and postgraduate degree programs in tourism (Okumus, 2003). The reason for this is that most tourism programs still award only generic tourism degrees (Dale & Robinson, 2001). Moving from generic tourism degrees to specialized and functional degrees is a challenging task that not only requires better teaching staff and more resources but also changes in the mindset of academics in the tourism field. It is also essential to develop a strategy for higher education in tourism that clearly defines the missions and objectives of associate, bachelor, and postgraduate programs and the distinctive aspects of each level of education.

Biggs (2003) stated that there should be constructive alignment in university level teaching. This would involve aligning the overall aims of a program with the curriculum and teaching and assessment methods. It is known that most of the tourism programs in Turkey do not have clearly defined program aims and intended outcomes. There is little justification for why certain subjects are included (or not included) in each program. Moreover, the main teaching method is the lecture with limited discussion, and the main assessment method is written exams that often force students to memorize facts and theories rather than to achieve deeper learning by applying, synthesizing, and evaluating theories and issues. Changes in the above areas should be discussed and agreed upon by all key stakeholders, including the government, the council of higher education, universities, industry partners, and students. Then, following Biggs' (2003) constructive alignment principle, program objectives can be identified by considering the types of skills, knowledge, and experience that tourism students should have at each stage. Further to this, the overall missions and objectives, curricula, as well as the teaching and assessment methods for associate, bachelor, and postgraduate degrees, should be revised as part of an ongoing process. Finally, a move from a teacher-oriented approach to a student-oriented learning strategy is essential.

Certifying Academic Staff

As discussed earlier, finding qualified and experienced teaching staff has been a challenge for associate, bachelor, and postgraduate programs in tourism higher education. Apart from programs at Gazi University, master's and doctoral programs in tourism do not require students to take any subject on teaching and learning during their studies. It is also worth noting that teaching staff at Turkish universities are not asked to provide any formal teaching certificates as part of the recruitment process or required to attend any courses on teacher training at the higher education level after they have been hired. Promotion to the positions of assistant, associate, and full professor is mainly based on research output. Good teaching skills and records are required, but not seen as a primary requirement for promotion. It would be beneficial for all parties if all teaching staff at tourism programs were to be certified as effective at delivering teaching and training activities. Such training workshops can focus on developing program objectives, intended subject outcomes, and syllabi, and on selecting teaching and assessment methods. These training workshops can discuss not only the importance of student-centered teaching and learning strategies, but also how to apply such approaches in tourism schools.

Auditing and Certifying Tourism Programs

There is no system of accreditation in Turkish higher education, only official recognition. In the 2003-2004 academic year, the "Regulations on Academic Assessment and Quality Control" in higher education was initiated by the Inter-University Board. The regulations state that all higher education degree programmes need to be evaluated. The aim is to obtain a transparent result, which should be posted on the web site of the university. This initiative is still relatively new, and if implemented successfully, the auditing of all associate, bachelor, and postgraduate programs in tourism would certainly indicate problematic areas and result in the elimination of weak ones in the long term. In the process of Turkey joining the European Union, the National Ministry of Education and the Council of Higher Education have started initiatives and projects to integrate the Turkish higher education system with that of the European Union in the areas of credit systems, and the design of certificates and transcripts. In the long term, the accreditation of tourism programs by international universities and institutions will bring major advantages to tourism programs and their graduates.

Collaboration

There are a number of areas for establishing collaboration. The first area is among tourism programs as well as among tourism academics. There is no formal association for tourism educators and their respective institutions. Forming an association for the tourism and hospitality educators would create a platform for collaboration and interaction between higher education programs in tourism. A further issue is that of the current structure of universities. Currently there is no direct or formal cooperation between two-year associate and four-year bachelor degree programs, particularly at the state universities. The two-year associate degree programs, and four-year degree programs, are run separately under different schools. It would be ideal if the two-year associate degree programs were moved to four-year tourism and hospitality schools where appropriate. However, given the legal structure for the running of the universities, this is not viable.

A further area for collaboration is with international universities. Some Turkish universities teach in English and their curricula are similar to those of tourism and hotel schools in the West. There are academics based in tourism programs in Turkey who have studied abroad and regularly publish in international tourism journals. Given the internationalization of tourism education, universities offering tourism programs could establish exchange programs for staff and students with universities in other countries. This collaboration could help the universities to certify and accredit their programs internationally in the long term. Finally, tourism programs also need to establish good collaboration with partners in the tourism industry. There has been a lack of collaboration and communication between industry members and tourism academics. However, over the years, graduates from two-year associate and four-year bachelor degree programs in tourism have gradually started occupying middle and higher managerial positions in tourism organizations. Compared to their earlier counterparts, they are more eager to collaborate with tourism schools in the areas of internship, employing tourism graduates, arranging joint training programs, and participating in academic and applied research. Forming advisory boards made up of these managers could be helpful to tourism programs in many ways.

Funding

The sources of income of universities in Turkey include annual budgetary allocations from the state, student fees, aid and donations, income from property, and profits from enterprises. However, the main source of income has been from student fees and state aid. The student fees for state universities are particularly low; therefore, most universities face major financial constraints in providing a good teaching, training, and research environment for their academic staff and students. This is also the case for most tourism programs at the associate and degree level. It is essential to note that the percentage allocated in government budgets for education, including primary, secondary, higher, and public education, has been around 3% (State Institute of Statistics, 2004). Given the fact that almost 50% of the country's population is younger than 30 years of age, this allocated amount is not sufficient if the country is to provide contemporary education and training for its young population.

Obtaining funding from external parties through consultancy work, through providing training or from donations is uncommon for tourism programs. However, in the long run, depending on the knowledge and skills of academics in tourism programs, getting external funding through consultancies and providing training can be a major source of funding for those tourism programs. To be able to deliver such services, tourism academics should be able to offer something valuable to tourism organizations and also establish good collaboration with them. Certainly, this requires them to employ a more professional business approach. Overall, solving the problem of funding can have a positive impact on many areas in tourism higher education in Turkey.

CONCLUSIONS

This paper has sought to discuss and evaluate the development of tourism higher education in Turkey. Based on the above discussions and evaluations, a number of conclusions can be drawn. Tourism higher education is undertaken at three levels: the associate, bachelor, and postgraduate degree levels. As tourism education mainly started in the early 1990s, it is still a relatively new phenomenon. The development of tourism education in Turkey has so far been in an ad-hoc and unplanned manner. Despite this, there have been some positive progress and good outcomes over the years. However, there are several challenges and problems at the associate, bachelor and postgraduate levels, although the associate degree programs seem to face more severe problems than the other programs. The main difficulties that tourism programs face include a lack of qualified academic staff, improperly designed curricula, limited practical training opportunities for students, and the difficulty of keeping qualified graduates in the industry. These problems are not unique to tourism higher education in Turkey, since previous studies in other countries also refer to similar issues and problems (e.g., Amoah & Baum, 1997; Barrows & Bosselman, 1999; Christou, 1999; Cooper et al. 1992; Dale & Robinson, 2001; Hobson, 1999; King, 1994; Knowles et al., 2003; Sigala & Baum, 2003; Theuns & Rasheed, 1991).

If Turkey is to gain more from tourism in the long run, it is essential to improve the standards of tourism higher education. A number of recommendations can be made. These include revising the curriculum, certifying teaching staff, auditing and certifying tourism programs, providing more funding, and finally, establishing collaboration not only between tourism programs but also between tourism programs and industry partners, and between tourism programs and international universities. However, the above problems are not unique to programs in the field of tourism and hospitality. In fact, university programs in all areas in Turkey face similar problems. Therefore, in order to achieve some significant improvements, some radical cultural and structural reforms are needed not only in tourism higher education but also in the country's higher education system as a whole. It is also important to underline that, when developing contemporary tourism higher education policies and plans, they should be part of the country's long-term tourism plans and strategies. Unfortunately, Turkey has so far neither developed sustainable tourism plans and strategies, nor has any genuine intentions to design and implement any in the near future. Although it is not desirable, tourism development and tourism higher education in Turkey will most likely continue to grow in an ad-hoc and unplanned manner.

This paper has looked only at the development and evaluation of tourism higher education in Turkey. At the secondary level education, there are vocational hotel and tourism schools run by the National Ministry of Education. Both the National Ministry of Education and the Ministry of Culture and Tourism organize training and educational programs and workshops for people who work in the industry, as well as for the general public. Future studies can further investigate tourism education in Turkey at all levels. It is hoped that this paper will provide some guidelines for tourism educators not only in Turkey but also in countries facing similar situations. It is also hoped that this study will succeed in stimulating further research into tourism higher education in developing countries. Comparative studies may perhaps also yield interesting findings.

REFERENCES

Amoah, V., & Baum, T. (1997). Tourism education: Policy versus practice. *International Journal of Contemporary Hospitality Management, 9*(1), 5-12.

Association of Travel Agencies. (2004). *Statistics [On-line].* Available: *http://www. tursab.org.tr*

Aymankuy, Y. (2002). *Önlisans ve Lisans Düzeyindeki Turizm Eğitimi Veren Yüksek Öğretim Kurumlarının Bulundukları Yerlerin Analizi ve Turizm Eğitimi İçin Öneri Bir Model* [Analysis of Associate Degree and Bachelor Degree Programs' Locations and Proposing a Tourism Education Model]. *Ministry of Tourism, Tourism Education Conference/Workshop* (pp. 29-42). Ankara, Turkey: Ministry of Tourism.

Barrows, C., & Bosselman, R. (Eds.) (1999). *Hospitality management education.* Binghamton, NY: The Haworth Hospitality Press.

Biggs, J. (2003). *Teaching for quality learning at university.* Buckingham: The Open University.

Boylu, Y. (2002). Türkiye'deki Örgün Turizm Eğitiminin Sistematik Olmayan Bir Açıdan Değerlendirilmesi [A non-systematic analysis of formal tourism education in Turkey]. *Eastern Mediterranean University Journal of Tourism Research, 3*(2), 66-75.

Brotherton, B., Woolfenden, G., & Himmetoglu, B. (1994). Developing human resources for Turkey's tourism industry in the 1990s. *Tourism Management, 15*(2), 109-116.

Christou, E. (1999). Hospitality management education in Greece–An exploratory study. *Tourism Management, 20*(6), 683-691.

Cooper, C., Scales, R., & Westlake, J. (1992). The anatomy of tourism and hospitality educators in the UK. *Tourism Management, 13*(2), 234-241.

Dale, C., & Robinson, N. (2001). The theming of tourism education: A three-domain approach. *International Journal of Contemporary Hospitality Management, 13*(1), 30-34.

Echtner, C. (1995). Tourism education in developing nations: A three-pronged approach. *Tourism Recreation Research, 20*(2), 32-41.

Ergin, A., & Yagci, Ö. (2003). An evaluation of the vocational school and short term higher education project of the ministry of education and higher education council. *Journal of Education, 25*(1), 256-264.

Harrison, D. (2001). *Tourism and the less developed countries: Issues and case studies.* Oxon: CABI.

Hobson, P. (1999). International perspectives: A comparison of U.S., U.K., and Australian hospitality education and their university systems. In C. Barrows, & R. Bosselman (Eds.) *Hospitality Management Education* (pp. 213-238). Binghamton, NY: The Haworth Hospitality Press.

King, B. (1994). Tourism higher education in island microstates: The case of the South Pacific. *Tourism Management, 15*(4), 267-272.

Kizilirmak, I. (2000). Meslek Yüksek Okulları Turizm ve Otelcilik Programlarının Günümüz Turizm Sektörünün Beklentileri Doğrultusunda Değerlendirilmesi. [An evaluation of tourism and hotel management programs in vocational high schools]. *Milli Egitim, 147*(Temmuz-Agustos-Eylul), 147-156.

Knowles, T., Teixeira, R., & Egan, D. (2003). Tourism and hospitality education in Brazil and the U.K.: A comparison. *International Journal of Contemporary Hospitality Management, 15*(1), 45-51.

Korzay, M. (1987). Tourism education in Turkey. *International Journal of Hospitality Management, 6*(1), 43-48.

Kusluvan, S. (2003). Characteristics of employment and human resource management in the tourism and hospitality industry. In S. Kusluvan (Ed.), *Managing Employee Attitudes and Behaviors in the Tourism and Hospitality Industry* (pp. 3-24). New York: Nova Science Publishers.

Kusluvan, S. & Kusluvan, Z. (2000). Perceptions and attitudes of undergraduate tourism students towards working in the tourism industry in Turkey. *Tourism Management, 21*(3), 251-269.

Ministry of Tourism. (1994). *Turizm Endüstrisi İşgücü Araştırması* [An investigation into labor force in the tourism industry]. Ankara: Levent Ofset.

Ministry of Tourism. (2002). 2nd *Tourism Forum, sub-commission reports, general assembly discussions and decisions.* Ankara: Author.

Ministry of Tourism. (2005). *Statistics* [On-line]. Available: *http://www.turizm.gov.tr.*

Okumus, F. (2003), *Türkiye de turizm eğitimi ve sorunları* [Tourism education and its problems in Turkey]. Paper presented at Mugla University Monthly Conferences, January 2003, Muğla, Turkey.

Okumus, F., & Kilic, H. (2004). Turizm İşletmeleri ve Merkezlerinde Rekabet Avantaji Geliştirilmesi ve Korunmasi [Creating and maintaining competitive advantage in tourism organizations and destinations]. *Seyahat ve Otel Isletmeciligi Dergisi, 1*(1), 10-17.

Sigala, M., & Baum, T. (2003). Trends and issues in tourism and hospitality higher education: Visioning the future. *Tourism and Hospitality Research, 4*(4), 367-376.

State Institute of Statistics (2004). *General Statistics [On-line].* Available: *http://www.die.gov.tr*

State Planning Organization. (2001). *Eighth five-year development plan: The tourism report.* Ankara, Turkey: Author.

Student Selection and Placement Centre. (2004a). *Öğrenci Seçme ve Yerleştirme Sistemi Yükseköğretim Programları ve Kontenjanları Klavuzu* [Student selection and placement system's higher education and quotas guide]. Ankara, Turkey: Author.

Student Selection and Placement Centre. (2004b). *The 2003-2004 academic year higher education statistics* (ÖSYM Publications, No: 2004-3). Ankara, Turkey: Author.

The Council of Higher Education. (2004a). *The Turkish higher education system* [On-line]. Available: *www.yok.gov.tr*

The Council of Higher Education. (2004b). *MEB-YÖK Meslek Yüksekokulları Projesi Değerlendirme Raporu.* [An evaluation report on the joint project of the Ministry of National Education and the Council of Higher Education's Vocational High Schools' development]. Ankara: Author.

Theuns, H., & Rasheed, A. (1991). Alternative approaches to tertiary tourism education with special reference to developing countries. *Tourism Management, 14*(1), 42-51.

Timur, A. (1992). Turkiye'de Turizm Eğitiminin Yapısı, Uygulanan Politikalar ve Sonuçları [Tourism education in Turkey: Structure, policies and results]. *Turizm Eğitimi: Konferans-Workshop* (pp. 44-52). Ankara, Turkey: Ministry of Tourism Education Publications.

Tosun, C. (2001). Challenges of sustainable tourism development in the developing world: The case of Turkey. *Tourism Management, 22*(3), 285-299.

Tosun, C., & Timothy, D. (2001). Shortcoming in planning approaches to tourism development in developing countries: The case of Turkey. *International Journal of Contemporary Hospitality Management, 13*(7), 352-359.

Turkish Tourism Investors Association. (1992). *Contribution of tourism investments to the economy.* Istanbul: Author.

World Tourism Organization. (2002). *Tourism and poverty alleviation.* Madrid: Author.

World Tourism Organization. (2003). *Tourism market trends* (2003 Edition). Madrid: Author.

Yagci, Ö (2001). Tourism education in Turkey, basic problems of employment and solution suggestions. *Journal of Commerce and Tourism Education Faculty, 4*(1), 23-39.

Tourism Higher Education in China: Past and Present, Opportunities and Challenges

Wen Zhang

Xixia Fan

SUMMARY. This paper first reviews the origins and development of tourism higher education in China, then elaborates on its present hierarchy of programs, regional distribution and mechanisms for operating schools. Based on an investigation, the paper also discusses the educational objectives, program setup, curriculum design, textbooks and reference materials. It summarizes the problems and challenges China's higher education studies in tourism are facing, and in conclusion, it explores development trends and offers suggestions for its future. *[Article copies available for a fee from The Haworth Document Delivery Service: 1-800-HAWORTH. E-mail address: <docdelivery@haworthpress.com> Website: <http://www.HaworthPress.com> © 2005 by The Haworth Press, Inc. All rights reserved.]*

Wen Zhang is Professor and Vice Dean, School of Tourism Management, Beijing International Studies University, #1 Dingfuzhuang, Chaoyang District, Beijing, P.R. China 100024 (E-mail: zhangwen@bisu.edu.cn).

Xixia Fan is a Postgraduate Student, School of Tourism Management, Beijing International Studies University, #1 Dingfuzhuang, Chaoyang District, Beijing, P.R. China 100024 (E-mail: dafanxi@163.com).

The authors would like to take this opportunity to express their great thanks to Miss Ming Zhang, who helped them collect data and information for this paper.

[Haworth co-indexing entry note]: "Tourism Higher Education in China: Past and Present, Opportunities and Challenges." Zhang, Wen, and Xixia Fan. Co-published simultaneously in *Journal of Teaching in Travel & Tourism* (The Haworth Press, Inc.) Vol. 5, No. 1/2, 2005, pp. 117-135; and: *Global Tourism Higher Education: Past, Present, and Future* (ed: Cathy H. C. Hsu) The Haworth Press, Inc., 2005, pp. 117-135. Single or multiple copies of this article are available for a fee from The Haworth Document Delivery Service [1-800-HAWORTH, 9:00 a.m. - 5:00 p.m. (EST). E-mail address: docdelivery@haworthpress.com].

doi:10.1300/J172v05n01_06

KEYWORDS. Tourism higher education, tourism industry, program, China

INTRODUCTION

China's higher education in tourism studies has a short history, less than 30 years. It came into being after China's opening-up in 1978 and implementation of economic reform, and has developed with the sustained growth of China's economy and the strengthening of its tourism industry. Today, China's higher education in tourism has made considerable achievements, not only in the number of schools and students, but also at different levels and in mechanisms for running programs.

In 1979, China's first tourism institution of higher learning–Shanghai Institute of Tourism–was founded, and offered a diploma program the same year. This marked the beginning of China's higher education in tourism studies. Since the early 1980s, China National Tourism Administration (CNTA) provided funds for several universities across the country to help establish tourism programs to meet the urgent needs for higher education for tourism professionals and to speed up the development of tourism higher education in China (Liu, 1996; Yu, 2003). Hangzhou University, Beijing Second Foreign Language University (now Beijing International Studies University) and Beijing Institute of Tourism then began to offer undergraduate tourism programs. In the late 1980s, the initial pattern of China's higher education in tourism took shape with CNTA acting as the steering body and Nankai University, Northwest University and Zhongshan University playing the key roles (Du, 2003). China's tourism higher education entered a period of fast development in the 1990s (see Table 1). With the deepening of reform in general higher education and the growing demand for tourism professionals with higher education due to the rapid growth of China's tourism industry, many institutions of higher learning across the country established tourism specialties or programs based on relevant existing programs.

Dong (1998) split the development of China's higher education in tourism into three phases, namely: exploring development, scale development and quality development. He said that, by 1995, China's higher education in tourism had acquired a considerable scale and entered the stage of quality development. Du (2003) stated that the development of China's tourism higher education could be divided into two stages. (1) Starting Stage from 1979 to 1990. The special feature of this stage

TABLE 1. Number of Institutions and Students of Tourism Higher Education in China 1990-2003

Year	Institutions	Students
1990	55	8,263
1991	68	7,567
1992	59	8,893
1993	102	12,266
1994	109	15,486
1995	138	20,121
1996	166	25,822
1997	192	28,566
1998	187	32,737
1999	209	54,041
2000	251	73,586
2001	311	102,245
2002	407	157,400
2003	494	199,682

Source: Adopted from CNTA (1990-2003; 2003).

was that many universities and colleges established tourism programs or specialties with the direct guidance of CNTA and funds provided by CNTA. This greatly alleviated the urgent needs of the tourism industry for professionals with higher education. (2) Fast Development Stage from 1990 to now. At this stage, the scale of China's tourism higher education has grown rapidly and the overall quality of teaching and teachers has improved. The feature of this stage lies in the diversification of institutions of higher learning that run tourism programs or specialties. According to the Personnel, Labor and Education Department of CNTA (1998), a great increase was seen in 1997 in China's higher education in tourism in the scale of development, hierarchy of programs, quality of teaching and distribution of schools. It should be mentioned that since 1997 the emphases of China's tourism higher education have shifted to: (1) educational reform, improvement of program facilities and research on the establishment of the tourism discipline; and (2) cooperation and exchanges with tourism institutions abroad, and the integration of international practice.

Over the past 26 years, China's higher education in tourism has fostered a large number of qualified professionals for the development of the nation's tourism industry. At the same time, tourism institutions of higher learning have made full use of their teaching resources and have played an active part in on-the-job training and continuing education for tourism industry practitioners, thus making great contributions to the improvement of the quality of the human resources of the tourism industry.

CURRENT STATE OF TOURISM HIGHER EDUCATION IN CHINA

Scale of Development

After 26 years of development, China's tourism higher education has expanded rapidly in the number of schools and enrollment of students (see Table 1). According to CNTA (2003), by the end of 2003 the total number of universities and colleges offering tourism programs or specialties had reached 494, with a total student body of close to 200,000 (which represents 9 and 24 times those of 1990, respectively). Higher education in tourism has become one of the fastest growing sectors in China's higher education as a whole.

Hierarchy of Programs

Tourism higher education in China has developed four levels, namely, diploma program, undergraduate program, postgraduate program and doctoral program. According to of some experts among the universities and colleges offering tourism programs, those having diploma programs take up about 70%; those offering undergraduate programs account for 35% and those running postgraduate and doctoral programs represent 10% (Yang, 2003).

Distribution of Schools

At present, there are tourism institutions of higher learning in all the provinces, autonomous regions and municipalities in China, excluding

Taiwan, Hong Kong and Macau. The regional distribution of schools, in general, complies with the development of tourism in the regions with only a few exceptions. That is: the more developed the regional tourism industry is, the more schools are and the larger the number of students is in the region.

Figure 1 shows the proportion of tourism employees, schools and students of higher learning in each of the 31 provinces, autonomous regions and municipalities in 2002. The number of employees in the tourism industry reflected the capacity of tourism reception and services in a region. Therefore, the number of schools and students should be in proportion to the number of employees, for students are the upcoming workforce for the industry. In Figure 1, the ups-and-downs of the three

FIGURE 1. Proportion of Tourism Employees, Schools and Students of Higher Learning in Each of the 31 Provinces, Autonomous Regions and Municipalities in 2002

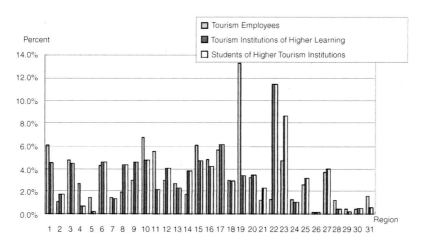

Source: Adopted from CNTA (1990-2003).
Regions:

1 = Beijing	2 = Tianjin	3 = Hebei	4 = Shanxi
5 = Inner Mongolia	6 = Liaoning	7 = Jilin	8 = Heilongjiang
9 = Shanghai	10 = Jiangsu	11 = Zhejiang	12 = Anhui
13 = Fujian	14 = Jiangxi	15 = Shandong	16 = Henan
17 = Hubei	18 = Hunan	19 = Guangdong	20 = Guangxi
21 = Hainan	22 = Chongqing	23 = Sichuan	24 = Guizhou
25 = Yunnan	26 = Tibet	27 = Shaanxi	28 = Gansu
29 = Qinghai	30 = Ningxia	31 = Xinjia	

figures are, in general, following the same trend with only a few exceptions. The exceptions indicate the shortage and surplus of human resource reserves in the regions.

Mechanisms of Running Schools and Programs

Over the past 26 years, China's tourism institutions of higher learning have actively explored the mechanisms of operating schools and
programs. They have found many ways of running institutions, including state-funded, partnerships between governments and enterprises,
private/enterprise-invested, and international cooperation. At present,
stated-owned universities and vocational colleges are still the main-
stream of tourism higher education in China. However, joint efforts and
enterprise/private invested schools and programs have developed rapidly in recent years.

The setup of China's higher education in tourism can be divided into
three types, namely independent institutions, tourism schools, and tourism departments/programs. (1) Independent institutions, such as the Guilin Tourism Institute, are independent educational entities with fully
independent utilization of educational resources and the flexibility of running programs. However, there are only a small number of these kinds of
institutions in China. (2) Tourism schools, such as the Tourism Management School of the Beijing International Studies University, are affiliated
with universities or institutions of higher learning. Although the educational resources of the university can be shared, there is less flexibility
and limited input for operating and developing programs. (3) Tourism de-
partments/programs, such as the Tourism Program of the Business School
of Chengdu University and the Tourism Department of the International
Business School of the East China Normal University, are within a school
of a university or institution of higher learning. This greatly limits program development in terms of facilities, teaching staff and input (Yang,
2003). In tourism higher education in China, tourism departments/pro-
grams are generally subordinate to schools of economics, management,
business, foreign languages, history, humanity, cookery, city planning,
gardening, geography or environmental resources.

Educational Objectives

With the strengthening of the function and position of the tourism industry in the national economy and social development, the educational
objectives of China's higher education in tourism have showed a trend

of diversification, aiming at fostering talents tailored to management, research and services as well as operation in the tourism sector.

In 1998, the Ministry of Education readjusted the specialties of undergraduate programs and merged the various existing tourism programs/specialties into tourism management. The Ministry of Education stipulated the educational objective of undergraduate studies of tourism management, as: 'to foster advanced tourism managerial talents who acquire basic tourism management knowledge and are capable of working in tourism enterprises or administrative departments.' The requirements of knowledge, and capability of graduates from tourism management programs are: (1) acquiring the basic theories and knowledge of the discipline of tourism management; (2) grasping qualitative and quantitative research methods in tourism management; (3) possessing the ability of analyzing and solving problems by using basic tourism management theories; (4) familiarizing with the laws, regulations and policies in developing tourism; (5) acquaintance with the development trends of China's tourism industry; and (6) mastering the basic methods of literature review and data collection. The Ministry of Education requested tourism institutions of higher learning to set up their specific educational objectives for undergraduate programs according to this stipulation and requirements, and to establish objectives for diploma and postgraduate programs accordingly.

The websites of 130 tourism institutions of higher learning in China were examined by the authors. The educational objectives for programs from these institutions are summarized as follows:

- *Diploma:* to train tour-guides and professionals for travel agencies, hotels or related businesses, to acquire basic knowledge of modern economic and managerial theories and to speak at least one foreign language.
- *Undergraduate:* to foster composite talents of tourism education, research or management, who are capable of working in tourism administrative departments, travel agencies, hotels or tourism schools; and who are to systematically acquire basic theories of tourism management; familiarization with the laws, regulations and policies in developing tourism; be acquainted with the development trends of China's tourism industry; master the operation of tourism enterprises; have creativeness and sociability; have the ability to analyze and solve problems in the workplace; and adapt to the needs of development of the tourism industry. Some universities

have special objectives to train students to have knowledge in eco-tourism development or management.

- *Postgraduate:* to foster advanced tourism managerial talents, who acquire solid and systematic knowledge of general as well as tourism economic and managerial theories, grasp the development trends of the tourism discipline, have rigorous scientific attitude and ability to do research independently, have creativeness and original views, master the basic methods of literature review and data collection, and can express their academic ideas and views in English. Some universities have special objectives to educate students to have knowledge in environmental protection and urban and rural planning and management.
- *Doctoral:* to foster theoretical researchers in tourism management.

Program Setup

In the Catalogue of Specialties for Undergraduate Programs at Institutions of Higher Learning stipulated by the Ministry of Education (1998), there is only one tourism related specialty–tourism management, classified as a branch of management, which is a "first-level category" discipline. However, the program setup (or program orientation) of tourism institutions of higher learning in practice is very complicated. In China, there are altogether about 30 tourism-related program titles (or program orientations), covering almost all the aspects of tourism activities and the tourism industry.

The program setup of most tourism universities and colleges was designed according to the structure of the tourism industry; for example, tourism economics, tourism management, tour-guiding and interpretation, hotel management, and food and beverage management. Some universities and colleges offer programs according to some applied disciplines in the tourism industry, such as tourism geography, tourism accounting, and tourism marketing. Tourism programs offered by some business and vocational schools give prominence to economics and management, and those offered by some foreign language schools attach importance to tour-guiding and interpretation.

To summarize, programs offered by the four levels of higher tourism education are mainly:

- *Diploma:* tour-guiding, tourism management, tourism service and hotel management, food and beverage management, hotel management, eco-tourism management, travel agency management, city planning, tourism information system, entertainment operation and management, and ethnic culture and tourism.

- *Undergraduate:* tourism management, tourism enterprise management, tourism economics, hotel management, travel agency management, tourist attraction management, eco-tourism management, tourism education, tourism development and planning, tourism marketing, international tour-guiding, tourism and air-transportation service, tourism accounting, tourism management and service, cookery and nutrition education, convention and incentive tourism management, geographic science, resource and urban and rural planning and management, garden and landscape planning and design, and environmental science.
- *Postgraduate:* tourism development and planning, tourism management, tourism enterprise management, tourism marketing, garden and landscape planning and design, tourism information management, tourism economics and strategic development, impact studies of tourism, environmental science, land resources management.
- *Doctoral:* tourism management, tourism enterprise management, tourism planning and management, tourism marketing, anthropology of tourism, natural and human geography, garden and landscape planning.

Curriculum Design

Tourism higher education in China has generally originated from programs such as management, economics, geography, foreign languages and history. Therefore, there is a great difference in curricula from different universities and colleges. Wu, Hu, and Zhang (1998) made a comparative study of the curricula of hotel management programs of three universities (Huadong University, Shanghai Communication University and Shanghai Institute of Tourism), and found that the differences between the curriculum had close relationships with the program setup, educational objectives and student recruitment of each school.

The Catalogue of Specialties for Undergraduate Programs at Institutions of Higher Learning (Ministry of Education, 1998) stipulated the major courses of tourism management programs. These are management, micro economics, macro economics, management information systems, statistics, accounting, financial management, marketing, economic law, introduction to tourism, tourism economics, basic theory of hotel management, and tourism resources development. It also required student internships in the tourism industry as well as social practice. The authors found that the requirements of student internship of different universities and colleges varied from one year to a few weeks for diploma programs and half a year to a few weeks for undergraduate programs.

Textbooks and Teaching Materials

Du (2003) stated that the development and construction of textbooks and teaching materials for China's higher education in tourism grew in three stages. (1) The stage of void. During the pioneering stage of China's higher tourism education, many of the teachers were transferred from other related disciplines to tourism programs. They managed to overcome the difficulties of lack of textbooks and teaching materials by writing and compiling their own teaching manuals. (2) The stage of import. During this stage, teachers and researchers of tourism introduced applicable theories and knowledge from other disciplines to tourism education on the one hand, and translated a number of foreign professional publications on the other hand. The achievements of this period laid a solid foundation for the development of tourism higher education in China. (3) The stage of self-development. During this stage, some established tourism institutions commissioned tourism scholars and experts to develop and publish a series of textbooks on the basis of their teaching manuals. These textbooks are now widely used by tourism programs in China.

Now China has domestically published textbooks on the following subjects: introduction to tourism, tourism economics, tourism marketing, tourism accounting, tourism enterprises management, tourism law, tour-guiding, tourism psychology, tourism culture, tourism literature, and foreign languages in tourism. With the development of the tourism industry and the deepening of tourism research, new textbooks have covered the areas of eco-tourism, tourism transportation, tourism and environmental protection, tourism development and planning, sustainable tourism development in China, hotel corporate identity (CI) design, public relations in tourism, history of tourism, and China's tourism and population, etc. The emphasis of textbooks compilation is shifting from theoretical and academic only, to both theoretical and practical. Recent publications by the Tourism Education Press include Classical Cases of Tourist Attraction Operation and Management, Manual of Tourism Laws and Regulations, Dynamic Approach to Tourism Resource Development and Planning, Manual of Tour Leaders, and

Case Analysis of Hotel Service (*www.tepcb.com*). China Travel and Tourism Press (*www.cttp.net.cn*) published the translations of the series of textbooks by the American Hotel and Lodging Association (AH&LA); of which 16 are now in circulation. They include International Hotel Management, Hospitality Industry Computer Systems, Supervision in the Hospitality Industry, Marketing in the Hospital Industry, Management of Food and Beverage Operations, Managing Front Office Operations, Managerial Accounting for the Hospitality Industry, Resort Condominium and Vocation Ownership Management, Convention Management and Service, etc.

PROBLEMS AND CHALLENGES IN TOURISM HIGHER EDUCATION IN CHINA

Over the past 26 years, tourism higher education in China has accumulated substantial successful experiences, but at the same time there are still many areas that need improvement. In general, the development of higher education in tourism studies in China has lagged behind the rapid growth of the tourism industry.

Rapid expansion but with low efficiency and limited improvement in educational quality (Du, 2003; Liu & Bi, 2001; Wang & Wang, 2001; Yu, 2003). Because of the great demand for tourism talents in China, tourism higher education has adopted a development pattern of quantity expansion since the 1980s, especially in the 1990s. Quite a number of universities and colleges established tourism departments/programs based on relevant disciplines as a response to the growing demand for talents for the tourism industry, while some institutions restructured themselves to create tourism departments/programs in order to find a solution for some declining programs. As shown in Table 1, the number of universities and colleges that offered tourism programs in 1995 was 2.5 times that of 1990, and the number in 2003 was 3.6 times that of 1995. There are now tourism institutions of higher learning in almost every province, autonomous region and municipality. However, such expansion has resulted in the scattering of educational input and duplicate investment. As a result, efficiency can barely be achieved in most of the universities and colleges, the limited educational input of the country cannot be fully utilized and the return on educational investment stays low.

A gap between the requirements of modern tourism higher education and the present tourism program setup, educational objectives and cur-

riculum design (Du, 2003; Liu & Bi, 2001; Wang & Wang, 2001; Xu, 1999; Yang, 2003; Zhang, 1998; Zhang & Gu, 2000). Tourism higher education needs a standardized and scientific approach towards program setup and curriculum design. Without a good understanding of the inherent laws and development trends of the tourism industry and the mission of higher tourism education, many of the universities and colleges that entered into tourism education since the 1990s are short of clear educational objectives. Their program setup and curricula were developed using existing resources of their previous disciplines and programs without rational design principles and feasibility studies. Their initiatives were blended with factors of blindness and vogue or survival and transference of the already-declining programs. Almost all normal universities (i.e., teacher training universities) have added tourism programs in geography, history or foreign language schools/departments; and some agriculture and forest, geology and water conservancy schools/departments have established tourism programs. Another obvious problem in tourism higher education in China is that programs are sometimes set up without careful thought. Tourism is a comprehensive industry embracing a variety of fields, therefore it needs professionals with comprehensive knowledge. The establishment of poorly prepared programs has resulted in students having a narrow scope of knowledge, an unsystematic knowledge structure, lack of skills in comprehensive analysis and coordination as well as poor adaptability to tourism-concerned occupations. What is more, programs were unclearly named. For example, "hotel management," "hotel service and management," and "tourism and hotel management" are in fact the same program.

Educational objectives are at the center of all the teaching activities of a school, whereas curriculum design reflects the all-rounded and concrete structure of knowledge and capability cultivation identified in the objectives. The present curriculum systems of tourism higher education in China lack standardization. As most of the tourism programs in China originated from relevant disciplines such as geography, foreign languages, economics or history, curricula of tourism programs of different universities and colleges vary greatly. Graduates from tourism programs of different universities or colleges may have acquired different ranges of knowledge: others are well acquainted with Chinese history and tourism biographies, while some are very familiar with the location of tourist attractions in China, and some even have chef certificates upon graduation. Furthermore, the features of the tourism industry requires its managerial professionals to have comprehensive expertise and general knowledge, while the present curriculum systems of China's tourism universities and colleges, in general, cannot embody the educational objectives of "solid foundation and high adaptability." In the present curriculum systems, courses in natural, cultural and social sciences are not adequately represented. Besides, some major courses, such as transportation management, are not offered in the tourism programs of many universities. Destination management is another important course in tourism programs, but few schools have this course in their curriculum. Furthermore, great attention is given to theoretical courses in most of the curricula, while practical courses are considered as less important. The percentage of courses that combine theory with practice is getting smaller, when the level of programs goes higher.

Needs for improvement in teaching methods and textbooks (Wang & Wang, 2001; Xu, 1999; Yang, 2003; Yu, 2003; Zhang & Gu, 2003). There are a number of institutions, and their teachers, who still follow the traditional "classroom-centered" teaching method (i.e., teachers give lectures and students take notes) and examinations are based on the content of textbooks and notes. This kind of teaching method is likely to result in students' being good at memorization of theories, but incapable in solving problems and a lack of creativity and original views. The authors have interviewed undergraduate students of tourism programs from several universities and colleges, and the majority of them stated that teaching was theoretically-oriented and teaching methods were mainly lectures in the classrooms.

As for textbooks, there are still quite a number of institutions that are blindly compiling and publishing textbooks for tourism programs despite their lack of teaching experience and research capability. As a result, duplication and plagiarism are often found in textbooks. These textbooks can hardly reflect the recent theoretical innovation and development in the tourism industry or innovative practices in tourism management and operations. The lack of quality textbooks and reference materials has restricted the improvement of the education standards of the tourism programs. Furthermore, textbooks of some institutions remain unchanged for many years, and the contents are out-of-date.

A lack of qualified instructors (Du, 2003; Wang & Wang, 2001; Yu, 2003). Because of the short history and rapid growth of tourism higher education in China, the lack of qualified instructors has become an obvious issue. The majority of the teachers and researchers currently involved in tourism education came from other disciplines (e.g., foreign languages, economics, history, and geography), and their educational backgrounds vary greatly. Most of them have never worked in or hardly understand the practice of the tourism industry, either at home or abroad.

Moreover, compared with the continuous occurrence of new phenomena and the rapid growth of China's tourism industry, the knowledge base of faculty members seems obsolete, the content of teaching out-of-date and the method of education outmoded. The level of expertise of most tourism educational professionals needs to be raised.

Although tourism programs have stronger fund-raising capability compared to conventional programs, the current relationship and cooperation between universities and the tourism industry is still far from being close, consistent, or regular. Therefore, professors of tourism programs are poorly informed of the current issues and practices in the industry, and most of their research achievements are largely academic and seldom gain recognition and support from the tourism industry.

Inadequate educational resources input (Du, 2003; Yu, 2003). At the early stage of tourism development, the Chinese government created a favorable environment for the development of the tourism discipline and programs by providing preferential policies and sufficient input. After the Ministry of Education (1998) stipulated the Catalogue of Specialties for Undergraduate Programs at Institutions of Higher Learning in 1998, many universities offering tourism programs restructured their schools and departments/programs according to the new catalogue of specialties. In these universities, the position and relative independence of tourism education decreased, input and support to tourism programs were reduced, and the development of tourism programs declined.

Due to tight budgets, most tourism programs have limited financial resources to improve teaching facilities and conditions. Tourism higher education in China is faced with inadequate input to construct teaching laboratories and internship bases, and has no close connection with the industry to provide enough opportunities for students to complete internships. Student internships are arranged randomly and inconsistently, so their effectiveness is not guaranteed.

A large percentage of are graduates employed outside the tourism industry (Wu, Hu & Zhang, 1998; Zhang & Gu, 2000; Zhou, 2001). Now in China, tourism higher education graduate output does not match the employment mechanisms of enterprises and government personnel systems. A large percentage of graduates of undergraduate and graduate programs find jobs outside the tourism industry.

In the job market, graduates from tourism diploma programs find it relatively easy to get jobs and stay in tourism enterprises. However, for the percentage of graduates from undergraduate programs and above, finding employment in the tourism industry is not satisfactory because of their lack of practical ability and experience. According to employment statistics, about 50% of the graduates from undergraduate tourism programs who entered the tourism industry after graduation quit their first job and found employment outside the industry (Zhou, 2001). This represents a significant waste of the output of tourism education.

It is unfair to blame the graduates for not working in tourism enterprises, because the employment mechanisms of the enterprises are not completely rational. For example, new employees in hotels, no matter what their educational background, have to work up from the lowest level. This is fine, if a different pathway is set up for people with different educational backgrounds. The practice of "management trainee" in other countries is a good system that should be considered as a reference. Tourist enterprises should set up an efficient mechanism for screening supervision and promotion opportunities for new employees in order to retain talents.

Tourism institutions of higher learning should, of course, enhance the proportion of practice and internship in their curricula to help their students become acquainted with the practice of the industry. After a short period of entry-level work, they could be promoted to supervisory or managerial positions. China's higher education in tourism needs to be integrated with the international tourism program practice, especially in curriculum design, internship, and opportunity for relevant working experiences.

DEVELOPMENT TRENDS AND PROSPECTS FOR TOURISM HIGHER EDUCATION IN CHINA

China's entry into the World Trade Organization (WTO) has brought about both promising opportunities and unprecedented challenges to its tourism industry. The new environment has made new requirements on the quality of Chinese tourism professionals. Hence, education has become an important factor affecting the development of China's tourism industry. Tourism higher education in China needs to keep pace with the world practice. However, there is still a long way to go in both standards and scale.

According to the prediction of the World Travel and Tourism Council (WTTC), the number of employees in China's tourism industry will increase at a rate of 3.2% per year in the next few years, with an annual average growth of more than one million (Wang & Wang, 2001). Beijing Tourism Administration (2001) projected that, in 2010, the total number of employees in the Beijing tourism industry will reach 650,000 from the current 346,000, and middle and advanced levels of managerial personnel will reach 70,000, up from the current 30,000. These figures show that tourism higher education in China has a demanding task in fostering talents for the 21st century.

Faced with the rapid development of China's tourism industry, the globalization of its economy and China's entry into WTO, tourism higher education in China should make efforts to develop in the following areas:

a. *To establish an association of Chinese tourism education.* The China Tourism Association has submitted an application to the Ministry of Civil Affairs to establish a sub-association of tourism education. The founding of this association could promote the improvement of the quality of higher tourism education and research, enhance exchanges between institutions of higher learning, enterprises and government departments and create a favorable environment for the upgrading of the academic position of the tourism discipline.

b. *To enhance the reputation of the tourism discipline.* By encouraging tourism research and striving for a "first level category" discipline position based on the stipulation of the Ministry of Education. Teaching and academic research are the two major tasks for institutions of higher learning. The development of higher tourism education is dependent upon its general capability of academic research, which supplements, as well as complements, the improvement of teaching. Tourism research in China has developed along with the growth of tourism education; however, compared to other more established disciplines, tourism research lags behind both in terms of strength and achievements. This undoubtedly affects the academic standing of tourism studies. According to the Catalogue of Specialties for Undergraduate Programs at Institutions of Higher Learning, China's higher tourism education belongs to the "second level category" of disciplines, under the first category of management. The development of tourism education is thus heavily hindered (Shen, 1998).

c. *To emphasize cooperation and interaction with the tourism industry.* Tourism institutions of higher learning have to make efforts to develop close relationships with industry practices by offering tailor-made training programs and participating in consultancy and management of tourism enterprises. In turn, institutions can gain financial support from the industry and form a win-win relationship with the tourism business (Du, 2003). In addition, reform is necessary for China's tourism higher education to establish a more rational teaching mode with integrated education as the base, technical training as the practical link, and research as the direction for future development. Such an educational system can optimize the allocation of resources and adapt to the law of the market (Ma & Shu, 1997).

d.   *To enhance weak existing programs and broaden the vision and adaptability of tourism graduates.* Now, the mode of teaching of tourism higher education in China is transforming from "knowledge-imparting" to "ability-cultivating," and will ultimately get to the stage of "quality-training" (Yuan, 1999; Zhang, 1998). Program setup and curriculum systems will need to be adjusted according to the educational goal of "solid foundation and high adaptability." The program setup of tourism higher education in Australia has two orientations: general tourism and hospitality management (Craig-Smith & Ding, 2001). This can serve as a reference for the restructuring of programs in China's tourism higher education.

e.   *To promote effective teaching methods.* The proportion of courses teaching practical skills ought to be appropriately increased, and students should be provided with more a favorable environment and conditions for self-study. Great development could be seen in areas such as continuing education, vocational education, multimedia education, internet education and other forms of distance education.

f.   *To build a force of qualified instructors with an advanced theoretical level and rich practical experience.* To realize this objective, three strategies could be adopted: (1) to strengthen and diversify the training of young and middle-aged instructors in order to enhance their knowledge base, both theoretical and practical, and increase their capability; (2) to recruit experts and professors from abroad; and (3) to invite practitioners from the industry and government departments as guest lecturers for tourism education (Dang & Chen, 1997; Yuan, 1999).

With the rapid growth of China's tourism industry, the developments of tourism higher education lies not only in being integrated with world practices, but also by establishing a mechanism for talent development and training adapted to Chinese conditions and market demands. Such development will provide the supply of talents suitable for the growth of the tourism industry in quantity and quality, setup, and distribution; and a solid human resources support to China's realization of being "a big tourism country in the world."

REFERENCES

Beijing Tourism Administration. (2001). *Projection of the development of Beijing tourism human resource.* Beijing: China Travel and Tourism Press.

China National Tourism Administration (CNTA). (1990-2003). *The yearbook of China tourism.* Beijing: China Travel and Tourism Press.

China National Tourism Administration (CNTA). (2003). *CNTA statistical report on China's tourism education in 2003.* Unpublished government document.

Craig-Smith, S. & Ding, P. (2001). University tourism education in Australia: Origin, development, difficulties and prospects. *Journal of Beijing International Studies University, 101,* 24-31.

Dang, J. & Chen, F. (1997). Features and task of China's tourism education in the new situation. *Tourism Tribune, 12*(Special Issue of Tourism Education), 32-33.

Dong, G. (1998). Research on higher tourism education in the era of information economy. *Tourism Tribune, 13*(Special Issue of Tourism Education), 6-9.

Du, J. (2003). Reforms and development of higher tourism education in China. In G. Zhang, X. Wei, & D. Liu (Eds.), *Green book of China's tourism development 2002-2004* (pp. 221-230). Beijing: Social Scientific Literature Press.

Liu, M. & Bi, D. (2001). Problems and measures of China's tourism education and training. *Journal of Adult Education of Hubei University, 19*(5), 9-12.

Liu, Z. (1996). Retrospect and prospect of China's tourism education. *Tourism Tribune, 11* (Special Issue of Tourism Education), 9-12.

Ma, Y., & Shu, B. (1997). A research on the 'trinity' model for tourism education. *Tourism Tribune, 12*(Special edition of Tourism Education), 42-45.

Ministry of Education (1998). *The catalogue of specialties for undergraduate programs at institutions of higher learning.* Unpublished government document.

Personnel, Labor & Education Department of CNTA (1998). *A report on China's tourism education.* Unpublished government document.

Shen, B. (1998). A few issues of higher tourism education. *Tourism Tribune, 13*(Special Issue of Tourism Education), 31-33.

Wang, W. & Wang, Y. (2001). On the development of China's higher tourism education. *Journal of Jinggangshan Normal Institute, 22*(6), 51-54.

Wu, B., Hu, X., & Zhang, L. (1998). A research on the structure of China's tourism education system. *Journal of Guilin Tourism Institute, 9*(3), 65-71.

Xu, C. (1999). A discussion on the curriculum of undergraduate tourism program. *Journal of Guilin Tourism Institute,* 1999 Supplementary Issue of Tourism Education, 143-145.

Yang, Z. (2003). *On China's higher tourism education* [On-line]. Available: www.cthy.com

Yu, C. (2003). *Development of tourism human resource.* Beijing: China Travel and Tourism Press.

Yuan, S. (1999). Development and reform of China's tourism education in the 21st century. *Tourism Tribune, 14*(Special Issue of Tourism Education), 39-42.

Zhang, H. (1998). On the higher tourism education in the 21st century. *Journal of Shanxi University, 21*(1), 91-95.

Zhang, W. & Gu, H. (2000). A survey on the hotel job intention of undergraduates majoring in tourism management. *Tourism Tribune, 15*(Special Issue of Tourism Education), 32-36.

Zhang, W., & Gu, H. (2003). Rethink of China's tourism education and research. *China Tourism Hotel, 15*(6), 53-55.

Zhou, G. (2001). When will the embarrassed hotel management graduates become unembarrassed. *North Economy and Trade, 203,* 158-160.

The Past, Present, and Future
of Hospitality
and Tourism Higher Education
in Hong Kong

Ada Lo

SUMMARY. Hospitality and tourism management programmes are widely available in Hong Kong. At present, there is no official publication on the history and development of higher education in hospitality and tourism management in Hong Kong. This paper aims to review the history and current status of hospitality and tourism higher education in Hong Kong, focusing on the programmes offered at sub-degree, degree, and post-graduate degree levels, and to explore future directions for its development. *[Article copies available for a fee from The Haworth Document Delivery Service: 1-800-HAWORTH. E-mail address: <docdelivery@ haworthpress.com> Website: <http://www.HaworthPress.com> © 2005 by The Haworth Press, Inc. All rights reserved.]*

KEYWORDS. Higher education, hospitality and tourism education, Hong Kong

Ada Lo is Lecturer, School of Hotel & Tourism Management, Hong Kong Polytechnic University, Hung Hom, Hong Kong (E-mail: hmada@polyu.edu.hk).

[Haworth co-indexing entry note]: "The Past, Present, and Future of Hospitality and Tourism Higher Education in Hong Kong." Lo, Ada. Co-published simultaneously in *Journal of Teaching in Travel & Tourism* (The Haworth Press, Inc.) Vol. 5, No. 1/2, 2005, pp. 137-166; and: *Global Tourism Higher Education: Past, Present, and Future* (ed: Cathy H. C. Hsu) The Haworth Press, Inc., 2005, pp. 137-166. Single or multiple copies of this article are available for a fee from The Haworth Document Delivery Service [1-800-HAWORTH, 9:00 a.m. - 5:00 p.m. (EST). E-mail address: docdelivery@haworthpress.com].

INTRODUCTION

Hong Kong is one of Asia's most popular tourist destinations. By 2020, Hong Kong will be the world's fifth most popular tourist destination (World Tourism Organization, 2000). Tourism is one of the major economic pillars of Hong Kong, alongside with logistics, financial and professional services. In 2003, tourism was its second-largest earner of foreign exchange with total tourism receipts amounting to HK$53,235 million (Hong Kong Tourism Board, 2004). Competition for visitors throughout the region is fierce and it is the strategy of the Hong Kong Special Administrative Region (SAR) government to promote the city as a top-class destination for leisure and business visitors by turning Hong Kong into "Asia's World City." Government efforts include the provision of additional infrastructure, improvement of existing facilities, enhancement of service quality, facilitation of visitors' entry and active promotion overseas. All these efforts, as well as the future of the tourism industry in Hong Kong, rely on the people who are employed in the industry. Certainly, higher education in hospitality and tourism education plays an important role in preparing future employees and executives for the tourism industry in Hong Kong and worldwide.

The Hong Kong SAR government's objective in the provision of education is to ensure that young people in Hong Kong receive an all-around quality education to prepare them for life and work and to provide them with an aptitude for life-long learning. The government provides nine-years free and universal basic education (Primary One to Secondary Three), beginning at the age of 6 up to 15 years of age. Under the current policy, subsidized senior secondary (Secondary Four and Five) or vocational training is provided for all Secondary Three graduates who have the ability and wish to continue their studies (HKSAR, 2004). Secondary Five graduates who have completed and passed the Hong Kong Certificate of Education Examination (HKCEE) may opt to continue with Secondary Six and Seven. Upon completion of the seventh year of secondary education, students will participate in the Hong Kong Advanced Level Examination (HKALE) and with the results of the examination students can apply for university undergraduate programmes. Highly subsidized university education is available to about 18% of the 17-20 age group. In addition, another 35% of the relevant age group has access to post-secondary education in other forms. A comprehensive package of student financial assistance is available to ensure that no students will be deprived of education for lack of financial means (Education and Manpower Bureau, 2005a).

At present, there are eleven degree-awarding institutions, eight of which are funded by the University Grants Committee (UGC). Of the eight, seven are fully self-accrediting degree-awarding universities–namely, City University of Hong Kong, Hong Kong Baptist University, Lingnan University, The Chinese University of Hong Kong, The Hong Kong Polytechnic University, The Hong Kong University of Science and Technology, and The University of Hong Kong. The other one is The Hong Kong Institute of Education which is a degree-awarding teacher training institute. In addition, there are three tertiary institutions not funded by the UGC–namely, the publicly-funded Hong Kong Academy for Performing Arts and the self-financed Open University of Hong Kong and the Hong Kong Shue Yan College. In addition, Caritas Francis Hsu College is a privately-funded approved post-secondary college (University Grants Committee, 2004).

Hospitality and tourism management programmes at various levels are widely available in Hong Kong. To the knowledge of the author, there is no official documentation on the history and development of higher education in hospitality and tourism management in Hong Kong. The purpose of this paper is to review the history and current status of hospitality and tourism higher education in Hong Kong, focusing on the programmes offered at sub-degree, degree, and post-graduate degree levels, and to explore future directions for its development. Internet and library searches, plus telephone and personal interviews, were used to collect information for this paper. Annual reports and prospectuses of institutions were also reviewed.

A BRIEF HISTORY OF HOSPITALITY AND TOURISM HIGHER EDUCATION IN HONG KONG

Hospitality and tourism higher education in Hong Kong has evolved from vocational-basis courses to programmes at various levels serving the needs of the different sectors of the industry. Initially all the programmes were funded by the government but with the increase in demand from the local population and from industry, non-government programmes began to emerge in the mid-1990s. The sections presented below are summaries of the development of hospitality and tourism higher education programmes over the past years.

Vocational-Based Programmes

In the 1970s, the hotel and tourism industry in Hong Kong was growing rapidly. The number of tourist arrivals and the number of hotel rooms available continued to grow every year. With the increase in demand for professionally trained staff by the hotels in Hong Kong, institutions began to offer vocationally based courses. The Haking Wong Technical Institute (HWTI), inaugurated in November 1977, was the first government institution to offer formal vocational hotel and catering training courses. The Hotel-Keeping and Tourism Studies Department at the HWTI started with only 80 students who were mainly secondary five graduates. These one-year courses were further developed into courses offered in different modes with various durations and at different levels to accommodate the requirements of the hospitality industry. Most of the courses offered were at Certificate level and mainly focused on the three main areas of hotel studies, tourism and travel agency operations, and food and beverage operations.

The Hong Kong Polytechnic was formally established in August 1972. Its goal was to provide application-oriented education to meet the community's need for professional manpower (The Hong Kong Polytechnic University, 2005). The Polytechnic closely followed the British Polytechnic system by mainly offering application-oriented diploma and higher diploma programmes with universities offering degree and post-graduate programmes (Hobson, 1999). The Department of Institutional Management and Catering Studies (IMCS) founded at The Hong Kong Polytechnic in 1979 was first conceived as a management level hotel school, running alongside a technical training centre, to meet the needs of the rapidly growing hotel industry in Hong Kong in the 1970s. It was felt that future management at department head level and above would need to be "home grown." The department not only focused on grooming hotel professionals but the scope was widened to include "institutional management" with the objective of improving residential and catering standards for the whole of Hong Kong, more specifically in public catering and residential care in sectors such as hospitals, prisons, school and industrial and commercial enterprises, airlines, marine, resorts, and restaurants.

A Higher Diploma (HD) programme in Institutional Management and Catering Studies (IMCS) and a Diploma programme in Catering Studies were created. The aim of the HD programme in IMCS was to provide a sound technical education for students who aspired to positions of responsibility in the food and accommodation industry. The programme was designed to be completed in three years, including a period of practical training undertaken in the industry. Students were required to complete a number of specified courses in the areas of accommodation operations, food preparation and processing, food and beverage service, applied science, applied accounting and control, psychology and sociology, facility planning, training procedures, sales and marketing, and English and communications.

The aim of the two-year Diploma programme was to provide students with the knowledge, skills, and attitude required to operate at technician/supervisory level in the food and accommodation industry. Compared to the HD programme, the diploma programme had a stronger emphasis on food and beverage courses but at the same time provided students with sufficient exposure in training and supervisory procedures.

The Hong Kong Hotels Association worked with the Department to develop a Career Internship Scheme for the graduates, providing them with certification for a one-year post-graduate development programme. A Higher Certificate (HC) programme in Institutional Management and Catering Studies, A Certificate programme in Catering Supervision, and a Certificate programme leading to Part A Examination of the Hotel Catering and Institutional Management Association were also created as part-time day release programmes for industry employees in the following year.

In consultation with the industry, these two institutions, HWTI and the Polytechnic continued to modify their programmes to better suit the needs of the industry. For example, in 1983, the Polytechnic realigned its resources to upgrade its full-time three-year HD in IMCS. With the growth in the number of hotels being built, the demand for professionally trained hotel employees increased. Therefore, the HD programme included a stronger emphasis in various aspects of hotel operations. Communication and language skills were emphasized in the programme in order to equip graduates with professional communication skills for front-line guest contact positions in the hotel industry. Students were required to take a number of courses in written and oral English, and workplace communication. In addition to English, French was also introduced as an elective course. The Diploma programme was dropped while the HC in Hotel, Catering, and Institutional Management was introduced as a three-year part-time day release programme designed to enable those in full-time employment in the hospitality industry to develop the abilities, skills, and attitudes which formed the basis of professional competence for line management in the industry. The two-year part-time day release Certificate in Hotel, Catering and Institutional Operations programme continued to be offered, aiming to develop professional competence at front-line management and supervisory level in the hospitality industry.

These two institutions took different directions in developing new programmes and courses. In the later part of the 1980s, HWTI continued to follow the vocational route, offering certificate programmes with its first Diploma course in Restaurant and Catering Operations (Chinese Style) in 1995. In 1993, the Department of Hotel, Service and Tourism Studies, was founded as part of the Hong Kong Technical College (HKTC). The Department offered HD courses combining theoretical and practical studies on campus, and application through work experience in industry. In 1999, the seven technical institutes and two technical colleges consolidated to form the Hong Kong Institute of Vocational Education (HKIVE). The Hong Kong Technical College was renamed Institute of Vocational Education (Chai Wan). The Department of Hotel, Service and Tourism Studies focused on offering Higher Diploma courses in Hotel and Catering, Travel and Tourism, Leisure Studies, Sports Management and Training Sciences. They also offered a Foundation Diploma in Hospitality Management which aimed to prepare young people to become supervisors, and eventually middle managers, in the hospitality- and tourism-related sectors (Hong Kong Institute of Vocational Education, 2002).

In the consolidation exercise, the Department of Hotel-Keeping and Tourism Studies of the HWTI was renamed as the Department of Hotel, Service and Tourism Studies and launched four full-time Diploma courses and seven Vocational Certificate Courses in part-time day release and part-time evening mode (Hong Kong Institute of Vocational Education, 2002). A one-year HD in International Hospitality Management was launched in 2003 to cater for their own Higher Diploma graduates who intended to further their studies in the respective areas of interest so as to enhance their employability.

The Polytechnic continued to run its HD programmes in full-time and part-time modes. Over the years, the programmes emerged from its original strong emphasis on vocational skills to the current credit-based HD in Hotel, Catering, and Tourism Management with increased emphasis in the general business discipline and supervisory skills training. Three specializations in Hotel Management, Catering Management, and Tourism Management are available for students to choose from.

Undergraduate Programmes

In 1986, the Department of IMCS at the Polytechnic was renamed as the Department of Hospitality Management to better reflect a wider focus on various sectors of the hospitality industry. In 1988, the Bachelor of Arts (BA) in Hospitality Management, the first undergraduate hospitality programme, was launched by the Department in addition to the existing HD programmes. The BA curriculum placed emphasis on providing education in professional concepts, general business principles, and quantitative and analytical decision-making. The BA was a four-year degree programme, and students were required to complete two phases of industry internship for a total of one year. The Department also introduced a BA (Hons) in Tourism Management in 1991 with the aim of developing students for tourism and travel related businesses. In 1992, the Department of Hospitality Management was renamed as the Department of Hotel and Tourism Management to better reflect the content and emphasis of the programmes offered. The Polytechnic received approval from the University and Polytechnic Grant Committee to offer self-accredited degree programmes and acquired full university status and named The Hong Kong Polytechnic University (PolyU) by the end of 1994 (The Hong Kong Polytechnic University, 2005). The BA in Hospitality Management programme was changed to BA (Hons) in Hotel and Catering Management in 1993, one year before the official change from polytechnic to university status. More emphasis was placed on catering and foodservice operations in addition to the hotel component of the programme. Later, both BA (Hons) programmes were aligned into three-year programmes, while students could opt for a four-year sandwich programme with a one-year industrial placement.

The new BA (Hons) in Hotel, Catering, and Tourism Management was introduced in 2000 immediately before the naming of the Department of Hotel and Tourism to School of Hotel and Tourism Management in 2001. As with the HD programme, students can choose to enrol in Hotel Management, Catering Management, or Tourism Management specialization. The most significant feature of the new BA (Hons) programme is that students are required to complete a range of business courses taught in the context of hospitality and tourism plus a suite of courses in their own specializations. In addition, students are allowed to choose other courses in any one of the three specializations in order to broaden their breadth of knowledge. Students are required to complete industrial placements for two 10-week periods in order to obtain industry experience. All first year students of the BA (Hons) and HD programmes are required to take a number of courses common to both programmes in their first year.

Up until 1998, PolyU was the only institution offering undergraduate programmes in hotel and tourism management funded by the University Grant Committee (UGC). In view of the strong demand for professionally trained graduates for the hospitality industry as well as the SAR Government's emphasis on developing tourism as one of the core industries for Hong Kong, The Chinese University of Hong Kong (CUHK) started a three-year Bachelor of Business Administration (BBA) (Hons) in Hotel Management in 1999. This programme was offered by the School of Hotel Management of the Faculty of Business Administration and featured a strong business administration focus in which students are required to complete general business-related courses with an emphasis on real estate and hotel management. The programme was renamed BBA (Hons) in Hotel and Tourism Management in 2002 to reflect the broader spectrum of the programme curriculum. Students majoring in Hotel and Tourism Management are required to take the core curriculum of business courses and other courses in hotel and tourism management, real estate and property investment, and hospitality strategic management. The programme also offers concentration areas for students to choose from once they have completed the required number of elective courses in one of the following areas: human resource management, real estate and finance, and marketing and tourism (Chinese University of Hong Kong, 2005).

A number of overseas institutions also saw the opportunity to offer hospitality and tourism higher education programmes in Hong Kong. For example, the Hong Kong Institute of Technology has offered a Victoria University of Australia off-shore Bachelor of Business programme since 1992. Students may opt for three-year full-time mode or four-year part-time mode, and may choose to major in Hospitality Management, Tourism Management, or Hospitality and Tourism Management. Structure of this undergraduate programme is very similar to the regular programme offered on campus in Australia. Students are also required to complete two 10-week internships during the course of study (Education and Manpower Bureau, 2005b). In addition to the traditional hotel, travel and tourism, and food service courses, institutions also address the need of the growing Meeting, Incentive, Convention, and Exhibition (MICE) sector of the industry by offering MICE related courses and programmes. Furthermore, some of the programmes even focus on a broader aspect of leisure and tourism management.

These overseas programmes are regulated by the Non-Local Higher and Professional Education (Regulation) Ordinance which came into effect in June 1997. The objective of the Ordinance is to protect Hong Kong consumers by guarding against the marketing of sub-standard non-local higher and professional education courses conducted in Hong

Kong. It also enhances Hong Kong's reputation as a community that values rigorous and internationally recognized academic and professional standards. It aims to monitor the standards and quality of all courses conducted in Hong Kong leading to the award of non-local higher academic qualifications (i.e., sub-degree, degree, postgraduate or other post-secondary qualifications) or registered professional qualifications. Three types of programmes are exempted from registration: (a) courses conducted in collaboration with specified local institutions of higher education; (b) purely distance learning courses; and (c) courses conducted solely by local registered schools or local institutions of higher education (Education and Manpower Bureau, 2005b).

Associate Degree Programmes

In the early 2000s, it was noticed that the higher education system in Hong Kong had started to deviate from the traditional British model to a form of the North American model by the introduction of the Associate Degree (AD) level awarded by non-government educational institutions. AD is a two-year programme commonly offered by the community colleges in the United States and, upon completion of the programme, graduates can choose to progress to complete the final two years at universities offering full degree programmes (Hobson, 1999). The Chief Executive of the Hong Kong SAR Government in his annual policy address proposed to support the progressive increase in post-secondary education. By the academic year 2010-2011, 60% of the senior secondary school leavers in Hong Kong will have access to post-secondary education (Education and Manpower Bureau, 2005a). The Government also encouraged tertiary institutions, private enterprises and other organizations to provide options other than traditional Secondary Six and Seven education, such as professional diploma courses, and allocate more resources by providing land and loans to those institutions interested in offering such courses. Therefore, a number of tertiary institutions and private organizations started to offer courses at AD level for the first time in 2002. According to the Education and Manpower Bureau of the Hong Kong SAR, the qualification of an AD award is described as follows (Education and Manpower Bureau, 2005c):

> As an exit qualification for further studies, an AD award is normally equivalent to 50% of a 4-year university degree (North American model) or one-third of a 3-year university degree (British model). In other words, AD graduates can articulate to Year 3

of a 4-year university degree (North American model) or Year 2 of a 3-year university degree (British model). As an exit qualification for employment purpose, AD should generally be considered as equivalent to that of a Higher Diploma.

Successful applicants with Secondary Five qualification are required to complete a pre-AD programme for at least one year before progressing to the two-year AD programme, while Secondary Seven graduates can enrol in the first year of the AD programme. The Hong Kong Community College (HKCC), formed by PolyU in 2002 as an independent, self-financed entity, was among the first tertiary institutions offering AD programmes, including AD in Business, specializing in hospitality and tourism, for young school leavers. Some institutions also offered specialized AD in hospitality and tourism related disciplines including the AD in Hospitality and Tourism Management offered by The School of Continuing Studies (SCS) of the CUHK, Advanced Diploma in Hospitality Management and Advanced Diploma in Tourism Management offered by the School of Professional and Continuing Education (SPACE) of the University of Hong Kong (HKU) in the same year.

Top-Up Degree Programmes

With the large numbers of HD graduates from PolyU, IVE Haking Wong, and IVE Chai Wan, saw the need to upgrade their academic qualifications, PolyU launched a top-up programme for BA (Hons) in Hotel and Catering Management in which HD holders who were working full-time in the industry could complete the required number of courses and obtain a Bachelor's degree. This top-up programme was first offered in part-time mode (three-year) in 1999. The full-time mode was launched in 2002 and attracted a number of recent graduates from HD hospitality and tourism management programmes who wanted to immediately upgrade their qualification after graduation. The PolyU's School of Professional and Executive Education Development (SPEED) also offered a BA in Travel Industry Management in 2003 delivered in both part-time and full-time mode.

More institutions began to offer non-government funded top-up degree programmes in 2004 since the first batch of AD graduates were looking for opportunities to upgrade their qualification. There was also an increase in the number of non-local institutions offering their hospitality programmes in Hong Kong. Some examples included the BSc (Hons) in Hospitality Management from Sheffield Hallam University of the United Kingdom through the Management Learning Institute, a local private training company, and the Bachelor of Arts in Hotel and Hospitality Management from the University of Strathclyde, Scotland, offered by HKU's School of Professional and Continuing Education (SPACE). Both programmes are offered in part-time mode.

Post-Graduate Programmes

Before 1990, higher education programmes in hospitality and tourism management were mainly offered at sub-degree and undergraduate levels. In 1991, the then Department of Hospitality Management at PolyU began admitting a handful of Doctor of Philosophy (PhD) and Master of Philosophy (MPhil) students. The objectives of these research-based programmes was to train future research personnel and educators for the industry. CUHK's School of Hotel Management also admitted MPhil and PhD students in 1999.

With the increasing demand for industry practitioners to upgrade their academic qualifications, PolyU began offering Master of Science (MSc) and Post-graduate Diploma (PgD) in Hotel and Tourism Management in 1994. These programmes mainly targeted local industry practitioners with supervisory or managerial experiences in the hospitality or tourism industry. The programmes have a stronger focus on courses related to business practices in the hotel and tourism sectors to prepare students who are full-time managers and executives in the hospitality and tourism industries and allows them to finish in three years for MSc and two years for PgD. Started in 2002, the programmes were also offered in one-year full-time mode and attracted students from overseas and Mainland China. The success of PolyU's MSc programme in Hong Kong also led the School of Hotel and Tourism Management to offer the programme in Hangzhou, China in 2000 via the University's Outpost Centre in Zhejiang University, in block study mode and taught by staff from the School. The content of the programme is the same as the programme offered in Hong Kong. Responses to the Hangzhou programme were overwhelming. The School also started to offer the same programme in Beijing in 2004 with the same content as the Hangzhou programme due to the increase in demand from Beijing.

As with the undergraduate programmes, a number of overseas institutions also offered graduate programmes in Hong Kong either via distance-learning mode, block delivery or part-time modes. For example, a MSc in Hospitality and Tourism Marketing was offered by Victoria University in Australia and managed by a local enterprise, Media

Learning (formerly Media Education Info-Tech Co. Ltd.), and a Master of Management (Hospitality and Tourism Management) offered by Macquarie University operated by the Hong Kong Management Association, were some of the early entrants into this non-local higher education market in the field of hospitality and tourism.

OVERVIEW OF CURRENT HOSPITALITY AND TOURISM HIGHER EDUCATION IN HONG KONG

There are many hospitality and tourism higher education programmes at different levels to train Hong Kong professionals for the industry. These can be categorized by the source of funding and types of programmes. The programmes included in this section were listed in the Education and Manpower Bureau website, and course brochures of individual programmes as of January 2005.

Government-Funded Sub-Degree Education

Sub-degree programmes include programmes leading to a qualification at AD, HD or Professional Diploma level (Education and Manpower Bureau, 2005d) mainly targeting secondary school leavers. Both AD and HD programmes equip students with generic skills, knowledge in specialised disciplines and practical vocational skills. In general, AD programmes put more emphasis on general education, while HD and Professional Diploma courses are more vocationally oriented.

As shown in Table 1, two institutions offer government-funded sub-degree programmes. They are all HD programmes in the hospitality and tourism-related discipline. These are the School of Hotel and Tourism Management of PolyU and the HKIVE (Chai Wan). The HD programmes mainly target Secondary 7 graduates with the emphasis on equipping the students with technical, operational and professional skills for the hospitality and tourism industry. These programmes specifically prepared students for entry-level supervisory skills essential for a career within the industry. These programmes have a stronger vocational component in which students are required to work in the industry for industrial placement for an extended period of time (between 6 to 12 months) prior to graduation.

TABLE 1. Government-Funded Sub-Degree Programmes

Programme/award	Mode and duration of study	Offered by
HD in Hotel and Catering	Full time: 3 years	Hong Kong Institute of Vocational Education (Chai Wan)
HD in Travel and Tourism	Full time: 3 years	Hong Kong Institute of Vocational Education (Chai Wan)
HD in Leisure Studies	Full time: 3 years	Hong Kong Institute of Vocational Education (Chai Wan)
HD in Hotel, Catering, and Tourism Management	Full-time: 3 years Part-time: maximum 6 years	The Hong Kong Polytechnic University, School of Hotel & Tourism Management

Non-Government Funded Sub-Degree Education

As shown in Table 2, universities, vocational institutions, private institutions, and organizations offered a variety of non-funded sub-degree programmes. These programmes are usually designed for Secondary 7 graduates or those who have completed a Diploma or Foundation Diploma in the related area of studies.

In terms of the specializations of study the non-government funded sub-degree programmes are very much driven by the demand from potential students and industry practitioners. Since the MICE sector of the tourism industry is one of the developing sectors of Hong Kong's tourism industry, a number of programmes are offered on MICE, events, and entertainment business. Studies in cultural tourism, eco-tourism and heritage tourism studies are also in demand. Most of the AD Programmes tend to be more general by either following a business-related or social science route with emphasis on tourism and hospitality.

Government-Funded Undergraduate (Degree) Education

Currently, there are only two government-funded undergraduate programmes offered by PolyU and CUHK as shown in Table 3. Secondary 7 graduates with HKALE results (past and/or current) can apply for these programmes through the Joint University Programmes Admission Systems (JUPAS).

The BA (Hons) programme offered by PolyU has three specializations–Hotel Management, Catering Management and Tourism Management. Students are admitted to one of the respective specializations they apply for and are required to complete a suite of required foundation courses in hotel, catering, and tourism and a number of required courses in their own specialization. Students can also enrol in elective

TABLE 2. Non-Government Funded Sub-Degree Programmes

Programme/award	Mode and duration of study	Offered by	Remarks
HD in International Hospitality Management	Full time: 1 year	Hong Kong Institute of Vocational Education (Haking Wong)	Targeting students with foundation diploma qualification
HD in Theme Park and "MICE" Tourism	Full time: 2 years	Hong Kong Institute of Vocational Education (Chai Wan)	
HD in Sustainable Tourism (Eco-Tourism, Culture, and Harbour Tourism)	Full time: 2 years	Hong Kong Institute of Vocational Education (Chai Wan)	
HD in e-Tourism	Full time: 4 years	I long Kong Institute of Vocational Education (Chai Wan)	
HD in Entertainment Business Operations	Full time: 4 years	Hong Kong Institute of Vocational Education (Chai Wan)	
HD in Tourism and Events Management	Full time: 2 years	The University of Hong Kong, School of Professional and Continuing Education	
Higher National Diploma in Travel and Tourism	Full time: 2 years	Hong Kong College of Technology	
HD in Business (Tourism)	Full time: 3 years	Hong Kong College of Technology	
Associate of Social Science (Tourism)	Full time: 2 years	The Hong Kong Institute of Education, Division of Continuing Professional Education	
AD of Business	Full-time: 2 years Part-time 32 months	Hong Kong Institute of Technology	Students can major in either Hospitality Management, Tourism Management, Hospitality and Tourism Management
Associate of Social Science (Tourism)	Part-time: 2 years	The Hong Kong Institute of Education, Division of Continuing Professional Education	
Associate of Business Administration (ABA) in Tourism and Marketing Management	Full-time: 2 years	Caritas Francis Hsu College	
Foundation Degree in Hospitality Management	Distance learning: 2 years	The Hong Kong University of Science and Technology, College of Lifelong Learning	This is a distance learning programme offered by University of Derby, Buxton, UK
Advanced Diploma in Hospitality Management	Part-time: 16-36 months	The University of Hong Kong, School of Professional & Continuing Education	
Advanced Diploma in Tourism Management	Part-time: 16-36 months	The University of Hong Kong, School of Professional & Continuing Education	
Professional Diploma in Tourism Studies	Part-time: 235 hours	The University of Hong Kong, School of Professional & Continuing Education	

TABLE 2 (continued)

Programme/award	Mode and duration of study	Offered by	Remarks
Professional Diploma in Hospitality Studies	Part-time: 240 hours	The University of Hong Kong, School of Professional & Continuing Education	
Professional Diploma in Management and Marketing of Business Events	Part-time: 36 sessions	Hong Kong Exhibition & Convention Industry Association Ltd and the Hong Kong Productivity Council	

TABLE 3. Government-Funded Undergraduate Programmes

Programme/award	Mode and duration of study	Offering institutions/organizations
BA (Hons) in Hotel, Catering, and Tourism Management	Full time: 3 years or 4 years sandwich mode	The Hong Kong Polytechnic University, School of Hotel & Tourism Management
BBA (Hons) in Hotel and Tourism Management	Full time: 3 years	The Chinese University of Hong Kong, School of Hotel & Tourism Management

courses outside their areas of specialization. The programme offered by PolyU is the only undergraduate programme in Hong Kong where students can specialize in catering and foodservice management. The BBA (Hons) programme offered by CUHK requires students to take the core curriculum of business courses as well as courses in hotel and tourism management.

Non-Government-Funded Undergraduate (Degree) Education

As shown in Table 4, there are two main types of non-government funded undergraduate (degree) hospitality and tourism programmes in Hong Kong–a top-up or articulation programme and a full undergraduate programme. With the increasing number of graduates from the sub-degree programmes offered by the different institutions over the years, the demand for top-up articulation programmes is relatively high. Industry practitioners are seeking for opportunities to upgrade their existing qualification to a recognized degree. Duration of study for these top-up programmes ranges from one to three years depending on the mode of study. A few of the programmes are Honours programmes while the majority are non-honours programmes.

PolyU's School of Hotel and Tourism Management offers a top-up programme, BA (Hons) in Hotel and Catering Management, in both

TABLE 4. Non-Government-Funded Undergraduate Programmes

Programme/award	Mode and duration of study	Offered by	Remarks
BA (Hons) in Hotel, Catering, and Tourism Management	Full-time: 1 year Part-time: 3 years	The Hong Kong Polytechnic University, School of Hotel and Tourism Management	Top-up degree programme for applicants with Associate Degree or Higher Diploma qualifications
BA in Travel Industry Management	Full-time: 1.5 years	The Hong Kong Polytechnic University, School of Professional Education and Executive Development	Top-up degree programme for applicants with Associate Degree or Higher Diploma qualifications
BA in Hotel and Hospitality Management	Part-time: 16-36 months	The University of Hong Kong, School of Professional & Continuing Education (SPACE)	Top-up degree programme for applicants with Associate Degree or Advanced/Higher Diploma qualifications. Graduates from this programme can progress to the Jointly offered by SPACE and The Scottish Hotel School, University of Strath-clyde
BA in Tourism Management	Part-time: 16-36 months	The University of Hong Kong, School of Professional & Continuing Education (SPACE)	Top-up degree programme for applicants with Associate Degree or Advanced/Higher Diploma qualifications. Graduates from this programme can progress to the Jointly offered by SPACE and The Scottish Hotel School, University of Strath-clyde
BA (Hons) in Travel and Tourism Management	Full-time: 10 months	The City University of Hong Kong, School of Continuing and Professional Education	Top-up degree programme for applicants with Associate Degree or Advanced/Higher Diploma qualifications. Offered by the University of Northumbria at Newcastle, United Kingdom
BA (Hons) in International Hospitality and Tourism	Full-time: 10 months	Vocational Training Council	Top-up degree programme for applicants with Associate Degree or Advanced/Higher Diploma qualifications. Offered by the University of Northumbria at Newcastle, United Kingdom
BSc(Hons) in Hospitality Management	Full-time 12 months	Management Learning	Top-up degree programme for applicants with Associate Degree or Advanced/Higher Diploma qualifications. Offered by the Sheffield Hallam University, United Kingdom
BSc (Hons) in International Tourism Business Management	Full-time: 12 months	Management Learning	Top-up degree programme for applicants with Associate Degree or Advanced/Higher Diploma qualifications. Offered by the Sheffield Hallam University, United Kingdom

Programme/award	Mode and duration of study	Offered by	Remarks
Bachelor of Commerce (Tourism Management)	Part-time: 2 years	Hong Kong Management Association (HKMA), Professional Institute of Management and Education	Top-up degree programme for applicants with Certificate/Diploma qualifications. Offered by Curtin University of Technology Australia in cooperation with HKMA
Bachelor of Arts (Hons) in Travel and Tourism Management	Part-time: 2 years	Hong Kong College of Technology	Top-up degree programme for applicants with Associate Degree or Advanced/Higher Diploma qualifications. Offered by the University of Ulster, UK
BA (Hons) Hospitality and Tourism Management	Part-time: 20 months	Caritas Francis Hsu College, Center for Advanced and Professional Studies	Top-up degree programme for applicants with Associate Degree or Higher Diploma qualifications. Offered by the Birmingham College of Food, Tourism & Creative Studies, UK
Bachelor of Business	Full-time: 3 years, Part-time: 4 years and 8 months	Hong Kong Institute of Technology	Offered by Victoria University Australia. Students can major in Hospitality Management Tourism Management, or Hospitality and Tourism Management

full-time and part-time mode. This programme is specifically tailor-made for the School's HD graduates and graduates of other AD programmes. The BA in Travel Industry Management is a top-up programme offered by the PolyU's SPEED. Students can specialize in either tourism management, convention and event management, or tourism retailing. The City University of Hong Kong, School of Continuing and Professional Education, offers a full-time top-up BA (Hons) in Travel and Tourism Management awarded by the University of Northumbria at Newcastle-upon-Tyne, United Kingdom. Its sister programme BA (Hons) in International Hospitality and Tourism is offered through the Vocational Training Council. The HKU's SPACE offers two BA programmes in collaboration with the Scottish Hotel School of the University of Strathclyde–BA in Hotel and Hospitality Management and BA in Tourism Management. Graduates from these two programmes can enter the Honours (final) year for the BA programme of the Scottish Hotel School.

Other institutions from the United Kingdom and Australia also offer their undergraduate top-up programmes in Hong Kong through some private organizations and education institutions, including the Hong Kong Management Association, the Caritas Francis Hsu College, Centre for Advanced and Professional Studies, Management Learning Institute, and the Hong Kong Technical College. In line with the postgraduate programmes offered by overseas institutions, these overseas top-up degree programmes are also regulated by the Non-Local Higher and Professional Education (Regulation) Ordinance.

In addition to top-up degree programmes, overseas institutions also provide their off-shore programmes in Hong Kong. The Victoria University in Australia offers a full Bachelor of Business through a private institute, Hong Kong Institute of Technology. The programme is offered in both full-time (3 years) and part-time (4 years and 8 months) mode in which students can choose to major in Hospitality Management Tourism Management, or Hospitality and Tourism Management.

Government-Funded Postgraduate Education

Since the early 1990s, institutions in Hong Kong began offering hospitality and tourism post-graduate programmes. The University Grants Committee (UGC) of Hong Kong is a non-statutory advisory committee responsible for advising the Hong Kong SAR Government on the development and funding needs of higher education institutions in the SAR. Under the current education funding system, PolyU and The CUHK are the only two government-funded institutions offering higher education in hospitality and tourism management. The government-funded post-graduate programmes that these two institutions offer are research-based MPhil and PhD programmes as listed in Table 5.

TABLE 5. Government-Funded Post-Graduate Programmes

Programme/award	Mode and duration of study	Offering institutions/organizations
MPhil in Business Administration	Full-time: 2 years	The Chinese University of Hong Kong, School of Hotel & Tourism Management
PhD in Business Administration	Full-time: 3 years Part-time: 5 years	The Chinese University of Hong Kong, School of Hotel & Tourism Management
Master of Philosophy in Hotel and Tourism Management	Full-time: 2 years Part-time: 4 years	The Hong Kong Polytechnic University, School of Hotel & Tourism Management
PhD in Hotel and Tourism Management	Full-time: 3 years Part-time: 6 years	The Hong Kong Polytechnic University, School of Hotel & Tourism Management

Non-Government Funded (Self-Financed) Postgraduate Education

With the increase in demand for hospitality and tourism professionals with higher academic qualifications, government-funded institutions started to offer self-financed post-graduate programmes. These programmes are coursework-based in which students are required to take a certain number of postgraduate level hospitality or tourism related courses in either taught mode or distance learning mode. Some programmes also have a thesis or dissertation component. The courses are mainly geared towards the needs of the industry in terms of the practicality of the content delivered. They include Post-graduate Certificate (PgC), Post-graduate Diploma (PgD), Master's level programmes in full-time or part-time mode and are summarized in Table 6. Most programmes have a hotel/hospitality and tourism focus, while others have a greater emphasis on travel and tourism.

TABLE 6. Non-Government Funded (Self-Financed) Post-Graduate Education

Programme/award	Mode and duration of study	Offering institutions/organizations
MSc in Hotel and Tourism Management	Full-time: 1 year Part-time: 3 years	The Hong Kong Polytechnic University, School of Hotel & Tourism Management
PgD in Hotel and Tourism Management	Part-time: 2 years	The Hong Kong Polytechnic University, School of Hotel & Tourism Management
MSc in Travel and Tourism Management	Distance learning: 2.5-3 years	The Hong Kong University of Science and Technology, College of Lifelong Learning
PgD in Travel and Tourism Management	Distance learning: 2 years	The Hong Kong University of Science and Technology, College of Lifelong Learning
PgC in Travel and Tourism Management	Distance learning: 1 year	The Hong Kong University of Science and Technology, College of Lifelong Learning
MSc in Hospitality and Tourism Marketing	Part-time: 2 years	Hong Kong Institute of Technology
Master of Management (MM) (Hospitality and Tourism Management)	Part-time: 18 months	Offered by Macquarie School of Graduate Management, Australia in cooperation with International College of Tourism and Hotel Management (ICTHM) and operated by the Hong Kong Management Association (HKMA), Professional Institute of Management and Education
MSc in Hospitality Management	Distance learning with classroom tutorials and lectures. Part-time: 2 years	Offered by the Sheffield Hallam University, United Kingdom and operated by the Management Learning Institute
Master of Arts in Hospitality Management	Part-time: 30 months	Offered by Birmingham College of Food, Tourism & Creative Studies and operated by the Caritas Francis Hsu College, Center for Advanced and Professional Studies

For the part-time programmes, applicants are mainly local managers and executives who are currently working in the hospitality and tourism industry, but there are also other applicants who may not have any working experience in the industry but intend to broaden their scope of knowledge in the booming tourism industry. They are delivered in either traditional taught-mode or distance-learning mode using Internet, CD-ROM or study packages without face-to-face interactions. Full-time MSc is only offered by PolyU's School of Hotel and Tourism Management. The programme has attracted not only local students but a good number of overseas and Mainland Chinese students as well. The MSc programme is also offered in Hangzhou and Beijing in collaboration with universities in the mainland serving the industry practitioners and executives in the region. Other postgraduate level programmes are offered by overseas institutions as franchised programmes in which a local organization or institution is appointed to administer the programme on their behalf while the curriculum and the degree awarded are the same as their domestic programme. These programmes usually combine the traditional taught-mode, delivered by the faculty members appointed by the overseas institutions, with distance learning components.

It is important to recognize the contributions made by the various parties over the years in offering a plethora of hospitality and tourism education programmes to meet the needs of the flourishing tourism industry of Hong Kong. It started with only a few vocational training programmes offered by the Technical Institute and has evolved into a wide spectrum of courses at various levels offered by government-funded institutions, its self-financed professional and continuing education units, and other private enterprises, organizations and associations. These programmes are mainly targeting different types of students as show in Table 7. In addition to the types of programmes available, students' choice of the individual programmes also depends very much on their economic and financial situation, availability of financial subsidies from the Government, their career aspirations and opportunities in the hospitality and tourism industry.

FUTURE DEVELOPMENTS OF HOSPITALTY AND TOURISM EDUCATION IN HONG KONG

In view of the continuous support from the government in developing the tourism industry as one of the major pillar of Hong Kong's economy, it is expected that the demand for professionally trained people

TABLE 7. Hospitality and Tourism Higher Education Programmes Targeting Different Types of Candidates

Programmes	Candidates
• Universities which offer hospitality and tourism management degree and sub-degree programmes • Overseas off-shore programmes • Self-financed Associate Degree programmes offered by different institutions and organizations	Secondary 7 graduates who seek admission to tertiary level education.
• Self-financed top-up degree programmes	Associate Degree and Higher Diploma graduates who would like to upgrade to a degree qualification
• Self-financed course-work based post-graduate programmes offered by universities and overseas programmes administered by local institutions • Government-funded research based post-graduate programmes offered by universities	Industry practitioners who are degree holders and would like to upgrade to a post-graduate level qualification

will continue to increase over the next decade. In addition, tourism in Mainland China is growing at a rapid pace. With the Beijing Olympics coming up in 2008 and the forecast from the World Tourism Organization that China will become the world's leading travel destination by 2020, more opportunities are available for Hong Kong people who are interested in developing a career in the field of hospitality and tourism in Mainland China. Therefore, the number of hospitality and tourism programmes will continue to grow. A number of trends are worthy of attention by the providers and end-users of these programmes.

The "Asian Wave"

Hospitality and tourism education has developed in three different stages. Beginning with European programmes emphasizing the practical training and apprenticeship, through U.S. programmes focusing on the management science of the hospitality and tourism industry to the Asian emphasis on innovation and service quality. Asia will emerge as a global centre for excellence in hospitality and tourism in the future. The growth and success of Asian-based multinational corporations in hospitality businesses are mainly due to the innovative strategies, modern technology and most importantly, the strong hospitality culture and human resources which are unique to the region (K. Chon, personal communication, February, 2005; School of Hotel and Tourism Management, 2005). This "Asian Wave" will continue to influence and shape the future of the hospitality and tourism industry in the future. Hospitality and tourism programmes in Asia are leading the world to experience this new wave (K. Chon). Programmes in Hong Kong have many advantages, since the development of the programmes are supported by high demand from the tourism industry and the strong hospitality culture brought in by the establishments of Asian-based hospitality organizations.

Increase in Demand for Hospitality and Tourism Programmes

Demand for hospitality and tourism management programmes at all levels will continue to grow since a series of support measures for both students and providers of post-secondary programmes have been intro-duced by the Hong Kong Government. For example, the provision of student grants and loans, as well as an interest free start-up loan to post-secondary education institutions, will encourage practitioners to enrol in courses to upgrade their qualifications. This will certainly en-courage more private organizations and self-financed and continuing education units of education institutions to offer more hospitality and tourism education programmes to fulfil the need. The market for these programmes has also become more competitive as students have more choices with the increase in the number of programmes offered at dif-ferent levels.

With the increase in the number of self-financed AD and HD programmes, there is certainly a need to provide more top-up degree programmes to satisfy the demands from this particular group. Articu-lation arrangements between the sub-degree programmes and top-up degree programmes will be an important consideration when students are considering enrolling in sub-degree programmes in the future. It is also important for institutions offering AD, HD, and top-up degree programmes to coordinate the design of their curricula so as to better ac-commodate the articulation from AD/HD to degree programme.

The Curriculum

In order to be more competitive, curriculum should be tailored to meet the needs of the hospitality and tourism industry in terms of the professional skills required. Universities, institutions, and other orga-nizations offering hospitality and tourism programmes should work closely with the industry in developing and reviewing the curriculum.

Universities offering degree and postgraduate degree programmes have been consulting the industry about the design of their curriculum through the advisory committees composed of industry practitioners and executives. Since the hospitality and tourism industry is operating in a rapidly changing environment, the curricula of these programmes have to be reviewed periodically in order to meet the changing needs of the industry. The two universities offering hotel and tourism management degree programmes are constantly reviewing and modifying their curricula in consultation with the industry representatives. There is now a greater emphasis on competence rather than transfer of theoretical knowledge for hospitality and tourism programmes.

PolyU's School of Hotel and Tourism Management has created new programmes and modified the curricula of the programmes over the years and will be introducing the latest version of its curriculum in September 2005. The award for the two bachelor degree programmes will be renamed Bachelor of Science (BSc) (Hons) in Hotel Management and BSc (Hons) in Tourism Management in order to reflect the scientific nature of hospitality and tourism management disciplines. The new curricula of these programmes reflect the growing demand for specialized education in specific sectors of the hospitality and tourism industry but still retaining the emphasis on integrating practical experience and theories. These specializations include Lodging Development, Foodservice Management, Convention and Exhibition Management, Aviation Services Management, and Theme Park and Attractions Management. In addition, the new programmes will incorporate liberal elements such as culture and sociology in the courses. This will help students generate new ways of thinking and a wider appreciation of world views on the concepts of hospitality and tourism (Morrison & O'Mahony, 2003). Changes will also be introduced to the School's MSc programme to allow students to specialize in one area such as Tourism Management, International Hotel Management, and Convention and Events Management.

Opportunities in Mainland China

Since the 1990s, Mainland China's national policy of accelerating reform and an open door policy to the outside world, has improved the living standards of the people. Tourism has developed rapidly in China. In 1998, an economic conference held by the Central Committee of the Communist Party of the Peoples' Republic of China recognized tourism as a new economic growth area. In 2000, the National Tourism Bureau set an objective to turn China from an Asian tourism power to a global tourism powerhouse. Twenty-four provinces and municipalities in China have since chosen tourism as their mainstay industry (He, 2004). It is estimated by the World Tourism Organization that China will become the biggest travel destination in the world by 2020. With the rapid development of tourism and China's accession to the World Trade Organization, high quality hospitality and tourism personnel are needed.

The China National Tourism Administration (CNTA) has always placed great emphasis on tourism education and training and regarded it as a key strategic task to promote tourism development. Under the framework of China's tourism master development plan, CNTA formulated a plan for tourism education and training every five years. The emphasis is to educate four categories of personnel, namely administrative leadership, business operational professionals, high demand personnel and tourism educators ("Knowledge in Tourism from the Top," 2003).

According to Prof. He Jian Wei of the Shenzhen Tourism College of Jinan University, the training of tourism personnel in Mainland China is lagging behind (He, 2004). Both the quantity and quality of tourism personnel fail to meet the demand of the fast development of the tourism industry. Most of the undergraduate programmes focus on vocational training while postgraduate programmes train "scholars" instead of professional managers with an international outlook which the industry is looking for. On a similar note, Mr He Guangwei, CNTA Chairman, expressed a view that the development of Chinese tourism needs a huge number of personnel with theoretical and professional knowledge, but also the experience of studying overseas ("Knowledge in Tourism from the Top," 2003). These aspects create tremendous opportunities for well-established universities in Hong Kong to cooperate with universities in the mainland in offering post-graduate programmes specifically targeting the mainland market as well as attracting mainland students for the programmes offered in Hong Kong.

The MSc programmes offered by PolyU's School of Hotel and Tourism Management in collaboration with Zhejiang and Beijing International Studies Universities are very successful examples. More collaboration with institutions in other cities for programmes at both post-graduate and undergraduate level is expected in the future. In view of the efforts made by Mainland Chinese tourism businesses to upgrade the academic qualifications of talented managerial and executive level staff, there are many opportunities for academic institutions to offer tailor-made postgraduate and undergraduate award programmes for these companies (R. Pine, personal communication, August, 2004).

International Strategies for University Programmes

Hong Kong's continued success as a destination in Asia owes much to its worldwide reputation for hospitality and quality services. As the hub of international tourism activities, the demand for professionally trained employees who have international exposure will continue to increase. Therefore, hospitality and tourism education providers should adopt international strategies in three different areas–encouraging international students to join the programmes, help students gain international exposure, and develop an international faculty.

With the increase in demand for hospitality and tourism courses, students' profiles may be more diverse. Local postgraduate programmes will continue to attract local industry executives who aim to upgrade their skills and qualifications. At the same time, self-financed programmes with a more established history will attract more students from overseas and mainland China as it is becoming more popular for students from the mainland to study full-time in Hong Kong, with support from their organizations. Universities offering hospitality and tourism management programmes are also aggressively recruiting high quality students from the mainland by participating in education exhibitions in major mainland cities.

Because of the international nature of the tourism industry, more international students are seeking opportunities to study outside their home country, and Hong Kong is one of their preferred choices. The number of international students enrolling in both undergraduate and postgraduate programmes will continue to grow in the coming years with the increase in reputation of the high quality hospitality and tourism programmes offered by the two universities in Hong Kong. In view of the increase in the diversity of the study body, there should be more balance between the needs of local and international students. The design of the curriculum, teaching and learning approaches, and the syllabus for individual courses should take into account cultural issues and diversity.

In addition, it is also critical for hospitality and tourism students to have a global view and understanding of the hospitality and tourism industry. Therefore, international academic collaborations through students and faculty exchanges will benefit the students. Through exchange programmes, students can gain an international perspective and improve their language and communication skills ("25 Years of Excellence," 2004). Study abroad and overseas work placements will continue to be important for students to acquire international experiences which will be beneficial for their personal development and future career progression (K. Chon, personal communication, February, 2005).

Furthermore, international exposure for local hospitality and tourism students is very important as well. Faculty members with an international background, industry experience, and excellent research ability are the cornerstone of a strong hospitality and tourism programme. In addition, the international experience of the faculty members can contribute to the design and delivery of programmes with a broader international and regional focus.

E-Learning

In addition to the traditional classroom delivery mode, a variety of approaches using the Internet and other information technologies to enable learning and teaching will continue to flourish. This is because e-learning offers a number of advantages for certain student populations over traditional single-site classroom approaches. E-learning will allow more student-centred learning rather than faculty-centred instruction. It also encourages interactive discussions involving all students. It can provide more flexibility for students to learn at their own pace and be geared more to the interest of continuous education and lifelong learning (Frechtling, 2003). Practitioners in the hospitality and tourism industry who are interested in upgrading their qualifications will benefit if more programmes are offered in e-learning mode since their job nature requires them to work shifts and long hours which may not be feasible for some of them to join traditional classroom-taught programmes on a regular basis.

This type of e-learning not only benefits programmes offered to the local community but to students overseas too. A good example of this type of successful "knowledge transfer" is the licensing of the BA (Hons) in Hotel and Catering Management top-up degree curriculum and teaching and learning material by PolyU to the Otago Polytechnic, Dunedin in New Zealand. Another example is the E-Learning Cooperation Model developed by the University of Quebec in Montreal and the George Washington University to deliver tourism education in developing countries in Africa (Frechtling, 2003). With the improvement in technology and the increase in access to personal computers and the Internet, this will encourage high quality undergraduate and post-graduate programmes offered by academic institutions in Hong Kong to be offered outside its territory. On a similar note, opportunities are available for overseas institutions to offer more distance learning hospitality and tourism programmes in Hong Kong.

Increase in Stakeholders' Participation

Education is the key to the development of human capital. Various stakeholders have an interest in ensuring that the provision of education is appropriate to meet the needs of the different parties. Greater acknowledgement of the role that stakeholders can play in the education process may assist the process of adaptation to the rapidly changing environment (King, 2004). In a traditional educational model, the key participants in the education process include the education institutions which provide the education, the students who are the recipients of education, and the tourism industry who are the future employers of the graduates. However, it is important for education institutions to work closely with other parties such as the government, non-government organizations, and the community as well (King, 2004).

There are several ways that more industry participation can be solicited. Traditional models of education in which funding from a single source, emphasis on curriculum-based learning, and teachers being recognized as figures of authority are no longer appropriate for education provision which is experiencing a period of rapid change (King, 2004). In view of the budget cuts from the Hong Kong Government, institutions currently enjoying government funding can no longer rely solely on this traditional funding source but need be more aggressive in obtaining funding from alternative sources to support their programmes. Therefore, universities can work closely with the industry as partners to contribute monetary support for research and education for advancement in academic knowledge and contributions to the industry. It is important to solicit industry's views about what needs be taught and what skills graduates should possess as industry will be the ultimate "end-users" (future employers) of the students. Advisory committees for education institutions which consist of industry members will continue to play an important role in guiding the development and modifications of the curriculum for hospitality and tourism programmes. In addition, industry's participation in selecting the candidates for hospitality and tourism programmes is a way to help the educational institutions in selecting the candidates with the appropriate attitude, personality, and passion for the industry. Currently, both universities offering degree programmes are inviting industry executives to participate in panel interviews for the applicants. The industry is very supportive of this initiative as they can contribute to the selection of future employees.

Another important stakeholder is the student. King suggests that greater emphasis on students as "clients" and "customers" is essential. Students' opinions about programme and curriculum matters should also be considered.

Universities need to work closely with government and non-government organizations in supporting tourism research and policy formulation. Since tourism is the key driver of Hong Kong's economy, the government is placing great emphasis in enhancing the growth of the industry. For example, the Hong Kong Government is committed to invest heavily in developing tourism attractions, such as Disneyland, the Cable Car System and the Hong Kong Wetland Park, and improving existing tourism facilities. Various initiatives have been taken by the government to strength heritage tourism in Hong Kong by inviting various parties to develop heritage tourism facilities. With its world-class infrastructure and tourism facilities, Hong Kong is well placed to become a regional cruise hub for North Asia, the South China Sea and the Far East. The government is committed to developing new cruise facilities in Hong Kong to capitalize on the rapid growth of the cruise industry worldwide and in particular in the Asia Pacific region ("25 Years of Excellence," 2005). Universities can play a more active role in tourism research from which the community, the industry, and the university can gain mutual benefits. The Public Policy Research Institute was formed by The Hong Kong Polytechnic University, and included tourism as one of its key research areas. This serves as a platform of collaboration between the University and the government, non-government organizations, and the industry ("Policy Makers," 2005).

CONCLUSION

Hospitality and tourism education in Hong Kong has grown from vocational training courses in the 1970s to a breadth of programmes offered by different institutions in different funding modes and various modes of study. The demand for these programmes will continue to increase in order to support the rapid growth of the tourism industry in Hong Kong, Mainland China, and the Asia-Pacific region. With more non-government funded sub-degree programmes offered by private organizations and educational institutions, it is important to ensure the quality of the programmes delivered by different parties. With more international students enrolling in degree and postgraduate degree programmes offered by the two universities in Hong Kong and an increase in opportunities for overseas exchange programmes, this will help the international exposure of local students to different cultures and improve their language and communication skills. Mainland China will continue to be a huge potential market and the hospitality and tourism programmes offered in Hong Kong or in collaboration with mainland education institutions will continue to be in demand. With all these developments and opportunities for Hong Kong's hospitality and tourism education, it is important to recognize that education institutions should involve the relevant stakeholders in the process of designing the programmes, providing teaching and learning experiences for students and giving support to the industry and government in research and development, and continuous professional and executive education.

REFERENCES

25 years of excellence. (2004). *Horizons, 4*(2), 3-7.

Chinese University of Hong Kong. (2005). Academic programs. Retrieved January 31, 2005, from the School of Hotel and Tourism Management of the Chinese University of Hong Kong Web site: http://htm.baf.cuhk.edu.hk/academic_shm.htm

Education and Manpower Bureau. (2005a). Expansion in post-secondary education opportunities. Retrieved January 30, 2005, from http://www.emb.gov.hk/index.aspx?langno=1&nodeid=1355#objective

Education and Manpower Bureau. (2005b). Non-local higher education and professional courses (2005). Retrieved January 31, 2005, from http://www.emb.gov.hk/index.aspx?nodeID=226&langno=1

Education and Manpower Bureau. (2005c). Common descriptors on Associate Degree. Retrieved January 31, 2005, from http://www.emb.gov.hk/index.aspx?langno=1&nodeid=1222

Education and Manpower Bureau. (2005d). Post-secondary and higher education. Retrieved February 1, 2005, from http://www.emb.gov.hk/index.aspx?langno=1&nodeid=2118

Frechtling, D. (2003). E-Learning cooperation model for tourism education in developing countries. *Tedqual, 6*(1), 116-118.

He, J. (2004, October). *Strategies on training high quality tourism personnel under the tourism industrialization in China.* Keynote presentation at the First PolyU China Tourism Forum: Latest Developments in China Tourism, Hong Kong.

HKSAR. (2004). Provision of education. Retrieved January 30, 2005, from http://www.info.gov.hk/info/education.pdf

Hobson, J. S. P. (1999). International perspectives: A comparison of U.S., U.K., and Australian hospitality education and their university systems. In C. W. Barrows & R. H. Bosselman (Eds.), *Hospitality management education* (pp. 213-238). Binghamton, NY: The Haworth Hospitality Press.

Hong Kong Institute of Vocational Education. (2002). *25 years of hospitality education.* Hong Kong Institute of Vocational Education (Haking Wong) Department of Hotel, Services & Tourism Studies.

Hong Kong Tourism Board. (2004). *A statistical review of Hong Kong tourism 2003.* Hong Kong Tourism Board.

King, B. (2004, July). Hospitality and tourism education in the Asia-Pacific region: Involving our stakeholders. *APETTIT News, 3*(2), 5.

Knowledge in tourism from the top. (2003). *Tedqual, 6*(1), 50-54.

Morrison, A., & O'Mahony, G. (2003). The liberation of hospitality management education. *International Journal of Contemporary Hospitality Management, 15*(1), 38-44.

Policy makers. (2005). *Horizons, 5*(1), 4-5.

School of Hotel and Tourism Management. (2005). *School of Hotel and Tourism Management, The Hong Kong Polytechnic University* [Brochure]. Hong Kong: Author.

The Hong Kong Polytechnic University. (2005). History of the university. Retrieved February 1, 2005, from http://www.polyu.edu.hk/cpa/anniversary/history.htm

University Grants Committee. (2004). *Hong Kong higher education: To make a difference to move with the times.* Retrieved January 25, 2005, from http://www.ugc.edu.hk/english/documents/UGCpubs/policy%20document%20(e).pdf

World Tourism Organization (2000). *Tourism 2020 Vision.* Madrid, Spain: Author.

Tourism and Hospitality Higher Education in Taiwan: Past, Present, and Future

Jeou-Shyan Horng

Ming-Huei Lee

SUMMARY. The binary system of tourism and hospitality higher education in Taiwan divides into academic higher education and technical/vocational(institute/university of technology, five-year junior college and two-year junior college). The development of tourism and hospitality higher education in Taiwan is closely related to the growth in the domestic tourist market and the social development of the country. The earliest tourism education began in 1965. This long process of development has given Taiwanese tourism and hospitality education a multifaceted outlook and is generally divided into three periods: the origination period (1946~1968), the growth period (1969~1991), and the competition and adjustment period (1990~present). Over the past years, tourism and hospitality higher education in Taiwan has witnessed rapid growth in numbers, increasing diversification in program names, and with junior colleges and

Jeou-Shyan Horng is Professor, Division of Hospitality Management & Education, Department of Human Development & Family Studies, National Taiwan Normal University, 162, Sec 1, Ho-Ping E. Rd., Taipei 10610, Taiwan (E-mail: t10004@cc. ntnu.edu.tw).

Ming-Huei Lee is President, Taiwan Hospitality & Tourism College, 268, Chungshin St., Fengshan Village, Shoufeng, Hualien 974, Taiwan (E-mail: mhlee@ tht.edu.tw).

[Haworth co-indexing entry note]: "Tourism and Hospitality Higher Education in Taiwan: Past, Present, and Future." Horng, Jeou-Shyan, and Ming-Huei Lee. Co-published simultaneously in *Journal of Teaching in Travel & Tourism* (The Haworth Press, Inc.) Vol. 5, No. 3, 2005, pp. 167-196; and: *Global Tourism Higher Education: Past, Present, and Future* (ed: Cathy H. C. Hsu) The Haworth Press, Inc., 2005, pp. 167-196. Single or multiple copies of this article are available for a fee from The Haworth Document Delivery Service [1-800-HAWORTH, 9:00 a.m. - 5:00 p.m. (EST). E-mail address: docdelivery@haworthpress.com].

167

institutes of technology transforming themselves into universities of technology. Current tourism and hospitality programs are boosting global competitiveness for the future hospitality market in Taiwan, with careful positioning clear goals, curriculum planning, integrating hospitality/tourism curriculum, alliances and collaboration, and strengthening tourism and hospitality research. *[Article copies available for a fee from The Haworth Document Delivery Service: 1-800-HAWORTH. E-mail address: <docdelivery@ haworthpress.com> Website: <http://www.HaworthPress.com> © 2005 by The Haworth Press, Inc. All rights reserved.]*

KEYWORDS. Hospitality education, tourism education, hospitality, tourism, higher education

ACADEMIC INSTITUTION OF TOURISM AND HOSPITALITY EDUCATION IN TAIWAN

With domestic compulsory education extending from six to nine years in 1968, the official divided between general and technical/vocational education in the education system of Taiwan now begins after the nine years of national education (but with technical arts exploration education during the 7th to 9th grade). The tourism and hospitality education at college level is aimed at cultivating midrange managers for the industry, while the university level of tourism and hospitality education is provided for the preparation of higher level managers. Universities of technology are more focused on the teaching of professional theories and practical skills of the industry, with particular emphasis on hands-on practices and internships for the development of high-level skilled professionals for the industry. The graduate institutes of tourism and hospitality are geared more toward the cultivation of top-level senior managers and researchers. Over the past few years, many of the junior colleges in the technical and vocational education system have converted into institutes of technology. Still, there are some institutions maintaining the five-year and two-year junior college systems, which serve as an extension of the senior high school technical and vocational education.

Hospitality and tourism education in Taiwan covers a wide range of program levels (junior college, undergraduate, graduate, postgraduate) and academic institutions (two-year and five-year junior colleges, two-year and four-year institutes/universities of technology, universities, graduate institutes, part-time master programs, day and evening divisions, advanced study divisions, and extension programs). Tourism and hospitality education in Taiwan is gradually moving upward with the passage of time. Both masters and doctoral programs are already available. The availability of teacher preparation education and in-service advanced training is also improving as tourism and hospitality education continues to shifting upward, which include full-time master's programs, part-time master's programs, and doctoral programs. However, with the number of hospitality and tourism-related departments rising sharply, the demand for teachers both at home and abroad is also quickly soaring, making the gap between demand and supply continue to widen.

At present, tourism education in Taiwan is mainly divided into higher education system and technical/vocational education system, as discussed below.

The Higher Education System

In Taiwan, the primary source of undergraduate students receiving tourism and hospitality education in universities is senior high school graduates with only a small fraction being senior vocational school graduates. These students are admitted through university entrance exam, application, or recommendation. The graduate school system is mainly comprised of PhD and Master of Arts (MA) degree programs and takes in primarily university undergraduates from domestic higher education institutions as well as some graduates of technology universities from the technical/vocational system as shown in Figure 1. Currently, only the Department of Human Development and Family Studies of the National Taiwan Normal University offers a PhD program, which was set up under its nutrition, food and beverage management section (now the hospitality management and education section) in 2001.

The Technical/Vocational System

Tourism and hospitality higher education in the technical/vocational system of Taiwan currently covers two levels (i.e., institute/university of technology and junior colleges), with each level containing several different academic institutions, as discussed below.

FIGURE 1. Educational System

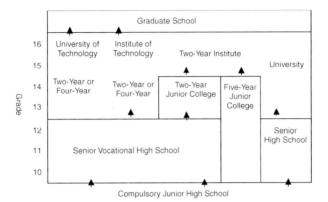

Institute/University of Technology

The tourism and hospitality education in the technical/vocational system of Taiwan can be divided into two major groups: universities of technology and institutes of technology. The undergraduate programs at universities/institutes of technology mainly contain two divisions.

One division is the four-year institutes of technology or universities of technology for senior high school and senior vocational high school graduates who passed the two-year and four-year Technological and Vocational Education (TVE) joint college entrance examination; students will obtain a bachelor's degree after successful completion of the four-year program. The other division is the two-year institute/university of technology, offering an opportunity of advanced study for two-year and five-year junior college graduates, who can receive a bachelor's degree upon completion of the two-year program.

Some of these universities even set up an affiliated two-year institute of technology, despite being part of the higher education system is similar to the aforementioned programs in terms of education goals. That is, to provide junior college or community college graduates a broader access to advanced studies.

Junior College

Traditionally, junior colleges included three different academic institutions of two-year, three-year, and five-year systems. Today, however, only the two-year and five-year junior college institutions remain. Each of these college institutions targets a different source of students, as illustrated in Figure 1.

Five-Year Junior College. The first five-year junior college department on tourism was established in 1965, which mainly admitted junior high school graduates and provided a complete five-year professional education on hospitality. This program was the main provider of professional training in the early days of Taiwan's tourism and hospitality education, and many of its graduates now working in the industry have received high appraisal for their strong professional capabilities. By the end of 1996, the Education Reform Committee of the Executive Yuan released its General Report on Educational Reform, which stressed that one of the higher education reform priorities was to separate the function of higher education from that of other educational systems so that educational resources could be fully and more effectively utilized. In response to the increasing demand for all kinds of higher education, the Committee proposed the establishment of more community colleges according to the domestic conditions in order to build a comprehensive and diversified system of higher education in Taiwan. The Committee also laid out its plans to set up community colleges across the country to ensure adequate and balanced access to higher education for community residents. After the release of the reform bill, the whole country seemed to be busy setting up colleges and universities. Due to the Chinese degree-chasing traditions and the deep-rooted value that liberal arts education is superior to technical or skill-oriented training, the cornerstone of junior college education (i.e., the five-year junior college system) was under serious threat. This is why junior colleges have been shrinking over the recent years. In replacement, many institutions have established a four-year institute of technology division to help fill this education gap.

Two-Year Junior College. Two-year junior colleges mainly offer further study for the graduates both from high school and vocational high school. Also, for those who in-service, these colleges provide them a continuing education opportunity as well. This indeed encourages many potential students willing to carry on two-year programs in tourism and hospitality.

Regretfully, the offer changes in 1996. Most of the colleges above are upgraded to four-year colleges. However, these colleges reserve the rights to affiliate two-year programs, according to the modified regulations made by the Ministry of Education in 1996. The impact occurs since most four-year colleges do not rely on or keep two-year programs due to competition in the free market. It can be seen the two-year program is diminishing. For those students wishing to take two-year programs, there are fewer and fewer choices.

Three-Year Junior College. The first three-year junior college was established in 1968, which mainly took in high school graduates and provided three-year comprehensive and professional training on tourism. Many of the graduates from these programs have taken leadership positions in today's tourism industry. Unfortunately, as many of these junior colleges continued to convert themselves into institutes, the three-year junior college system has ceased to admit new students since 1989.

DEVELOPMENT
OF TOURISM AND HOSPITALITY HIGHER EDUCATION
IN TAIWAN

The development of tourism and hospitality higher education in Taiwan is closely related to the growth in domestic tourist market and the social development of the country. The earliest tourism education began in 1965, with the establishment of a tourism department by Hsing Wu College. The Chinese Culture University soon followed suit, first setting up a tourism department, then a graduate institute, which is the first graduate study facility dedicated to tourism education in Taiwan. This tourism education and hospitality trend continued and gradually evolved into the incorporation of a sandwich-style instruction with the founding of National Kaohsiung Hospitality College. Driven by the overall economic development of Taiwan and the continuous growth of the local tourist business, the tourism and hospitality education has grown over the past forty years from scratch to the birth of two tourism schools under universities and expanded from junior colleges to universities, and from technical and vocational institutions to graduate schools including masters and doctoral programs, and even a hospitality college that provides the most comprehensive tourism and hospitality education. This process of development has given Taiwan's tourism and hospitality education a multifaceted outlook and is generally divided into the following three periods:

The Origination Period (1946~1968)

The first government-run tourism and travel agency in Taiwan was established in 1946, and the first large hotel with guest rooms exceeding

20 in number was set up in 1956, the same year when the government appointed a Tourism Commission to take the overall responsibility of managing tourism related affairs including the scenery, hotels, promotional efforts, planning, supervision, and coordination. At that time, the domestic tourism industry also began to take off. With the Japanese government lifting the ban on personal international travel in 1964, Taiwan began to receive foreign tourist groups, thereby infusing momentum into the local tourism and travel market. In 1965, Taiwan's ideal geographical location, abundant tourist resources, good social stability and security, low prices, and adequate tourist hotels and recreational facilities, began to attract American soldiers stationed in Vietnam for the Vietnam War to visit Taiwan for pleasure during holidays. On the catering front, this period also witnessed remarkable diversification of business types and models. The two drivers behind this change were: Internally, the integration of Chinese cuisines of various regional styles, and externally, the transformation and structural adjustment from a traditional agriculture-based society to a manufacturing industry-concentrated economy.

To cope with the increasing demand of the tourism industry for highly-trained professionals, Hsing Wu College established the first tourism department in Taiwan in 1965 and began to recruit and cultivate young talents for tourism (Table 1). In 1966, the Chinese Culture College, now the Chinese Culture University, also set up a tourism department. The college was converted into a university in 1968 and the name of the department was changed to Tourism Management. In 1989, the Chinese Culture University further established a graduate institute for tourism, giving tourism education an official status in the university system of Taiwan. The Chinese Culture University has since played an important role in the promotion of tourism education in Taiwan and has so far produced the most tourism graduates among domestic higher education institutions, many of them now taking leadership positions in local tourism businesses. During this period, Tamkang College and Ming Chuan College also joined in to provide tourism education in 1966 and 1968, respectively, marking the official beginning of tourism and hospitality higher education in Taiwan.

The Growth Period (1969~1991)

Before 1967, American tourists accounted for the largest share of all visitors to Taiwan. Japanese tourists ranked second, but later caught up from behind. The number of foreign tourists to Taiwan grew by 30-fold

TABLE 1. Milestone Events During the Origination Period

Year Founded	Original Institution Name	Original Department Name	Original Duration of Study (yrs)	Milestone Events
	Current Institution Name	Current Department Name	Current Duration (yrs)	
1965	Hsing Wu Junior College	Department of Tourism	5	• 1965: Five-year junior college.
	Hsing Wu College	Department of Tourism	4	• 1981: Added 2-year junior college program (evening division). • 1998: Added a supplementary school for advanced study. • 2000: Promoted into an institute of technology (includes: 4-year institute, 2-year junior college, 2-year institute, and 5-year junior college programs).
1966	Chinese Culture College	Department of Tourism Management	4	• 1968: Promoted into a university (the first university to have a department in tourism). • 1990: Established a graduate school for tourism (also the first of its kind).
	Chinese Culture University			
1966	Tamkang College	Department of Tourism	5	• 1966: Five-year junior college. • 1968: Added a 3-year junior college division.
	Aletheia University	School of Tourism (Tamkang Campus)	4	• 1994: Promoted into Tamsui Oxford College (Institute of Technology). • 1996: Added a leisure and recreation management department, under the 2-year institute of technology division.
		Department of Leisure and Recreation Management (Matou Campus)		• 1998: Added the Department of Airline Services Management and the Department of Leisure and Recreation Technology (under the 4-year institute of technology division).
		Department of Hotel & Restaurant Management (Matou Campus)		• 1999: Name changed to Aletheia University. • 2001: Established a school of tourism, which consisted of a department of tourism, department of hotel and restaurant management, and department of leisure and recreation management (includes: 4-year institute and 2-year institute programs).
		Department of Airline Service Management (Matou Campus)		

Year Founded	Original Institution Name	Original Department Name	Original Duration of Study (yrs)	Milestone Events
	Current Institution Name	Current Department Name	Current Duration (yrs)	
1968	Ming Chuan College	Department of Tourism	3	• 1968: Established a 3-year junior college division.
	Ming Chuan University	Ming Chuan School of Tourism	4	• 1970: Added an evening division. • 1971: Added an evening 5-year program. • 1990: Promoted into Ming Chuan College of Management–Institute of Technology.
		Department of Tourism		• 1995: Added a part-time student class under the 3-year junior college division.
		Department of Leisure & Recreation Administration		• 1996: Relocated to Taoyuan. • 2000: Established the school of tourism, which consists of a department of tourism, a department of leisure and recreation administration, and a department of hospitality management. (4-year institute program)
		Department of Hospitality Management		• 2001: Established a graduate institute of tourism.

between 1956 and 1970, contributing to the 86-fold increase in foreign reserves. In 1972, the Taiwanese government pushed the passage of a revised law to set up a tourism bureau to manage all businesses and affairs relating to tourism to facilitate growth and development of the domestic tourism industry. Lured by the rising demand in the tourist and travel market of Taiwan, international hotel chains began to enter this country to provide relevant services at the same time. The first international hotel chain to enter Taiwan was the Hilton Hotels, which opened its first chain hotel in Taiwan in 1973.

In 1979, in order to build a positive country image in the international community and to cope with the social development trends, the government finally shifted from the previous overseas travel restriction that allowed only international travel for business, by invitation, and for family visitation to an open policy for individual tourists to travel overseas. In the meantime, the rigid international travel requirements and formalities of the past were either eliminated or much simplified. Since then, every citizen of Taiwan with means and time can go abroad for travel at any time. In 1987, Taiwan further lifted the restriction on family visitation to Mainland China, which helped fuel the increase in the number of outbound travelers. This, coinciding with a global economic boom, has triggered a full-scale economic prosperity in Taiwan. Under such environmental stimuli, the domestic tourism industry enjoyed a substantial growth, similar to that of inbound and outbound tourism. This was also the time when the Taiwan stock market soared the highest in history. "Stock-price watching in the mornings, tea drinking in the afternoons, and restaurant dining in the evenings" was becoming like a routine across the island; and the speculative madness of the crowds stunned the world. The food service industry was also rapidly growing and diversifying amidst this money-chasing game. The entrance of the fast-food chain, McDonald's, into the Taiwan market in 1984 made a profound impact and fueled the development of international restaurant chains on the domestic market. Within six months in the second half of 1990, three world-renowned multinational hotel groups (i.e., Grand Hyatt, Regent, and Sherwood) all set up their chain hotels in the city of Taipei. The entrance of these global hotel chains not only shook the entire landscape of the domestic hotel industry, but their international influence made them the benchmark of hotel management for local catering and restaurant operations.

In response to this rapid surge in the demand for tourism and hospitality professionals, tourism/hospitality related programs and departments mushroomed in domestic education systems, including senior high and senior vocational schools and junior colleges. Later in this period, even colleges and universities joined in, with World College of Journalism (Shih Hsin University), Providence University, Tung Fang College of Commerce and Technology (Tung Fang Institute of Technology), Jing Zhong College of Commerce (Taiwan Hospitality & Tourism College) and Jin Wen College (Jin Wen Institute of Technology) all setting up tourism/hospitality departments (Table 2). Hospitality and tourism became the hottest field in the higher learning institutions, competing neck-to-neck to establish their leader position in tourism education. In the meantime, the private sector also began to realize the importance of tourism education.

TABLE 2. Milestone Events During the Growth Period

Year Founded	Original Institution Name	Original Department Name	Original Duration of Study	Milestone Events
	Current Institution Name	Current Department Name	Current Duration of Study	
1976	World College of Journalism	Department of Tourism and Promotion	3	• 1976: Established a 3-year junior college division program for tourism and promotion (the only institute that contains a sound facility for tourism internships). • 1991: Established a tourism section under the department of public communications during the World College of Journalism period. • 1993: Added a department of tourism (4-year institute program). • 1997: Promoted to Shih Hsin University. • 1998: Added a graduate institute of tourism. • 1998: Divided the tourism department into hospitality management section and travel and recreation management section.
		Department of Tourism	4	
	Shih Hsin University	Hospitality Management Section		
		Travel & Recreation Management Section		
1987	Providence University	Department of Tourism	4	• 2000: Established a graduate institute of tourism.
1989	Jing Zhong College of Commerce	Department of Tourism	2 5	• 1989: Established department of tourism (2-year and 5-year junior college programs). • 2002: School name changed. • 2003: Added department of hotel management, department of travel management, department of leisure management, and department of food and beverage management.
	Taiwan Hospitality & Tourism College	Department of Hotel Management		
		Department of Travel Management		
		Department of Leisure Management		
		Department of Food & Beverage Management		
1990	Tung Fang College of Commerce and Technology	Department of Tourism	5 2	• 1990: Established department of tourism (5-year junior college). • 1993: Added a 2-year junior college division. • 2003: Converted into an institute of technology. (includes: 4-year institute, 2-year institute, 2-year junior college, and 5-year junior college programs).
	Tung Fang Institute of Technology		4	

The Competition and Adjustment Period (1990~Present)

Entering into the 1990s, the prosperity in economy and in tourism continued, and Taiwan has established itself as one of the developed countries, with tourist activities growing exponentially and the tourism industry facing its first transition in its development. The tourist market of Taiwan was now no longer comprised of only inbound and outbound tourism. As the private sector continued to invest in domestic tourist market and relevant tourist facilities, local excursion travel, now with much improved travel quality and much higher public awareness began to surge. To meet the demand of an increasingly diverse tourist market, the cultivation of professional manpower, both in terms of quality and quantity, also needed to be diversified.

The Chinese Culture University led the pack by establishing the first graduate institute of tourism with a master's program in 1990, and thereby ushered in an era of academic research on tourism in higher education institutions. The other universities soon followed suit, with Shih Hsin University, Chaoyang University of Technology, Dong Hwa University, Providence University, Da Yeh University, Ming Chuan University, Southern Taiwan University of Technology, National Taiwan Normal University, and Fu Jen Catholic University, all setting up master's degree programs for tourism or related fields (Table 3). The Human Development and Family Studies Department's Section on Hospitality Management and Education of the National Taiwan Normal University even established a PhD program in 2001.

In the meantime, the long-awaited National Kaohsiung Hospitality College finally received approval in 1995 after over a decade of lengthy discussion and planning. As the first professional tourism and hospitality institution in Taiwan, the establishment of this college marked a major step forward in the history of tourism education in Taiwan. The halo that traditionally surrounded tourism higher education in technical and vocational systems has officially shifted to the newly emerged "sandwich-style instruction," which has become a whole new system powerful enough to rival the technical and vocational systems since 1995.

What is "sandwich-style instruction"? Generally speaking, the instruction is based on the theory "Doing by leaning, learning by doing." It is thus schemed that students need to spend one semester or more practicing their skills in the fields to connect what they learn at school. Overall, the results show that the sandwich-style instruction does help students better adapt to their occupational career later on. With the joint effort of the industry, the academia, and the government, Taiwan's tour-

TABLE 3. Milestone Events During the Competition and Adjustment Period

Year Founded	Original Institution Name	Original Department Name	Original Duration of Study	Milestone Events
	Current Institution Name	Current Department Name	Current Duration of Study	
1991	Jin Wen College	Department of Tourism Department of Food & Beverage Management Department of Hotel Management Department of Travel Management	2	• 1991: Established a department of tourism (2-year junior college program). • Sandwich-style instruction. • 1997: Divided the department into department of tourism, department of food and beverage management, department of hotel management and travel management (the so-called sandwich-style instruction; 2-year junior college program). • 1999: Promoted into Jin Wen Institute of Technology and established a department of tourism (4-year institute and 2-year institute programs). • 2001: Department of food and beverage management, department of hotel management and travel management started 4-year programs (includes: 4-year institute, 2-year institute, and 2-year junior college programs).
	Jin Wen Institute of Technology	Department of Tourism Department of Food & Beverage Management Department of Hotel Management Department of Travel Management	4	
1992	Southern Taiwan College of Commerce and Technology	Department of Tourism	2	• 1992: Established a department of tourism (2-year junior college division program) • 1996: Promoted into Southern Taiwan Institute of Technology. • 1997: Changed to Department of Tourism Technology (2-year institute) under Southern Taiwan Institute of Technology. • 1998: Name changed to Department of Tourism. • 1999: Promoted into Southern Taiwan University of Technology. • 2000: Department of Tourism was name changed to the Department of Leisure, Recreation, and Tourism Management (4-year institute and 2-year institute programs). • 2003: Established a graduate institute for Leisure, Recreation, and Tourism Management.
	Southern Taiwan University of Technology	Department of Leisure Management	4	
1993	Kaohsiung Institute of Marine Technology, Penghu Campus	Department of Tourism	2	• 1993: Established department of tourism, National Kaohsiung Marine Academy-Penghu Campus (2-year college program). • 1995: National Pengh Marine Management College. • 1999: The Department of Tourism withdrew. Added a department of hospitality management and department of leisure management. • 2000: Promoted as National Penghu Institute of Technology (4-year institute program). • 2002: Department of Tourism was restored. • 2004: Established department of marine sports and management.
		Department of Tourism	4	
	National Pengh Marine Management College	Department of Leisure Management		
	National Penghu Institute of Technology	Department of Hotel Management Department of Marine Sports & Management		

TABLE 3 (continued)

Year Founded	Original Institution Name	Original Department Name	Original Duration of Study	Milestone Events
	Current Institution Name	**Current Department Name**	**Current Duration of Study**	
1995	National Kaohsiung Hospitality (Junior) College National Kaohsiung Hospitality College	Departments of Food & Beverage Management Department of Hotel Management Department of Travel Management Department of Airline Management Department of Chinese Culinary Arts Department of Western Culinary Arts Department of Baking Technology & Management Department of Hospitality Marketing Management Department of Leisure Recreation Tourism Department of Hotel & Restaurant Management	2 4	• 1995: Kaohsiung Hospitality College was established (2-year junior college). • 1995: Established department of hotel management and department of food and beverage management. • 1996: Established department of travel management. • 1997: Established department of airline service, department of Chinese culinary arts, department of western culinary arts, and baking technology and management. • Sandwich-style instruction. • 2000: Promoted into Kaohsiung Hospitality College (Institute of Technology, include: 4-year institute program, except Department of Hotel & Restaurant Management maintained 2-year junior college programs). • 2002: Established department of hospitality marketing management. • 2002: Name changed department of airline service to department of airline management. • 2003: Established a graduate institute of hospitality management. • 2004: Established a graduate institute of travel industry management.
1996	Da Yeh University	Department of Leisure Management	4	• 2000: Added a graduate program.
1996	National College of Physical Education and Sports	Department of Physical Education Management --- Department of Recreation & Leisure Industry Management	4	• 2003: Department name changed to department of recreation and leisure industry management.
1997	Chaoyang University of Technology	Department of Leisure Management	4	• 1997: Established department of leisure management (include: 4-year institute and 2-year institute program). • 1998: Established a graduate institute (the first private university of technology).
1997	Deh Yu College of Nursing and Management Ching Kuo Institute of Management and Health	Department of Food & Beverage Management Department of hotel and restaurant management	2 4	• 1997: Established department of food and beverage management (2-year junior college). • Sandwich-style instruction. • 2002: Promoted and changed the name to Ching Kuo Institute of Management and Health. • 2004: Department name changed to hotel and restaurant management (includes 4-year institute and 2-year institute programs).

Year Founded	Original Institution Name	Original Department Name	Original Duration of Study	Milestone Events
	Current Institution Name	Current Department Name	Current Duration of Study	
1997	Ling Tung College of Commerce	Department of Tourism	5 2	• 1997: Established Department of Tourism (5-yr junior college program).
	Ling Tung College	Department of Tourism & Leisure Management	4	• 1999: Promoted to Institute of Technology. • 2000: 2-year junior college program. • 2003: Name changed to department of tourism and leisure management (4-year institute program).
1998	Chung Hua University	Department of Hotel & Restaurant Management Department of Leisure & Recreation Management	4	• 1998: Established department of hotel and restaurant management. • 2004: Added a department for leisure and recreation management.
1998	Ming Hsin Institute of Technology	Department of Hotel Management	4	• 1998: Established department of hotel management. • Sandwich-style instruction.
	Ming Hsin University of Science & Technology	Department of Leisure Management		• 2000: Added department of leisure management. • 2002: Promoted to university of science and technology.
1998	Fu Jen Catholic University	Department of Applied Life Science: Food & Beverage Management Section	4	• Department of Applied Life Science converted from Department of Home Economics & Nutrition. • 1998: Established a food and beverage management section.
		Department of Restaurant, Hotel and Institutional Management		• 2002: Restaurant, Hotel and Institutional Management became an independent department and added a graduate program.
1998	Shih Chien University	Department of Tourism Department of Applied Life Science (Taipei Campus)	4	• 1998: Established department of tourism. • 1999: Changed the department name to tourism management (Kaohsiung Campus).
		Department of Tourism Management (Kaohsiung Campus) Department of Food and Beverage Management		• 2004: Food and beverage management became an independent department from department of applied life science. (Department of Applied Life Science converted from Department of Home Economics.)
1998	Yuanpei Institute of Science & Technology	Department of Food & Beverage Management	4	
1998	Taipei Physical Education College	Department of Recreation & Sport Management	4	
1999	National Kaohsiung University of Applied Science	Department of Tourism Management	4	

TABLE 3 (continued)

Year Founded	Original Institution Name	Original Department Name	Original Duration of Study	Milestone Events
	Current Institution Name	Current Department Name	Current Duration of Study	
1999	Shu-Te Institute of Technology Shu-Te University	Department of Leisure, Recreation & Tourism Management	4	• 2000: Promoted to university of science and technology.
1999	Tajen Institute of Technology	Department of Food and Beverage Management Department of Recreation Sports Management Department of Hotel & Restaurant Management Graduate Institute of Leisure & Health Management	2 4	• 1999: Established department of food and beverage management 2-year junior college program. • 2000: Added department of recreation sports management. • 2002: Added department of hotel and restaurant management (4-year institute and 2-year institute programs). • 2003: Added department of food and beverage management 2-year institute programs. • Sandwich-style instruction. • 2004: Added graduate institute of leisure and health management.
1999	Hung Kuang Institute of Technology Hung Kuang University	Department of Hotel & Restaurant Management	4	• 1999: Added a department of hotel and restaurant management. • 2003: Promoted to Hung Kuang University.
1999	National Dong Hwa University	Graduate Institute of Tourism & Recreation Management	2	• 1999: Established a graduate institute of tourism and recreation management (the first master's degree program in a national university).
1999	Nanhua University	Graduate Institute of Tourism Management	2	
1999	Chia Nan College of Pharmacy & Science Chia Nan University of Pharmacy & Science	Department of Hotel & Restaurant Management Department of Recreation and Health Care Management Department of Tourism Management	4	• 1999: Established department of recreation and health care management. • 2000: Promoted to university. • 2001: Added department of hotel and restaurant management.
1999	Si Hai College of Industry & Commerce De Lin Institute of Technology	Department of Hotel Management Department of Leisure Management	2 4	• 1999: Established department of hotel management (2-year junior college program). • 2001: Promoted to institute of technology and name changed to De Lin.
1999	National Taiwan Normal University	Graduate Institute of Sport & Leisure Management	2	
2000	Tunghai University	Department of Hospitality Management	4	

Year Founded	Original Institution Name	Original Department Name	Original Duration of Study	Milestone Events
	Current Institution Name	**Current Department Name**	**Current Duration of Study**	
2000	Kai Nan University	Department of Tourism, Restaurant, and Hotel Management	4	
2000	Transworld Institute of Technology	Department of Leisure, Recreation and Tourism Management	2 4	• 2000: two-year junior college division program (admission in both spring and fall, sandwich-style instruction). • 2001: Added a 2-year institute program. • 2004: Added a 4-year institute program.
2000	Leader College of Management	Department of Leisure Management Department of Hotel Management Department of Food & Beverage	4	• 2000: Established department of leisure management. • 2002: Added department of hotel management and department of food and beverage.
2000	Diwan College of Management	Department of Tourism & Leisure Department of Hospitality Management	4	• 2000: Established department of tourism and leisure and department of hospitality management.
2000	Ta Hua Institute of Technology	Department of Tourism Management	4	
2000	China College of Marine Technology and Commerce	Department of Marine Leisure and Tourism	2	• 2-year junior college program.
2000	National Yunlin University of Science & Technology	Graduate Institute of Leisure and Exercise	2	• Master's program.
2000	National Pingtung Institute of Commerce	Department of Leisure Management	4	
2001	National Taiwan Normal University	Department of Home Economics Education: Nutrition, Food & Beverage Management Section (MA and PhD programs) Department of Human Development and Family Studies: Hospitality Management and Education Section (MA and PhD programs)	2 4	• 1996: Established a PhD program under the department of home economics education. • 2001: Established a PhD program containing separate sections on nutrition and food services (the first nutrition, food and beverage management PhD program). • 2004: Established a nutrition, food and beverage management undergraduate section. • 2005: Master and doctoral program of hospitality management and education section became an independent section.

TABLE 3 (continued)

Year Founded	Original Institution Name	Original Department Name	Original Duration of Study	Milestone Events
	Current Institution Name	Current Department Name	Current Duration of Study	
2001	National Pingtung University of Science and Technology	Department of Applied Life Science	4	• 2001: Department of hotel and restaurant management became an independent department.
		Department of Hotel & Restaurant Management		
2001	National Taipei College of Nursing	Graduate Institute of Tourism and Health Science	2	
2001	Ming Dao University	Department of Hospitality Manage-ment	4	• 2003: Added a department of holistic wellness.
		Department of Holistic Wellness		
2001	Taichung Healthcare & Management University	Department of Leisure & Recreation Management	4	• 2001: Established 4-year institute and master programs.
2001	Far East College	Department of Food & Beverage Management	2	• 2001: Established 2-year junior college program. • 2002: Added 5-year junior college program. • 2003: Added 2-year institute program.
2002	Yu Da College of Business	Department of Leisure, Recreation and Tourism Management	4	
2002	ToKo University	Department of Leisure & Recreation Management Department of Hospitality Manage-ment	4	
2002	National University of Kaohsiung	Department of Kinesiology, Health & Leisure Studies	4	
2002	National Chiayi University	Graduate Institute of Recreation, Tourism, & Hospitality Management	2	
2002	National Chung Cheng University	Graduate Institute of Sport and Leisure Education	2	
2003	Feng Chia University	Graduate Institute of Landscape & Recreation	2	
2003	Chang Jung Christian University	Department of Sport and Leisure Management	4	
2003	Vanung University	Department of Sports Health & Leisure	4	

Year Founded	Original Institution Name	Original Department Name	Original Duration of Study	Milestone Events
	Current Institution Name	Current Department Name	Current Duration of Study	
2003	Chung Hwa College of Medical Technology	Department of Hospitality Management	4	
2004	National Formosa University	Department of Leisure Planning	2	• 2004: Established 2-year institute program.
2004	Nan Jeon Institute of Technology	Department of Hospitality Management	4	
2004	Lan Yang Institute of Technology	Department of Health and Leisure Management	4	
2004	China Institute of Technology	Department of Food & Beverage Management Department of Tourism & Hospitality Management	4	

ism education experienced a total rebirth with the opening of this hospitality college, which not only helped rid local tourism education of what once had been a drag on its development, including low recognition, labor intensity, low technicality, and low entry barrier, but more importantly, helped attract wide media coverage. With large crowds of foreign and domestic visitors flooding in, the Kaohsiung Hospitality College's reputation surged to as high a level in Asian as that of Swiss hospitality schools in the world.

During this period, all kinds of programs and departments of tourism, hospitality, leisure, and recreation rapidly burgeoned in Taiwan, with the tourism and hospitality education itself quickly diversifying both in name and in substance. The only common thread underlying this diversification trend was that in almost all tourism education institutions, electives were increased while required courses were reduced. And this constituted the most revolutionary change in the talent cultivation approach of Taiwan's tourism and hospitality education.

Taiwan has seen a marked increase in the number of hospitality related programs and departments in higher education institutions since 1998. The increase is even steeper from 2000 onward. As of academic year 2003, universities and colleges have established a department or graduate institute for hospitality, tourism, or leisure and recreation, of which 64 are bachelor degree programs, 17 are master degree programs, and one is a PhD degree program (Table 4). Despite a relatively new

TABLE 4. Increasing Number of Leisure, Hospitality, and Tourism Programs

Year	1968-95	1996-97	1998-99	2000-01	2002-03	Total
Undergrad	7	3	10	18	26	64
Master	1	1	5	6	4	17
PhD	0	0	0	1	0	1
Total	8	4	15	25	30	82
Percentage (%)	9.8%	4.9%	18.3%	30.4%	36.6%	100%

discipline, hospitality and tourism education in Taiwan has grown rapidly as it has been in other countries. The employment opportunity created through the provision of hospitality and tourism education has made the Government realize the value and scale of tourism and hospitality related professions, and in the meantime, tourism and hospitality has also developed from a versatile business into a full-blown industry.

ACADEMIC INSTITUTION EVOLVEMENT IN TOURISM AND HOSPITALITY

Over the past years, the tourism and hospitality higher education in Taiwan has witnessed rapid growth in number and increasing diversification in program names and in curriculum design, as explained below.

Department Name Changes and Naming Diversification

The hospitality education in Taiwan was originated from tourism and home economics departments under business schools but has gradually evolved into food/beverage and restaurant/hotel studies. This is similar to the hospitality education migration trend in the U.S. between 1992 and 1997, as reported by Rappole (2000). Among existing hospitality departments in the U.S., the majority adopts a business program model (34.75%); followed by home economics model, or home economics turned program (25.53%), such as Purdue University's Department of Hospitality and Tourism Management (under School of Consumer and Family Sciences), Iowa State University's Department of Apparel, Educational Studies, and Hospitality Management (under College of Family and Consumer Sciences), Kansas State University's Department of Hotel, Restaurant, and Institution Management and Dietetics (under College of Human Ecology), and Penn State University's Department of Hotel, Restaurant, and Recreation Management (under College of Health and Human Development). Independent departments that distinguish themselves as dedicated hospitality education providers with proprietary equipment, learning environment, expertise, and teaching staff with industry experiences (e.g., Cornell University, University of Nevada Las Vegas, and University of Houston) are constantly on the rise. Business and home economics model-based programs and facilities, however, have experienced a decline first before going up again.

The tourism and hospitality department name change over time in Taiwan suggests that earlier names, such as "tourism" and "home economics," that covers a relatively large scope are no longer in tune with the social pulse of Taiwan. As the workforce of domestic economy is gradually moving toward specialization, home economics (applied life sciences) is also splitting into food and beverage management, hotel and restaurant management, hospitality management, and healthcare, while tourism is breaking into hotel management, travel, leisure, and recreation, or reintegrating into leisure and sport, leisure and healthcare, tourism and recreation management, and tourism and hotel. Despite the diversity in name, it is clear that both domestic and foreign higher education institutions of tourism and hospitality follow a similar track in department naming. Just like in the U.S., the naming system in tourism and hospitality higher education in Taiwan is highly diversified with many of the names used by only one single institution. Under such a diversification trend, therefore, it is certainly worth further investigation into whether departments that are similar in nature need to develop a core curriculum to maintain the education quality and turn out professional talents that meet international hospitality standards.

Up to 2003, of the 82 tourism and hospitality related higher education departments and institutes in Taiwan, 34 are hotel and restaurant related, 18 tourism related, and 30 leisure and recreation related. There are altogether 36 different names, with the majority of them being hospitality management (13.4%), followed by leisure management (12.2%), restaurant management (8.5%), tourism (8.5%), hotel management (3.7%), tourism management (3.7%), leisure and health care management (3.7%), travel management (2.4%), and airline management (2.4%). Also, 21 names are adopted by only one single institution, such as tourism, restaurant, and hotel management; leisure and recreation management; leisure and recreation business management; leisure industry/business management; leisure and sport management; sport, health, and leisure; airline service management. Up to 2004, fifty-four universities, universities of technology and institutes of technology have tourism and hospitality related departments and programs that increase continuously (Horng, 2003).

Curriculum and Instruction

The tourism education in Taiwan was originally established for inbound tourist reception, particularly in response to the surge in the number of foreign tourists since 1970s. Therefore, in curriculum design, the focus had been to provide travel management, language skill, and tourism administrative regulation training. The travel and hotel management courses were developed to train students about the operation procedures for receiving inbound foreign tourists. The language courses were designed to equip students with the necessary communication skills for delivering hospitality services, while the administrative regulation courses helped promote students' understanding of relevant government policies and regulations. Most of the culinary arts courses also focused on Chinese cuisines, together with some Western cooking and Japanese food preparation.

After the lifting of the ban on international travel for domestic individual tourists in 1979 and the opening of family visitation by Taiwanese residents to Mainland China in 1987, tourism related courses in education institutions began to shift their focus of training from foreign tourist reception to overseas travel activity organization in order to cope with the growing trend of international travel by Taiwan's citizens. In the meantime, to respond to the call from the industry for better integration of practical training with theoretical teaching in school education, various institutions began to collaborate with the industry and required students to take on internships outside of school for two months during any of the summer vacations or for at least 400 hours over the course of the four-year program. Since then, schools began to work more closely with the industry and were finally able to better reflect the needs of the industry in the school curriculum.

In 1995, the National Kaohsiung Hospitality College (NKHC) was established and was the first to adopt the sandwich-style instruction in the country. Under this new curriculum design, students are required to take not only school courses, but also to participate in on-campus and off-campus internships, as well as overseas visitation activities. In other words, throughout the course of the program, students will have to fulfill the hours with the various on-campus internship arrangements during regular school period, and in the meantime complete a six-month internship in the industry through school assistance to familiarize themselves with the industrial practices. Prior to graduation, the students will have to visit relevant operations in a foreign country through school arrangement in order to gain an international perspective and to get in touch with the global trends and industrial pulses of tourism and hospitality. After the launch of this curriculum by the National Kaohsiung Hospitality College, the popularity of this new curriculum quickly soared. Today, the overseas visitation component has been widely adopted by education institutions in the technical/vocational system. Some even include overseas visits in the graduation requirements for master programs. In culinary arts, the NKHC employs a foreign chef and a local teacher as co-instructors in courses such as western culinary arts to help students acquire the conventional knowledge of western cuisines, and to facilitate teacher-student interaction in English and boost students' understanding of international hotel operations, thereby cultivating world-class hospitality professionals for the international tourism market.

In general, Taiwan's tourism and hospitality higher education places more emphasis on industry-oriented skill and ability training in the technical/vocational system and on management capability development in the general university system. One thing the two systems have in common is their emphasis on practical experience, and therefore both systems have incorporated off-campus industrial learning components into their curriculum design.

Due to the lack of forward-looking analytical data on occupational ability requirements for the hospitality industry, the majority of domestic institutions have based their curriculum on existing courses offered by similar programs at home or abroad, with some modifications according to the school development characteristics. Therefore, it is difficult to tell whether such curricula can really address the current and future needs of the industry. The first author of this paper has undertaken a National Science Council (NSC) funded three-year integrated research project by the name of An Analytical Study of the Integrated Curriculum for Hospitality Curricular Group in the Technical/Vocational System, which was aimed at constructing occupational profiles for the various components of restaurant management, culinary arts, and hotel management in the tourism and hospitality curricular group, and identifying the required general and specialized capabilities for hospitality professionals. The study found that the lower the level of a job, the more important the industry-specific skills become, and that the higher the level of the job, the more important it is to possess general managerial abilities. In other words, the planning of hospitality curriculum should match the need for ability development and should include the teaching of general knowledge, professional ethic, and general courses that embrace a multicultural perspective, as well as basic managerial courses, industry-specific professional courses, and internships, in order to gradually deepen and broaden the knowledge and competency of students (Horng, 2004; Horng & Wang, 2003; Horng & Wu, 2002). In 2000, the Ministry of Education has also started to develop an integrated curriculum for the tourism and hospitality curricular group in the technical/vocational system. The purpose was to help provide some guidance for future school-based curriculum design.

Teaching Faculty

Taiwan did not have teaching faculty specialized in tourism and hospitality in the 1960s. Most of the teachers back then were officials from tourism administrative authorities or lecturers recruited from the industry. Teachers from tourism authorities mainly taught administrative regulation courses, while those with an industrial background lectured mainly on inbound tour reception and restaurant/hotel practice. Full-time instructors in tourism programs of the schools focused on the teaching of social studies, transportation, geography, economics, and foreign language courses. For culinary arts, teachers from home economics departments mainly taught food preparation principles/food preparation courses. After the government lifted the restriction on overseas travel by individual citizens, which enabled the public to travel or study overseas in greater numbers and at higher frequency, the source and quality of domestic teaching faculty for tourism and hospitality began to change. With an increasing number of master's degree holders in tourism, recreation, hotel management, restaurant and hotel, and hospitality management returning home, local schools began to see a mixture of both domestically and internationally trained teachers with tourism related degrees. Take the National Kaohsiung Hospitality College as an example, to enhance the quality and professionalism of its teaching staff, the school would select teachers already holding a master's degree in tourism and hospitality to go overseas for six to twelve months of professional training.

Over the past five years, the number of higher education institutions rapidly increased and junior colleges and institutes of technology continued to convert themselves into general or technology universities; as a result the number of tourism, hospitality, and leisure related programs has grown at an unprecedented pace. After the promulgation of the revised University Law, higher education institutions are now demanding a PhD degree when recruiting new teachers. However, the number of

PhD-degree programs offered by domestic and international hospitality institutions is rather limited, and tourism related programs offer PhD programs mainly in park and leisure/recreation studies. As regards the composition of teaching faculty, teachers from areas such as geography, forestry, landscape, urban planning, food science, and food nutrition are gradually entering into the field of hospitality. Although the percentage of teachers with a PhD degree has increased, the professionalism and practical experience of these teachers still has much to be desired. In order to further enhance the quality of the overall tourism and hospitality education therefore, more needs to be done in terms of teacher preparation and re-education.

IMPORTANT ISSUES OF CURRENT TOURISM AND HOSPITALITY EDUCATION IN TAIWAN AND FUTURE DEVELOPMENT TRENDS

Tourism and hospitality is gradually becoming an important industry for Taiwan in the 21st century. In order to enhance the competitiveness of domestic tourism and hospitality education in the international community, it is important to construct the knowledge body of tourism and hospitality and to integrate education with industrial needs. Therefore, the industry, government, and academia should work closely to develop and decide on future reform directions for tourism and hospitality education and to carefully examine all the important issues surrounding existing tourism and hospitality education in Taiwan, and make meaningful recommendations for future development.

Boosting Competitiveness for the Global Hospitality Market

With the tourism and hospitality education in Taiwan still on the rise, one cannot but wonder whether the industry has enough capacity for this rapidly increasing number of graduates, and whether the schools are turning out students that meet the expectations of the industry. Tourism and hospitality education are international by nature; therefore the curriculum will continue to move toward the direction of international hospitality management (Mok & Noriega, 1999), and will focus more on preparing students for a hospitality workplace that is gradually internationalized. Since Taiwan began its tourism and hospitality education relatively late it has the benefit of the experiences of other advanced countries to learn from. In the meantime, Taiwan should also actively seek recognition by international hospitality education programs, collaborate with foreign higher education institutions, and promote teacher and student exchanges to help broaden students' horizons and cultivate their employability for the global job market. By enhancing the quality of domestic human resources through cultivating students' foreign language skills and multicultural perspectives, Taiwan can boost the competitiveness of its own tourism and hospitality industries on the international market (Hsu, 2002; Horng, 2003).

Careful Positioning Under Clear Goals

Different levels of hospitality education should focus on the preparation of different types of human resources in order to meet the various levels of manpower requirements of the industry. The curriculum design should strive to match the professional and career development of their respective target students. The hospitality higher education in particular should carefully examine its overall strengths for development and form a close tie with the industry in order to foresee market trends and demands. Instead of following the fashion blindly, higher education institutions should develop a clear positioning for technical or academic training in their curriculum planning. Under the globalization trend in the 21st century, the biggest challenge facing domestic hospitality education is to balance between the need for the cultivation of truly international professionals of hospitality and the demand for promoting the characteristics of the local hospitality culture. To achieve this, Taiwan should set up clear education goals for hospitality education according to the development trends of the 21st century, and should learn from past experiences of advanced countries in order to infuse an international element into the hospitality curriculum and to establish standards for quality education. In other words, hospitality education should be managed in the same way a business is managed in the industry, in order to export domestic hospitality education and ensure a brighter future for the development of hospitality education in Taiwan (Horng, 2003).

CURRICULUM PLANNING

Meeting the Demands and Trends of Our Time

In the U.S., the majority of tourism/hospitality departments or programs fall under such disciplines as commerce, applied economics, tourism, leisure/recreation, health and human ecology, family and consumer sciences, and hotel management, with each having a different emphasis in the course design (Chen & Groves, 1999). Curriculum development can be a highly complicated task, involving not only the teachers' backgrounds and understanding, but also school traditions, administrative systems, and development priorities. However, relying on the teachers' effort for curriculum design can be problematic because the teachers' excessive self-centeredness can put a major constraint on the curriculum thus designed. Moreover, this type of curriculum design often lacks a systematic development and sustainable management view, because personnel changes can cause undesirable shifts in the departmental development direction and in the course content. One of the continuous challenges facing hospitality educators is to develop a curriculum that meets the constantly changing needs of the industry and to strike a balance between the needs of academic institutions and those of the industrial organizations in order to fill the expectation gap in the industry. Therefore, in addition to academics, the involvement of other stakeholders, including industrial leaders, alumni, and parents, are also important in curriculum development in order to produce a curriculum that meets the needs of the customers–students. Such a curriculum should be student-centered and process-oriented and one that is regularly reviewed according to industrial demands, graduates' employment status, and economic changes in order to stay in tune with social pluses and the changes of our time (Nelson & Dopson, 2001; Horng, 2003).

Standardizing the Core Curriculum and Diversifying Professional Courses

The increasingly diversifying hospitality and tourism education has resulted in a highly mixed naming system. In order to achieve vertical integration and international alignment, domestic hospitality curricula should incorporate both general and professional courses as well as theoretical and practical components and should strive to maintain a balance between them. International hospitality/tourism educators and industry players both feel the urgency and importance of hospitality/tourism core curriculum development, which specifies the minimum requirement of core skills and abilities that each student of hospitality should be equipped with. The British Council for Hospitality Management Education, for instance, proposed to align and standardize core curricula while diversifying professional courses at the same time. Schools can develop their own curricula tailored to specific market segments according to their resource availability and characteristic development, but should be subject to education quality evaluations using such indicators as course design, course content and structuring, students' progress and achievement, support and guidance received by students, learning resource availability, and quality management and enhancement (Cooper & Westlake, 1998; Rimmington, 1999; Horng, 2003).

Integrating the Hospitality/Tourism Curriculum

The technical/vocational tourism and hospitality education in Taiwan extends from crafts and arts education at junior high level to senior vocational schools, junior colleges, institutes of technology, and universities, forming a rather complete system. Hence, the integrated curriculum planning for the technical/vocational education should strive to ensure seamless connection and transition, competence orientation, curriculum alignment, and school-based development. In curriculum design, the emphasis should be on full development of students' potential and meeting the demand for in-service lifelong learning of the society. In addition, a sound curriculum evaluation system should be established as soon as possible in order to ensure the quality and connectivity of curricula at different levels of education.

Alliance and Collaboration

It is important to extend current efforts on setting up tourism and hospitality curricular groups and promote interdisciplinary, interschool, and even international collaborations for curriculum planning through strategic alliances between the teaching, research, and industry sectors. It is also important to strengthen industry-academia cooperation in order to create a rich and flexible learning environment, to facilitate the cultivation of an international perspective and professional capabilities in students (Jayawardena, 2001). Tourism and hospitality is a relatively new field of academic study. However, the tourism and hospitality education is already facing a rapid upward shift. Just like in other advanced countries, domestic colleges and universities also have a strong demand for PhD-degree holding faculty. And apparently, the demand has exceeded the supply in most cases. In the past, tourism and hospitality were often considered a "subject" rather than a "study." Hence the idea of cultivating "classic" doctors of philosophy in tourism and hospitality was very difficult to sell. Many faculty members were recruited from related academic fields. According to the 1999 U.S. tourism/hospitality department faculty member statistics, the number of teachers holding a PhD degree in hospitality/tourism was only close to one-third of the total. One problem with these teachers switching from a relevant field was that they usually lacked practical experience in the hospitality/tourism industry. Therefore, a close cooperative relationship between the industry and the academia will help these teachers to acquire the desired practical experience, thereby closing the gap between their theoretical understanding and the industrial realities. In the meantime, the industry can also send their personnel to receive in-service education in schools through such collaboration relationships. This should be able to enhance bilateral exchange and create more room for future collaboration between the industry and the academia (Baum, 1998; Tepeci, Seo, Upneja, & DeMicco, 2002; Horng, 2003).

Tourism and Hospitality Research

Tourism and hospitality lends itself to interdisciplinary integration because the tourism and hospitality industry itself is highly dynamic and diverse; and the management of tourism and hospitality transcends the boundaries of many disciplines. Therefore, the tourism and hospitality education should be multi-disciplinary in nature. Educators face the increasing concern over the issue of tourism and hospitality internationalization and the growing complexity of tourism and hospitality problems. Thus, educators and researchers must be able to think outside the box to break through the longstanding constraints of this study in order to really appreciate the comprehensive nature of tourism and hospitality education. In other words, a pluralistic angle and the perspective of interdisciplinary integration, as well as a diverse approach, a sound theoretical basis, and a heuristic standpoint, are necessary in order to gain a comprehensive understanding of the various problems and phenomena of tourism and hospitality and to better integrate knowledge and experiences under the support of both the industry and the academia to eventually produce innovative research results. Many countries are now vigorously developing the framework and network for the tourism and hospitality education research. In addition to the basic efforts to set up departments and programs for talent cultivation, it is also important for the tourism and hospitality education to build a good working relationship with the industry in order to jointly embark on active hospitality/tourism research activities, construct academic and industrial research databanks, and promote sound development of various societies and associations and of high-quality journals to provide resources for research (Horng, 2003).

REFERENCES

Baum, T. 1998. Mature doctoral candidates: The case in hospitality education. *Tourism Management, 19*(5), 463-474.

Chen, K. C., & Groves, D. (1999). The importance of examining philosophical relationships between tourism and hospitality curricula. *International Journal of Contemporary Hospitality Management, 11*(1), 37-42.

Cooper, C., & Westlake, J. (1998). Stakeholders and tourism education: Curriculum planning using a quality management framework. *Industry & Higher Education, 12*(2), 93-100.

Horng, J. (2004). Curriculum analysis of foods and beverage management in technological and vocational education. *Asia Pacific Journal of Tourism Research, 9*(2), 107-119.

Horng, J. (2003). The development of Taiwan's hospitality education from the hospitality education models in the U.S. and Australia. *Journal of Taiwan Normal University Education, 48*(2), 125-150.

Horng, J. & Wang, L. (2003). Competency analysis profile of F&B managers in international hotel managers in Taiwan. *Asia Pacific Journal of Tourism Research, 8*(1), 26-36.

Horng, J. & Wu, B. (2002). Competency analysis profile of managers of chain restaurants. *Journal of Chinese Home Economics, 32*, 1-15.

Hsu, C. H. C. (2002). The curriculum reform and trends of hospitality higher education development in United States. In *Proceedings of 2002 Hospitality Education International Conference* (pp. 41-46). Taipei: National Taiwan Normal University.

Jayawardena, C. (2001). Challenges in international hospitality management education. *International Journal of Contemporary Hospitality Management, 13*(6), 310-315.

Mok, C., & Noriega, P. (1999). Toward a cross-cultural diversity perspective in hospitality curriculum development. *Journal of Hospitality & Tourism Education, 11*(1), 30-34.

Nelson, A. A., & Dopson, L. (2001). Future of hotel education: Required skills and knowledge for graduate of U.S. hospitality programs beyond the year 2000–Part one. *Journal of Hospitality & Tourism Education, 13*(5), 58-66.

Rappole, L. C. (2000). Update of the chronological development, enrollment patterns, and education models of four-year, master's and doctoral hospitality programs in the United State. *Journal of Hospitality & Tourism Education, 12*(3), 24-27.

Rimmington, M. (1999). Vocational education: Challenges for hospitality management in the new millennium. *International Journal of Contemporary Hospitality Management, 11*(4), 186-191.

Tepeci, M., Seo, W. S., Upneja, A., & DeMicco, F. (2002). Supply and demand for hospitality/tourism management faculty in the United States. *Journal of Hospitality & Tourism Education, 14*(2), 38-45.

Travel and Tourism Education in Thailand

Manat Chaisawat

SUMMARY. The main principles of the tourism policy as established by the Ministry of Tourism and Sports during 2003-2006 is to develop Thailand to be Tourism Capital of Asia within 3 years starting from 2004 to 2006. To achieve the ambitious government target, the success of any tourism development strategy will be determined to a large extent by human resources, which can deliver efficient, high quality services. The travel and tourism education in Thailand at an undergraduate level was offered in the Faculty of Commerce and Accountancy, Chulalongkorn University in 1955 under the Bachelor of Commerce Degree with a major field of study in "Travel Management." Prince of Songkla University (PSU) brought the concept of community college from the U.S.A. to put into action by setting up Phuket Community College by offering 2-year diploma program in Hotel and Tourism Management to meet the staff requirement of tourism industry in Phuket in 1977. The findings of 'Baccalaureate and Graduate Degrees in Tourism and Hospitality Studies in Thailand: The Current Situations, Problems and Future Development' studied by Chaisawat (1997) and Chaisawat (2000) found that the situation of the universities/institutes that offered programs in hospitality and tourism had changed with a lot of quantity improvement in terms of institutions, number of staff, and number of input/output students as well as research projects. But the very important issues that relate directly to

Manat Chaisawat is Associate Professor, Prince of Songkla University, Phuket Campus, Phuket, Thailand (E-mail: manat@fsi.psu.ac.th).

[Haworth co-indexing entry note]: "Travel and Tourism Education in Thailand." Chaisawat, Manat. Co-published simultaneously in *Journal of Teaching in Travel & Tourism* (The Haworth Press, Inc.) Vol. 5, No. 3, 2005, pp. 197-224; and: *Global Tourism Higher Education: Past, Present, and Future* (ed: Cathy H. C. Hsu) The Haworth Press, Inc., 2005, pp. 197-224. Single or multiple copies of this article are available for a fee from The Haworth Document Delivery Service [1-800-HAWORTH, 9:00 a.m. - 5:00 p.m. (EST). E-mail address: docdelivery@haworthpress.com].

doi:10.1300/J172v05n03_09

the quality of graduates, problems and constraints running in the hospitality/tourism programs still existed. The National Economic and Social Development Board (NESDB) (2004) did an in-depth study of the labour force situation among middle- and high-level personnel within the tourism industry in order to increase productivity and capability of the national competitiveness. Chaisawat and Boonchu (2005) did another study on Baccalaureate and Graduate Degrees in tourism and hospitality studies in Thailand in 2003. Both studies also found that the quantity of graduates from the educational institutions was sufficiently to serve the demand of the industry. However, there were problems in terms of quality since graduates' qualifications were not up to the standards required by the employers. Finally the paper recommended that Thailand should be positioned as a centre for hospitality and tourism studies and training, locating at major tourism destinations. In terms of strategic implementation of tourism development, tourism educations and training institutions should play the catalyst and coordinating roles with the stakeholders in each region or destination. *[Article copies available for a fee from The Haworth Document Delivery Service: 1-800-HAWORTH. E-mail address: <docdelivery@haworthpress.com> Website: <http://www.HaworthPress.com> © 2005 by The Haworth Press, Inc. All rights reserved.]*

KEYWORDS. Tourism Capital of Asia, Hospitality and Tourism Education in Thailand, quantity of graduates, quality of graduates, strategic implementation of tourism development

INTRODUCTION

The Asia-Pacific region is the world's fastest growing tourism area in terms of visitor arrivals. Thailand is one of the countries in the Asia-Pacific region that has experienced tourism growth since the first Thai tourism plan was set up in 1976 at the end of the third National Economic and Social Development Plan (NESDP) (1972-1976). Even in the years after the financial crisis of 1997, the number of international tourist arrivals increased from 7.22 million in 1997 to 7.76 million in 1998 and up to 10.80 million in 2002. In 2002, the tourism industry became the top foreign currency earner when compared to other industrial sectors such as computers and parts, electronic components and textiles (Tourism Authority of Thailand, 2002). The year 2003 was the first time that the number of tourist arrivals to Thailand decreased–to 9.70 million because of the outbreak of bird flu in Asia.

The major factors that contributed to the increase of tourist arrivals to Thailand in the past were a favourable currency exchange, safety from natural disasters, a stable political situation, tax refunds for tourists, and a cooperation between public and private sectors in promoting the 'Amazing Thailand Years' in 1998-1999 (Tourism Authority of Thailand, 1999). The devaluation of the Thai Baht and the extended 'Amazing Thailand Years' campaign to 2000 have had a positive impact on Thailand's tourism industry. The devaluation of the Thai Baht allowed tourists to gain more value from the exchange rate, which enabled them to make more purchases at lower costs. Therefore, the costs of travelling to Thailand were more attractive than usual.

The aggressive marketing promotion of the 'Amazing Thailand Years' created a lasting awareness of the various types of tourist attractions in Thailand, specifically cultural and natural attractions, Thai food, and shopping. The growth rate of tourist arrivals kept growing even after the regional and world crises such as 9/11 in the United States, the bombing in Bali and the SARS epidemic (Porter, 2003). But revenues received from the industry in dollar terms were decreasing as opposed to the Thai Baht . . . Thailand generates less revenue per tourist than leading competitors, for example Indonesia; and Thailand has not been able to increase the revenue per tourist over time. Even after the 1997 devaluation, revenues in terms of Thai Baht only remained stable, while tourists reduced their spending in terms of U.S. Dollars.

HISTORICAL DEVELOPMENT AND EVOLUTION OF TOURISM HIGHER EDUCATION IN THAILAND

The first major field of study in "Travel Management" was offered in the Faculty of Commerce and Accountancy, Chulalongkorn University in 1955 under the Bachelor of Commerce Degree. The program was not a popular choice for students for their professional degree, because the opportunities for jobs in this area were very limited, and most students paid more attention to majors in Accounting, Finance, or Marketing.

Prince of Songkla University (PSU) brought the concept of the community college from the U.S.A. and put this into action by setting up the Phuket Community College in 1977. PSU offered a 2-year diploma program in Hotel and Tourism Management to meet the staff requirements of the tourism industry in Phuket. The program was run very successfully in terms of employment. Songkhla Teacher College, in co-operation with Phuket Community College, had extended the 2-year program in Hotel and Tourism Management and now offers it in Songkhla Province, the southern part of Thailand.

After Songkhla Teacher College was renamed the Rajabhat Institution, the program was developed into a 4-year degree program in Tourism. This program was then offered at 35 other campuses of the network of Rajabhat Institution throughout the country. The 2-year program at PSU Phuket Campus later became less popular among students because it was a terminal program for employment in the tourism industry. There was no opportunity for students to pursue further study for a bachelor's degree in any of PSU's campuses.

In 1993, PSU set up the Faculty of Hotel and Tourism Management at the Phuket Campus to offer an international 4-year degree program, a Bachelor of Business Administration (BBA) in Hotel Management for the 1994 academic year. It was the first international program in Hotel Management offered by a faculty of hotel and tourism management in Thailand, especially for the well-known tourism destination, Phuket.

The findings of 'Baccalaureate and Graduate Degrees in Tourism and Hospitality Studies in Thailand: The Current Situations, Problems and Future Development' by Chaisawat (1997) concluded that the universities/institutions offering hospitality/tourism programs could not produce qualified graduates, both in terms of quantity and quality, to meet the manpower needs of the country required to achieve the target of the Eight Tourism Plan, specifically regarding quality tourism. The recommendations of the study were:

1. The government should give top priority in allocating resources to quality hospitality and tourism education;
2. There is a need to unify and standardize the hospitality and tourism programs at all levels of study so that we can compete in terms of quality with those of other countries;
3. There is an urgent need to set up graduate programs in hospitality and tourism to develop teaching staff for colleges and universities;
4. There is a need for co-operation and support from related businesses in the hospitality and tourism industry as a source of guest instructors, practical training places for students, and on-the-job training for teaching staff; and last, but not least;
5. There is a need to set up an academic association among hospitality and tourism educators in the country for the purposes of strengthening the development of hospitality and tourism programs.

Chaisawat (1997) indicated that by the end of December 1995 at the level of bachelor degree, nineteen programs offering degrees in tourism and hospitality were available in state universities, private universities and colleges, and 18 Rajabhat Institutes also offered bachelor degrees leading to Bachelor of Arts in Tourism Industry. Rattanavirakul (1996) reflected the problems of shortages of administrators and marketers in the hotel business as well as the need for general managers (GM) to manage hotels in the age of globalization.

The Thai Hotels Association Annual Report 1995-1996 revealed that there were 81 non-Thai GMs from 259 hotels, or 31.27%. The same figure for Phuket was 17 out of 38, or 44.74%. Reggie Shiu, Accor Asia Pacific's chief executive for Thailand, Cambodia, Burma, and Laos (Thailand Traveller, 1996), said that "the most important problems of human resources is to recruit and to keep good people. One problem facing Accor Asia Pacific at the Bangkok office is the inability to develop Thai management staff. Now, there is only one Thai, Assistant Chief Executive and Director, working with the company."

The Changing Situation from 1996-1999

The Economic Crisis and Thai Tourism Industry: Thailand has confronted a strong financial and economic crisis since July 1997. The country had negative economic growth (Gross Domestic Products: GDP) at -0.4% and -7.0% in 1997 and 1998, respectively. The Baht lost more than 30% of its value against the U.S. dollar since the July 1997 devaluation. During these troubled years, the tourism industry was a major foreign-exchange earner and job provider.

In 1997 and 1998, the number of tourist arrivals to Thailand topped 7.22 million and 7.64 million at the growth rate of 0.7% and 7.53%, respectively. Earnings in 1997 and 1998 were U.S.$ 7.048 billion and U.S.$ 5.934 billion, down 19% and 16%, respectively, in dollar terms but slightly up in terms of local currency. In the first eleven months of 1999, tourist arrivals to Thailand grew by 11.29% due to the economic recovery in Asian markets and solid growth from many Western countries (TAT, 1993).

The Eighth National Plan set the growth rate of international tourist arrivals at 6% annually during 1997-2001. At the same time, tourist arrivals to East Asia and the Pacific (EAP) continued to fall by 1.2% over previous years both in 1997 and 1998. In this region, only Thailand, the Republic of Korea and China showed increases in the number of tourist arrivals.

International World Tourism and Regional Prospects, 1995-2020. Xu (1999), an officer of the World Tourism Organization (WTO) Asia and Pacific Section, briefly forecast that Europe would remain the leading tourism destination in 2020. However, its rate of growth would be less than the expected world growth rate. Even though it was in the midst of a financial crisis, EAP was expected to regain its second position in the world in terms of market share by 2020 with an average growth rate of 6.5 percent. All the EAP sub-regions would grow strongly at rates of between 5.5 percent a year and 6.8 percent a year, but the growth in intra-regional tourism would be slightly higher at 6.7 percent a year–despite the short term downturn. WTO's latest forecast indicated that Thailand would receive 36.9 million tourist arrivals by the year 2020 with an average growth rate of 6.91 percent between 1995 and 2020.

World Trade Organization. Thailand joined the World Trade Organization under specific commitments to the General Agreement on trade in services in April 1994 to liberalize services. These include professional, telecommunication, construction and engineering, wholesale and retailing, education, environmental management, banking and financial service, tourism, entertainment and transportation. Within 10 years, these services, specifically education and tourism, are in the competitive international market economy. This economic liberalization under this commitment to the World Trade Organization will allow international tourism related businesses and international educational institutes to enter the Thai tourism and the education marketplace unchecked.

Thai Tourism Promotion and Development Policies 1997-2003. The Eighth Tourism Development Plan (TDP) 1997-2001 had set its targets to promote tourism development in terms of quality and sustainable development. The main goal would focus on developing human resources throughout all levels of the industry. To balance economic, social, political and environmental development, plans would be developed for the management of tourism resources.

After the economic crisis of 1997, the Tourism Authority of Thailand (TAT) announced the 'Amazing Thailand 1998-1999' campaign in late 1997 to support the efforts of the government to earn more foreign-exchange and to achieve the targets of the national tourism plan. The two-year Amazing Thailand campaign ended with the growth rate of tourist arrivals as planned. The growth rate of tourist arrivals could not be claimed as the result of the campaign solely. The Baht devaluation, together with social and economic instability in Indonesia, were the key issues that made the tourists avoid Bali, Indonesia, and come to Thailand, specifically to Phuket.

In response to the changing situations, TAT set tourism promotion and development policies beyond the year 2001 up to 2003. Two of the eleven policies related directly to human resource development. The first, was to encourage the general public to help preserve and maintain tourism resources and the environment, as well as to be hospitable and cordial to tourists from elsewhere. The second, related to education, was to promote the development of personnel in the tourism industry in sufficient numbers, and of international quality standards, to meet market demand and to cater to the opening of trade in services, as well as to support the employment of more Thai manpower in the industry.

During 1997-1999, the Thai tourism industry had played the very important role in helping solve the economic crisis of the country in terms of foreign exchange earnings and maintaining or increasing jobs in the industry to absorb unemployed labor from other sectors. As the industry kept growing, the major problems in deterioration of natural resources and local cultures as well as other social problems, such as AIDS and organized sex tourism, still existed. The external forces from international organizations forced the country to open service industries, specifically tourism and education, to global competition. 'Quality tourism development' was the name of the game for international competition in the 21st century. The quality of manpower for the industry was the major factor to support quality tourism development.

Mr. Ryuji Yamakawa (2000), Chief, Tourism Unit, Transport, Communications, Tourism and Infrastructure Development Division, ESCAP and the coordinator of the Network of Asia Pacific Education and Training Institutes in Tourism (APETIT), also addressed the major problems and constraints facing human resource development in the tourism sector as follows:

1. Shortage of qualified manpower, particularly at the managerial level, which poses a major obstacle in the overall development of the tourism sector.
2. Shortage of qualified and experienced teaching staff.
3. Shortage of training materials and facilities.
4. Lack of strategies and policies for human resources development in the tourism sector.
5. Difficulty of keeping pace with rapidly changing technological innovation and dynamic changes in the global marketplace.
6. Complexity of multi-disciplinary nature of tourism studies.

7. Gap between training/education institutes' training capacity and industry's actual needs.
8. Shortage of the higher-level programs for management development.
9. Shortage of certain sub-sector's occupation and for entrepreneurship.

The Changing Situation After the Year 2000

National Tourism Plan. The proposed tourism action plans under the 9th NEEDS (2002-2006) (Tourism Authority of Thailand, 2001) were set to achieve: (1) the accessibility to tourism is the basic right of all Thai people with no discrimination; (2) the management of tourism must be in a united and integrated manner for the preservation of national tourism heritage for Thai younger generation; (3) tourism as a means to educate the younger generation, for continuing education for people and as the means to preserve, not destroy, natural culture and identity; (4) tourism is a means to offer employment opportunities, revenue generation and a process to strengthen the community; and (5) to maintain international competitiveness, to increase the quality of management standard in both private and public sectors and to increase personal skills for the quality of international service standards.

The main principles of the tourism policy as established by the Ministry of Tourism and Sports during 2003-2006 included (Brickshawana, 2003): (1) develop as well as promote sustainable tourism with the least environmental, natural, social and cultural impact, so as to preserve the existing national resources for the benefits of later generations; (2) enhance the quantitative expansion of the tourism industry through the development as well as management of potential tourism resources in a manner that generates the maximum benefits; (3) standardize tourism products in order to attract quality tourists; (4) use Thai uniqueness as the country's selling point while establishing a brand image for each region and push them to be developed accordingly; (5) present the products from different points of view in order to meet the tourists' demands due to the fact that 51 percent of tourist visitors to Thailand are repeaters; (6) promote international sporting events as a major tourist activity; and (7) develop an integrated management of information, public relations and customer relations through the use of information technology. The topmost target set by the government was that Thailand would become the Tourism Capital of Asia within 3 years, starting in 2004.

The Thaksin government, which took office in 2001, initiated many agreements and forums relating to tourism development, such as:

ASEAN Tourism Agreement. The ASEAN Tourism Agreement signed by the Heads of Government/State of the Association of Southeast Asian Nations (ASEAN) at Phnom Penh, Kingdom of Cambodia on the 4th of November 2002 aimed to recognize the strategic importance of the tourism industry for sustainable socio-economic growth of the ASEAN Member States and the diversity in cultures, economy, and the complementary advantages across the region, which would benefit the tourism development of ASEAN in the pursuit of improved regional quality of life, peace, and prosperity.

The objectives of the agreement are: (1) to cooperate in facilitating travel into and within ASEAN; (2) to enhance cooperation in the tourism industry among ASEAN Member States in order to improve its efficiency and competitiveness; (3) to substantially reduce restrictions to trade in tourism and travel services among ASEAN Member States; (4) to establish an integrated network of tourism and travel services in order to maximize the complementary nature of the region's tourist attractions; (5) to enhance the development and promotion of ASEAN as a single tourism destination with world-class standards, facilities and attractions; (6) to enhance mutual assistance in human resource development and strengthen cooperation to develop, upgrade and expand tourism and travel facilities and services in ASEAN; and (7) to create favorable conditions for the public and private sectors to engage more deeply in tourism development, intra-ASEAN travel and investment in tourism services and facilities.

Asia Cooperation Dialogue (ACD) Tourism Business Forum. The idea of an Asia Cooperation Dialogue was initiated by Prime Minister Thaksin Shinawatra. Dr. Thaksin Shinawatra addressed the first ACD Ministerial Meeting during 18-19 June 2002 in Cha-Am, Thailand, with the vision to see Asian countries coming together and combining their inner strengths and resources to create a synergy of win-win state of affairs for the betterment of Asia and Asian peoples. Thailand and Cambodia proposed to be a prime mover for cooperation in the tourism area. The ACD Tourism Business Forum was developed to build a high-level of cooperation and collaboration among its countries including Bahrain, Bangladesh, Brunei, Cambodia, China, India, Indonesia, Japan, Lao PDR, Myanmar, Malaysia, Pakistan, Philippines, Qatar, Singapore, South Korea, Vietnam, and Thailand.

Asian countries recognize the importance of tourism as a major social and economic development tool for increasing foreign exchange earnings, creating jobs and encouraging cultural and social exchanges and understanding. The objectives of the ACD Tourism Business Forum included:

- To allow member countries to jointly promote their tourism products.
- To establish a network between ACD public and private sectors.

To meet policy and strategic planning gaps in regional tourism development, the ACD Tourism Business Forum was held the first time in Phuket during May 22-24, 2003. In its first forum, under the current situation in Asia the ACD Tourism Business Forum identified four major issues to be discussed:

- Intra-Regional Promotion Initiatives.
- Safety and Security.
- Human Resource Development.
- Small and Medium-Sized Tourism Enterprises.

Economic Cooperation Strategy (ECS): The Bagan Declaration, the brainchild of the Economic Cooperation Strategy or ECS initiated by Thai Prime Minister Thaksin Shinnawatra, was signed on 12 November 2003, in Bagan, Union of Myanmar. The four signatories, Cambodia, Laos, Myanmar, and Thailand, agreed to promote cooperation in five areas: trade and investment, agriculture and industry, transportation, tourism, and human resource development. Under tourism cooperation, Thailand is now promoting the idea of "four countries, one destination," encouraging tourists who come to Thailand to also visit Cambodia, Laos, and Myanmar. A new project, CLMT Tourism Cooperation Bicycle Tour, was initiated by Thailand's Ministry of Tourism and Sports to promote the concept.

To achieve the topmost target set by the government that Thailand would become the Tourism Capital of Asia within three years, starting in 2004, human resources development was the key issue that Thailand mentioned in all agreements and forums with the neighboring countries to coordinate and cooperate with the education and training institutions and industry to produce a qualified and well trained workforce for the future development of the tourism industry.

TOURISM EDUCATION IN THE 1990s AND 2000s

Tourism Education: 1996-1999

Chaisawat (2000) studied Baccalaureate and Graduate Degrees in Tourism and Hospitality Studies in Thailand: The Comparative Studies Between 1996 and 1999, and found that the number of universities/institutes offering hospitality/tourism programs in 1999 were 11 state universities, 15 private universities and 25 institutes/colleges. The total number of all institutions offering hospitality and tourism programs increased from 42 in 1996 to 51 in 1999, at a growth rate of 21.43% over the three years.

The degrees offered by those institutions were Bachelor of Arts (BA) in Tourism Industry (19), Hotel and Tourism Management (12), Tourism Management (3), Tourism and Hotel (2), Hotel Management (1), Hotel (1), and Travel and Tourism (1). The Bachelor of Business Administration degree was offered in 13 universities with a major in Hotel and Tourism Management (7), Hotel Management (5), and Travel Management (1). The total number of degrees increased from 41 in 1996 to 52 in 1999.

In terms of student inputs and outputs, the yearly inputs increased from 3,939 students in 1996 to 5,136 students in 1999 (30.39% over 3 years). The yearly outputs from the programs increased from 1,737 students in 1996 to 2,485 students in 1999 (43.06% over 3 years). The total number of graduated students from the hospitality/tourism programs up to 1999 were 15,728 (38.52% over 3 years). There were 65 overseas students who attended the programs during this period. The proportion of male to female students remained 0.28 to 0.72 in these two periods.

In terms of teaching staff for the hospitality/tourism programs, the total staff increased from 324 in 1996 to 429 in 1999 (+32.41% over 3 years). The number of staff who were educated in hospitality/tourism disciplines increased from 96 in 1996 to 204 in 1999 (+112.5% over 3 years). The proportion of male to female staff was 0.30/0.70 in overall staff and 0.34/0.66 in hospitality/tourism staff.

The unsolved problems founded in the 1999 study were: lack of qualified teaching staff (48.33%), lack of financial support from the government (15.00%), low quality of input students (15.00%), insufficient practical training places in the industry for students (8.33%), lack of textbooks (8.33%) and the rest were negative attitudes of the students/parents to the industry, lack of overseas staff, and the need for a high investment in this program.

Chaisawat (2000) found that the situation of the universities/institutes that offered programs in hospitality and tourism education in 1999 as compared to those in 1996 had changed, with many quantity improvements in terms of number of institutions, number of staff, and number of input/output of students as well as research projects. But the very important issues that related directly to the quality of the graduates, and the problems and constraints of the hospitality/tourism programs still existed.

The study suggested that there is an urgent need to set up a graduate program in hospitality and tourism to develop teaching staff for colleges and universities. This study found that there was only one master program offered in 1999 at Chiang Mai University. The other one was the signing of agreement between the School of Tourism and Hospitality Management, Southern Cross University, Australia with Silpakorn University to offer a Master of International Tourism and Hotel Management in 2000 at Silpakorn University, Nakhornpathom Campus.

The study also suggested that in the future, the tourism industry and education will be a world business, competing in a free market economy or globalized economy. There will be many players or stakeholders involved in regulation, for example the World Trade Organization, World Tourism Organization, the players in information technology, regional competitors, and domestic and international competitors. The competition in the tourism industry follows the same pattern as in other industries, changing from the competitive advantage of the natural resources and low wages, to knowledge of working methods, finding smarter ways of doing the work as well as the capability of using and designing information technology as part of their work.

The following recommendations are made on the assumption of what can be done by the hospitality/tourism program managers/directors themselves, as the politicians and bureaucrats are only planning or speaking, but have no clear plan of action.

1. The need for curriculum development. From the study, Thailand had two types of degree (BA & BBA) with eight majors of study. Some were broad (tourism industry, tourism and hotel, travel and tourism) and some were narrow and highly specialized (hotel management, tourism management, travel management). The curriculum was designed to follow the curriculum of foreign institutions or take after other institutions. But the requirement of the industry now is for graduates who are more versatile. These graduates must have communication, critical thinking and problem solving skills, strategic management, and marketing, and other functional skills for surviving and doing well in the global economy. Therefore, the urgent issue was to set the concept of designing a new curriculum that can produce the graduates to shape the quality and sustainable tourism development of the country. This recommendation was trying to set the standard of hospitality and tourism by starting with the curriculum design.

2. *Joint-program for staff development.* The major problem of the hospitality and tourism programs was lack of qualified teaching staff. To solve this problem, in the past, some institutions had sent their teaching staff abroad for further study. This can cost over one million Baht (approximately U.S.$ 25,000) for a graduate study per year per person in some countries. It is now time for the universities/institutions to discuss this problem together to find a more efficient and economic way to solve the problem.

3. *The need for an association for coordination and development of the programs.* Different institutions under different ministries ran the hospitality and tourism programs. Under the constraints of financial support from the government and international competition, it requires a coordinating body to set guidelines of operation in terms of input/output of the students, curriculum development, and quality assurance as well as accreditation of the programs. This is to ensure that the universities/institutions can produce graduates capable of excelling in any service-based sector within the Thai tourism industry to compete in the world market economy. The recommendation clearly suggests that it needed a strong and efficient organization to support the program development.

The other reason that it needed an organization at a national level was to have a national representative to participate in the regional or international hospitality and tourism organizations, such as Asia Pacific Tourism Association (APTA), Asia-Pacific Education and Training Institute in Tourism (APETIT) established by ESCAP in September 1997, and other country national tourism associations, such as the Council of Australia University Tourism and Hospitality Educators (CAUTHE), Tourism Sciences Society of Korea (TOSOK), and Chinese Tourism Management Association, in Taiwan, ROC.

The Current Status, Structure, Characteristics and Trends of Tourism Education

Chaisawat and Boonchoo (2005) did another study on Baccalaureate and Graduate Degrees in Tourism and Hospitality Studies in Thailand in 2003 to find the number of institutions/universities and size of graduate output in the discipline of hospitality and tourism management at bachelor degree level and above, as well as problems and obstacles in producing graduates in this field of study. A structured questionnaire was adopted as a tool for study by sending to all universities/institutions in Thailand, both public and private universities/institutions. Sources of names and addresses of universities/institutions were found from secondary data, the Ministry Education and Ministry of universities Affairs website, Tourism Authority of Thailand, Thai Tourism Research Website, and Thailand Research Fund (TRF). The total population of 194 institutions comprised of 51 Public and Private Universities, 64 Public and Private Educational Institutions/Colleges, 41 Rajaphat Universities and 38 Rajamangala Institutions of Technology.

The questionnaire was designed according to general information of each university/institution and detailed information about programs offered in hospitality and tourism. The first part of the questionnaire included general information of name and address of each university/institution, program offering, number of student inputs and outputs and number of teaching staff; and the second part included information about number of research and projects completed and problems and suggestions for the program. The secondary data was obtained by searching from the Internet and related web sites that show names and addresses of universities and institutions in Thailand, searching documents and journals about hospitality and tourism education, and searching information about development strategies in hospitality and tourism education.

The findings of a study in 2003 and Chaisawat's study in 1997 are compared as follows:

During 2000-2003 the number of universities/institutes that offered hospitality and tourism programs increased from 51 in 1999 to 78 in 2003 (+52.94%). Ten universities/institutes planned to offer a program during 2004 to 2006. The number of public universities increased from 11 in 1999 to 16 in 2003 (+45.45%), private universities increased from 15 to 17 (+13.33%), and institutes/colleges increased from 25 to 45 (+80.00%) (Including Rajabhat University) (Table 1).

Table 2 indicates that Bachelor of Arts (BA) increased from 39 in 1999 to 67 during 2000-2003 (+71.79%). The BA in Hospitality increased from one in 1999 to three during 2000-2003, the BA in Tourism increased from one in 1999 to 12 during 2000-2003, the BA in Hospitality and Tourism increased from two in 1999 to three during 2000-2003, the BA in Hospitality/Tourism Management decreased from 16 in 1999

TABLE 1. Number of Universities/Institutes Offering Hospitality/Tourism Programs in 1999 and 2003

Types of University/ Institute	1999	2003	Percent Change
Public University	11	16	+45.45
Private University	15	17	+13.33
Institute/College*	25	45	+80.00
Total	51	78	+52.94

*Including Rajabhat University.

TABLE 2. Hospitality/Tourism Degree Offered by Universities/Institutes in 1999 and 2003

Majors of Studies/Degrees	1999		2003				
	B.A.	B.B.A.	B.A.	B.B.A.	M.A.	M.B.A.	Others
Hospitality	1	0	3	1	0	0	0
Tourism	1	0	12	3	0	0	0
Hospitality and Tourism	2	0	3	2	0	0	1
Hospitality/Tourism Management	16	13	12	13	3	2	0
Service Industries	0	0	1	2	0	0	0
Tourism Industries	19	0	34	0	0	0	0
Others	0	0	2	0	1	0	1
Total	39	13	67	21	4	2	2
Percent Change			+71.79	+61.54	-	-	-

to 12 in 2003, the BA in Tourism Industries increased from 19 to 34 during 2000-2003.

There were new majors offered in this period, these are the BA in Service Industries, the BA Tourism Development and the BA in Food Business. The Bachelor degree of Business Administration increased from 13 in 1999 to 21 in 2003 (+61.54%) in four years. There were new majors offered in this period, these are one BBA degree in Hospitality, three BBA degrees in Tourism, two BBA degrees in Hospitality and Tourism, and two BBA degrees in Service Industries. Hospitality/Tourism Management remained at the same level at 13. There were four new majors offered at master degree level, Master of Arts (MA), Master of Business Administration (MBA), and others. Two new majors were offered: one PhD in Architecture Development for Tourism and one BA and BSc in Hospitality and Tourism.

Table 3 shows characteristics of hospitality and tourism degrees offered by universities/institutes, 14 new Advance Certificates programs were offered during 2000-2003, a new Graduate certificate program was launched, Bachelor degrees increased from 50 in 1999 to 89 during 2000-2003 (+78.00%), Master degrees increased from one to six (+500.00% over 4 years), and a new Doctorate degree was offered in 2003. International and English programs increased from six in 1999 to 15 in 2003 a 150% over four years and Thai programs increased from 47 to 63 (+34.04%).

In terms of students inputs and outputs, as shown in Table 4, the yearly input increased from 5,136 students in 1999 to 6,279 students in 2003 (+22.25%). The yearly output from programs increased from 2,485 students in 1999 to 4,155 students in 2003 (+67.20%). The total numbers of graduated students from hospitality and tourism programs up to 2003 were 23,117 students (+46.98% over the last four years). The proportion of male to female students was 0.24 to 0.76 in 2003, changed from 0.28 to 0.72 in 1999. This means that the number of female students increased more than male students.

In terms of teaching staff for the hospitality and tourism programs, as shown in Table 5, the total staff increased from 429 in 1999 to 442 in 2003 (+3.03%). The number of staff who were educated in hospitality

TABLE 3. Other Characteristics of Hospitality/Tourism Degree Offering by Universities/Institutes in 1999 and 2003

Types of Degrees	1999	2003	Percent Change
Advance Certificate	0	14	-
Graduate Certificate	0	1	-
Bachelor Degree	50	89	+78.00
Master Degree	1	6	+500.00
Doctorate Degree	0	1	-
Thai Program	47	63	+34.04
International/English Program	6	15	+150.00

TABLE 4. Student Figures of Hospitality/Tourism Degrees Offered by Universities/Institutes in 1999 and 2003

Characteristics	1999	2003	Percent Change
Number of yearly entrants	5,136	6,279	+22.25
Proportion of male to female students	0.28/0.72	0.24/0.76	-
Number of yearly graduates	2,485	4,155	+67.20
Accumulative number of graduates	15,728	23,117	+46.98

and tourism disciplines increased from 204 in 1999 to 251 in 2003 (+23.04%). The proportion of male to female staff was 0.32 to 0.68 in overall staff, and 0.30 to 0.70 in hospitality and tourism staff. Teaching staff qualifications in terms of proportion of academic background and academic rank as well as monthly remuneration and academic work in these two periods, the overall figures showed that more qualified teaching staff with master and doctorate degrees increased significantly during 2000-2003 when compared to those in 1999. However, in terms of academic rank the major proportion were in the position of lecturer. More research had been done or was in progress during 2000-2003.

The average salary received increased 24.53% or 6.10% annually. The overall staff/student ratio increased from 1:46.62 in 1999 to 1:56.82 during 2000-2003. In terms of teaching staff with hospitality and tourism qualification, the ratio still increased from 1:98.04 to 1:100 during the same period. The ratio implied that the workload of teaching staff was not up to a generally accepted level at 1:20.

Table 6 suggests that, in the opinion of the director/manager of hospitality and tourism programs, the unsolved problems and constraints in running hospitality and tourism programs in universities/institutes still existed, but the priority had changed. The issue of insufficient financial support from the government was ranked first during 2000-2003 at 35.76% as opposed to 8.33% in 1999. The shortage of qualified and experienced teaching staff ranked the second at 22.52% during 2000-2003 from the first priority in 1999 at 48.33%. Low quality of students maintained the third priority at the similar figure of 15.00-15.23%. The inadequate curriculum was a new issue that emerged from this study.

The implication of the study from the supply side of the labour force indicated that during 2000-2003, the output of the graduates from hospitality and tourism programs yearly increased from 2,485 in 1999 to 4,155 in 2003 (+67.20%) over four years or 16.8%/year. The question

TABLE 5. Teaching Staff for Hospitality/Tourism Programs in Universities/Institutes in 1999 and 2003

Characteristics/Year	1999	2003	Percent Change
Male	145	143	−1.38
Female	284	299	+5.28
Total	429	442	+3.03
Proportion of male to female staff	0.34/0.66	0.32/0.68	-
Number of staff with hospitality and tourism qualifications			
Male	72	76	+5.56
Female	132	175	+32.57
Total	204	251	+23.04
Proportion of male to female staff	0.35/0.65	0.30/0.70	-
Degree achievement			
Pre-Bachelor degree	3	0	-
Bachelor degree	150	79	−46.67
Master degree	262	321	+22.52
Doctorate degree	22	43	+77.27
Proportion Ph.D.:M:B:B-	1:11.9:6.8:0.14	1:8.26:2.06:0	
Academic rank			
Lecturer	369	378	+2.44
Assistant Professor	41	40	−2.44
Associate Professor	14	19	+35.71
Professor	0	3	-
Monthly compensation (Baht)			
Average salary	14,833	18,471	+24.53
Maximum salary	24,875	23,602	−5.12
Minimum salary	9,117	10,739	+17.79
Academic work			
Research completed	26	332	+1,176.92
Teaching staff/Students ratio			
Estimated 4-year students	20,000	25,000	
Total staff (1)	429	440	
Staffs with H&T qualification (2)	204	250	
Ratio (1)	1:46.62	1:56.82	
Ratio (2)	1:98.04	1:100	

TABLE 6. Problems and Constraints in Running Hospitality/Tourism Programs in Universities/Institutes During 1996-1999 and 2000-2003

Issues	1996-1999	Percent	2000-2003	Percent
1. Shortage of qualified and experienced teaching staff	29	48.33	34	22.52
2. Shortage of overseas staff	1	1.67	4	2.65
3. Insufficiency of financial support from the government	9	8.33	54	35.76
4. Low quality of students	9	15.00	23	15.23
5. High investment for this program	1	15.00	13	8.61
6. Gap between training/education institutions' training capacity and industry's actual needs	-	-	8	5.30
7. Inadequate curriculum	-	-	15	9.93
8. Negative attitude of the students/ parents to the industry	1	8.33	-	-
9. Insufficient practical training places for students	5	1.67	-	-
10. Lack of textbooks in this area of study	5	1.67	-	-
Total	60	100.00	151	100.00

is, does the supply of the labour force in hospitality and tourism sufficiently meet the requirement of the labour force of the tourism industry both in terms of quantity and quality?

The study of the employment of the workforce in the hotel and tour operator businesses by the Thailand Development Research Institute (TDRI) in 2001 indicated that the labor force at medium- and high-levels requirement in hotel and tour operator businesses were forecasted at 3,912, 5,976, 6,363, 6,724, 7,307 and 7,263 in 2004, 2005, 2006, 2007, 2008 and 2009, respectively (Table 7). The average growth rate of requirement is about 14.60%. With the assumption that the hotel and tour operator businesses are the biggest employers for graduates at bachelor degree level and above, it is obvious in terms of quantity that the supply of higher degree graduates sufficiently meets the demand of those two sectors of business. The growth rate of future supply at 16.8% is also greater than industry demand at 14.60% annually.

In terms of the quality of graduates from the hospitality and tourism programs, Chaisawat (2000) mentioned that the quality of graduates was a question mark because the major factors contributed to the quality

TABLE 7. Workforce Requirement at Medium- and High-Levels in Hospitality and Tourism: Forecast Between 2004 and 2009

Business Types	Forecasted figures for labor force needed during 2004-2009					
	2004	2005	2006	2007	2008	2009
Hotel Business						
Medium level	2,471	1,978	2,063	2,153	2,375	2,354
High level	2,906	3,491	3,638	3,898	4,180	4,163
Tour Operator Business						
Medium level	(233)	173	190	179	208	206
High level	(1,232)	334	472	494	544	540
Total Medium level	2,238	2,151	2,253	2,332	2,583	2,560
Total High level	1,674	3,825	4,110	4,392	4,724	4,703
Grand Total	3,912	5,976	6,363	6,724	7,307	7,263
Growth rate (%)	-	52.76	6.48	5.67	8.67	−0.60

Adapted from: Thailand Development Research Institute (TDRI) in NESDB (2004).

of the product, such as the quality of teaching staff, staff-student ratio, the quality of input students, the curriculum that would produce graduates best fit to the requirements of the industry and program accreditation, are unsolved problems.

The National Economic and Social Development Board (NESDB) (2004) did an in-depth study of the labor force situation among middle- and high-level personnel within the tourism industry in order to increase productivity and capability of national competitiveness. The study employed a combination of research methods, including document research or existing survey, analysis of education curriculum, and in-depth interviews with selected tourism business organizations, educational institutions, graduates working in the tourism industry, and tourism experts.

The study indicated that "the quantity of graduates from the educational institutions was sufficient to serve the demands of the industry. However, there were problems in terms of quality, since graduates' qualifications were not up to the standards required by the employers. Their English language and second language proficiency were not acceptable, thus making them unable to communicate and function effectively and efficiency. Furthermore, their unfavorable attitude, inability to solve problems at work, as well as lack of service-mindedness, practical skills, flexibility and versatility, resulted from the education systems' overemphasis on theoretical training, rather than practice. Besides, graduates' managerial skill deficiency also adds to their poor quality" (NESDB, 2004, p. xiii).

NESDB (2004) also revealed that from a thorough analysis of the curriculum, courses or degree programs offered by most educational institutions emphasized too much on grammatical aspects of foreign languages, rather than the necessary practices or uses in real-life situations. Students received very little training in their respective fields because of inadequate training facilities and training at certain educational institutions was not up to real business standards. Similarly, for the internship programs, students were not trained to their fullest capacity by trainers. This was due to the fact that employers did not want to take risks with the trainees for fear that they might cause damage to business and the reputation of their establishments. The NESDB (2004) study concluded that the factors described above clearly affected the quality of graduates from tourism educational institutions, which is a basic foundation for the country's sustainable competitiveness in the tourism industry.

NESDB (2005) proposed a strategy to develop curriculum for educational institutes to fit with the direction of industrial development. The Ministry of Education was assigned to be the principal organization to look after this strategy with the support from the Commission of Higher Education, the Commission of Vocational Education, educational institutes, professional institutes and private enterprises. The guidelines for curriculum to be developed at higher education are:

- To develop the clustering curriculum and to increase the proportion of professional subjects fit to the requirement of the entrepreneurs as well as integrated subject learning grouping;
- To develop multi-campus curriculum by using consortia or excellence centers as an operating mechanism in order to satisfy the needs of the industry with different knowledge and skills;
- To develop a specialized graduate curriculum by adding one year more in-depth study to increase competitiveness;
- To establish a broader educational institute in the form of a corporate school to balance conceptual learning and professional experiences; and
- To develop and extend the time of internship training in different forms including a practice school, by aiming to develop the teaching methods to include more project work and to extend the intern-

ship period by having a staff advisor to follow up and advise students.

In recent years, there has been a positive trend for the government to support tourism education in terms of scholarship for teaching staff in public universities. All universities and institutions in higher education are under the supervision of one organization, the Commission of Higher Education, in the Ministry of Education. The positive trend to support the quality of hospitality and tourism education from the findings of Chaisawat and Boonchoo's (2005) study are the increase of teaching staff with hospitality and tourism qualifications, the reduction of teaching staff with bachelor degrees and the increase of master and doctorate degree level teaching staff.

With regard to curriculum development in hospitality and tourism, during the Sixth Asia Pacific Tourism Association (APTA) Annual Conference in Phuket, Thailand, June 28-July 1, 2000, around 30 department-program managers/program directors in the hospitality and tourism area from public and private universities and Rajaphat Institute in Thailand met informally at PSU, Phuket Campus to set up a forum to discuss the problems of hospitality and tourism program development. At the second meeting on Friday 6th October 2000 at Rangsit University, Bangkok, the forum agreed to set up a working committee to draft a standard curriculum in hospitality and tourism. The Ministry of University Affairs (MUA) (2001) approved the proposal by appointing the working committee chaired by Associate Professor Manat Chaisawat.

The working committee was comprised of a group of advisors and working committee members. The advisors were comprised of the Governor of Tourism Authority of Thailand, the President of Thai Hotels Association, the Director of Office of Higher Education and the Director of Curriculum and Standard Division, MUA. Members of the working committee come from public and private universities, Rajaphat Institutions, and Rajamangala Institution of Technology. The presidents of professional associations, such as Professional Guide of Thailand, Association of Thai Travel Agency, and others, are also members of the working committee.

Results of the curriculum development by the working committee were presented at the meeting, "Higher Education Revolution: Curriculum Development for Higher Education to Excellence," September 26, 2003, organized by MUA at the Ambassador Hotel in Bangkok. Ten subjects were approved at the meeting for adoption as core courses of the hospitality and tourism curriculum at bachelor degree level. After the Commission of Higher Education, Ministry of Education (2004), took over the role of MUA, a working Committee on the Development of Hospitality and Tourism Discipline was set up to further develop the electronic courseware for the ten core courses of the hospitality and tourism curriculum.

The other development of the hospitality and tourism program is the setting up of the Tourism Academic Association of Thailand (TAAT). This process was supported by the Thailand Research Fund (TRF), a national research funding agency. TAAT was officially set up with the approval of the Ministry of Interior on 27th May 2005. Its main objectives are: to develop and exchange the body of knowledge in the tourism discipline and related field of studies, to liaise between teaching staff in the tourism area and related organizations both within and outside the country, to promote and develop the potential of teaching staff, to promote and develop curriculum and research activities of tourism and related areas and to disseminate and provide academic information to public and related organizations.

FUTURE DEVELOPMENT

As for the situation of higher education in Thailand, Professor Suchada Kiranandana (2004) said that higher education was becoming increasingly global and borderless, creating new challenges for university leadership. These changes are both domestic and international in nature. For example, within the next year or two, state funds will be allocated on the basis of performance, thereby putting increased pressure on how these institutions manage their resources.

In addition, competition from foreign universities in the domestic market is looming on the horizon as a result of the increasingly free global trade in services, including educational services, as well as the rapid advancement and spread of information and communication technologies.

> In response to the government's new budgeting method [under which state universities will be given money based on the number of students they serve], we'll have to radically adjust our mentality to optimize the outcome in terms of both the quality of our education and the quantity [measured in numbers of students]. I think that will be tough, even though we should expect increased efficiency if we succeed, but there will have to be a lot of changes in the way we operate first. (Kiranandana, 2004, p. 9A)

Referring to the liberalization of trade in services, which will eventually allow foreign universities to set up campuses in Thailand and provide programs in one form or another directly to local students, Suchada said both opportunities and threats lay in the emerging education environment. For students or consumers, there will be more choices since several of the world's leading universities, such as Harvard and the University of Chicago, may one day be operating locally.

The Human Resources Development Strategy to Achieve a Sustainable Tourism Development in Thailand

To achieve the objective of Tourism Capital of Asia within 3 years starting from 2004, Chaisawat (2003) proposed a scenario of tourism planning and policies in Asian countries due to the fact that globalization has changed the rules of the game from comparative advantages in natural resources to tourism products. Strategic thinking needs to be applied to tourism policy and planning in order to differentiate tourism products and to compete with other regions by improving the quality of tourism products and the efficiency of the tourism operation.

In terms of the diversity in cultures, economies, and natural resources of the nations in the Asian region, countries must take advantages of these diversities to create complementary advantages across the region. This leads to positioning tourism destinations according to the diversity of each nation. In terms of competition among nations in the region, each nation has to compete in the light of *competitive differentiation, service quality, and productivity.*

In order to form strategies for Thailand, there are two major issues to be considered. The first is the involvement of local people. According to the Constitution of The Kingdom of Thailand B.E. 2540 (1997), Chapter III, Rights and Liberties of the Thai People, Section 56, "the right of a people to give the State and communities participation in the preservation and exploitation of natural resources and biological diversity and in the protection, promotion and preservation of the quality of the environment for usual and consistent survival in the environment which is not hazardous to his or her health and sanitary condition, welfare or quality of life, shall be protected, as provided by law." Therefore, planning is for the benefit of the people, and they should be involved in the planning and development of tourism in their areas.

The second issue is human resources development because the success of any tourism development strategy will be determined to a large extent by human resources, which can deliver efficient, high quality services. As a consequence of Thailand's rapid growth in tourism, the need to develop required human resources in various segments of the industry has become imperative.

Because of the importance of human resources development in the process of strategic implementation of Thailand's tourism product policy and planning, a model was proposed by putting human resources as the focal point of the implementation. Anna Pollock, in her keynote speech at the 53rd Annual Conference of the PATA in Jeju Island, South Korea, (Muqbill, 26 April 2004) mentioned: There is an implicit understanding that "command and control" structures cannot cope with the new realities. In this world, top down planning is replaced by simulation and experimentation. In a loosely coupled world of distributed intelligence, the infrastructure is almost more important than the marketing plan. Success depends on ensuring that those frontline individuals in daily contact with guests are able to share what they are learning about them with the rest of the "body corporate" as the learning occurs. Success depends on enabling each of those frontline sensors to adapt and respond in real time. . . . Modern commerce and economics are based on an assumption that is now proving false–that the value is created from things, and that things are scarce, and that we must compete for a share of those limited resources to survive. But we live now at a time when value is associated with ideas, with knowledge, innovation and creativity of which there is no shortage. The scarcity principle that underlines all economics is replaced with an abundance principle that requires us to share and to collaborate, rather than withhold and compete.

Chaisawat (2004) proposed a model for the implementation of tourism development strategy to achieve the 'Tourism Capital of Asia' by saying that "to compete and survive in the current global environment, we must understand the rules and scope of competition, the competitors involved. To improve the competitiveness of the Thai tourism industry, we have to identify specific target markets we want to serve and to create more value added product and service to satisfy our customers. Market segmentation, target market and product positioning; quality and efficiency; and human resources development are the key strategies for the competition within the Asian region" (Chaisawat, 2004, p. 20). One of the proposed strategies (Strategy 1) is explained in Figure 1.

Thailand should be positioned as a center for hospitality and tourism studies and training, with centers located at major tourism destinations. Human resources development is especially important in tourism because service activities depend in a large part for their success on the quality of personnel working in tourism. Persons working in the many

FIGURE 1. The Strategic Implementation of Planning and Policy for Thai Tourism Product Model

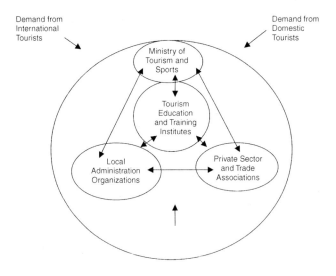

aspects of tourism must be properly trained. The general public and people living in tourism areas must be educated about tourism. Even the tourists themselves must be informed about their destination–its geography, history, cultural patterns and society–and encouraged to respect it. In terms of strategic implementation of tourism product development, tourism education and training institutions should be the catalyst and have a coordinating role with all stakeholders in each region or destination.

CONCLUSION

This paper has four main parts. The first part explained the overview of the tourism industry of Thailand. The second part described historical development and evolution of the tourism higher education in Thailand, especially, the changing situations affecting higher education. The third part described the status, structure, characteristics and trends of tourism education in Thailand. The final part dealt with the future development with regard to human resources development strategy to achieve a sustainable tourism development in Thailand.

REFERENCES

Brickshawana, A. (2003, December). *Tourism policy of Thailand.* Paper presented at the seminar held by Chulalongkorn University, Bangkok, Thailand.

Chaisawat, M. (1997, August). *Baccalaureate and graduate degrees in tourism and hospitality studies in Thailand: The current situation, problems and future development.* Proceedings of the APTA'97 Annual Conference, Taipei, Taiwan.

Chaisawat, M. (2000, June-July). *Baccalaureate and graduate degrees in tourism and hospitality studies in Thailand: The comparative studies between 1996 and 1999.* Proceedings of the Sixth Asia Pacific Tourism Association Annual Conference, Phuket, Thailand.

Chaisawat, M. (2003, December). *Policy and planning for tourism industry in Asian countries.* Paper presented at the seminar held by Chulalongkorn University, Bangkok, Thailand.

Chaisawat, M. (2004, June). *A model of policy and planning of tourism product development in Thailand.* Proceedings of the 6th ADRF General Meeting, Bangkok, Thailand.

Chaisawat, M., & Boonchoo, D. (2005, April 16). *Baccalaureate and graduate degrees in tourism and hospitality studies in Thailand in 2003.* Proceedings of 2005 PATA Educators' Forum, Institute for Tourism Studies, Macau, China.

Constitution of the Kingdom of Thailand B.E. 2540. (1997). Sutra Paisal Law Media.

Kiranandana, S. (2004, August 22). *Higher education.* The Nation, p. 9A.

Muqbill, I. (2004). *Executive travel impact newswire* (Edition 48). Retrieved April 26, 2004, from imtiaz@travel-impact-newswire.com

National Economic and Social Development Board (NESDB). (2004, September 9). *The In-depth study of the labor force situation among middle- and high-level personnel within the tourism industry in order to increase productivity and capability of the national competitiveness.* Prepared by Innovation Policy Center, Phra Chom Klaow Thonburi Technology University.

National Economic and Social Development Board (NESDB). (2005). *The strategies for human resources development to increase competitiveness in main industries.* Retrieved May, 2005, from http://www.nesdb.go.th

Porter, M. E. (2003, May). *Thailand's competitiveness: Creating the foundations for higher productivity.* Paper presented at Thai Cabinet Meeting, Bangkok, Thailand.

Rattanavirakul, K. (1996, June). *Arthit Vikroh, 16*(82).

Thailand Traveller. (1996, February). *Interview Reggie Shiu by Jennifer Sharples, 6*(51).

Tourism Authority of Thailand (TAT). (1993, February). *Tourism master plan: A review, sectoral economics program.*

Tourism Authority of Thailand (TAT). (1999). *1997-2003 Tourism promotion and development policies.*

Tourism Authority of Thailand (TAT). (2001, September). *Action plans for national tourism development under the 9th National Economic and Social Development Plan (BE 2545-2549).*

Tourism Authority of Thailand (TAT). (2002). *Statistical report 2002.*

Xu, J. (1999, May 30). *Tourism marketing for the new millennium.* Paper presented at the seminar held by Tourism Authority of Thailand (TAT), Bangkok, Thailand.

Yamakawa, R. (2000, June-July). *The role of the network of Asia-Pacific Education and Training Institutes in Tourism (APETIT) in promoting cooperation in human resources development in the tourism sector.* Paper presented at Asia Pacific Tourism Association 6th Annual Conference, Phuket, Thailand.

Past, Present, and Future of Tourism Education: The South Korean Case

Mi-Hea Cho

Soo K. Kang

SUMMARY. Tourism education in Korea, mandated by the Higher Education Act, has evolved rapidly in response to the tourism industry's growth and labor demands for the last four decades. As tourism education has matured and become increasingly recognized as a legitimate academic field of study, the Korean tourism education has attempted to generate future quality workforce and to establish the status of tourism as a prominent research oriented discipline. The purpose of this paper is to present an overview of the Korean tourism industry and tourism education over the past four decades and to suggest future directions for Korean education in the 21st century. By improving current curricula according to today's fast changing tourism business environment and cooperating with the tourism industry with the aid of the government on policies and

---

Mi-Hea Cho is Assistant Professor, Hospitality and Tourism Management, Sejong University, 98 Kunjadong, Kwangjinku, Seoul, South Korea (E-mail: chomihea@hotmail.com).

Soo K. Kang is Assistant Professor, Restaurant and Resort Management, Department of Food Science and Human Nutrition, Colorado State University, Ft. Collins, CO 80523-1571 (E-mail: skang@cahs.colostate.edu).

[Haworth co-indexing entry note]: "Past, Present, and Future of Tourism Education: The South Korean Case." Cho, Mi-Hea, and Soo K. Kang. Co-published simultaneously in *Journal of Teaching in Travel & Tourism* (The Haworth Press, Inc.) Vol. 5, No. 3, 2005, pp. 225-250; and: *Global Tourism Higher Education: Past, Present, and Future* (ed: Cathy H. C. Hsu) The Haworth Press, Inc., 2005, pp. 225-250. Single or multiple copies of this article are available for a fee from The Haworth Document Delivery Service [1-800-HAWORTH, 9:00 a.m. - 5:00 p.m. (EST). E-mail address: docdelivery@haworthpress.com].

Available online at http://www.haworthpress.com/web/JTTT
doi:10.1300/J172v05n03_10

regulations, Korean tourism education will continue to contribute to the Korean tourism industry as a legitimate partner. *[Article copies available for a fee from The Haworth Document Delivery Service: 1-800-HAWORTH. E-mail address: <docdelivery@haworthpress.com> Website: <http://www. HaworthPress.com> © 2005 by The Haworth Press, Inc. All rights reserved.]*

KEYWORDS. South Korea, tourism industry, tourism education, Asia Pacific Region, tourism labor

INTRODUCTION

South Korea (hereafter referred to as 'Korea'), officially Republic of Korea (ROK), is 99,313 sq. km (38,345 sq miles) with a population of 48.2 million and reported a gross national income (GNI) per capita of US$12,020 in 2003 (World Bank, 2003). Korea is divided into 9 provinces and 7 independent metropolitan areas, with 77 cities and 88 counties. Mountains cover 70% of Korea's land mass with beautiful scenery, making it one of the most mountainous regions in the world.

Korea has gone through a drastic economic transformation in the past few decades. Like many developing countries, Korea experienced sharp growth in the service industries in the 1990s, particularly in the tourism industry (OECD, 2002). After the 1997 financial crisis, the Korean economy recovered quickly with growth rates of 9.3% and 3.0% in 2000 and 2001, respectively. The share of the service industries, including hotels, restaurants, and real estate services, was 51.5% in 1997, by far the greatest growth sector in the economy (National Statistics Office, 2001). Between 1993 and 2002, the average growth rate in the restaurant and accommodation services ran as high as 37.4% annually, which was double the overall industry average of 19.8% during the same period. As the tourism industry has evolved, it has produced growing interest in education and training for tourism-related professions.

THE HISTORY OF THE TOURISM INDUSTRY

It is expected that tourism will play a vital role in the development of the Korean economy. The tourism industry accounted for approximately 4.72% of the gross domestic products (GDP) in 2001 and employed 13% of the nation's workforce. It is estimated that tourism will create an additional 400,000 jobs annually through 2008 (OECD, 2002).

In accordance with such increased attention to the tourism industry, the tourism education in Korea has undergone a period to reflect and accommodate the different interests of stakeholders involved in the scope of the tourism industry. It is important to understand that how the Korea tourism education has evolved throughout the last decades in response to the development of Korea's tourism industry. This paper, therefore, presents a comprehensive review of the chronological changes in the tourism education system in conjunction with the changes in tourism industry. The paper enumerates the wide range of factors in influencing tourism education and offers suggestions that can be helpful to design and plan the Korean tourism education in the future. Table 1 shows a summary of highlights in the Korean tourism industry and education over the last four decades.

The 1950s-1960s

Governmental policies and plans for tourism development were first proposed in 1954 with the establishment of the Tourism Bureau under the supervision of the Ministry of Transportation (D. Kim, 2001a). The tourism policy goals in the 1950s and 1960s were to promote the tourism industry as an earner of foreign exchange dollars and to construct tourism infrastructures throughout the nation.

The first governmental law to promote the tourism industry was the passage of the Tourism Industry Promotion Act in 1961 (D. Kim, 2001a; S. I. Kim, 2001b). The Tourism Industry Promotion Act mandated all tourism employees, including hotel employees, managers, tour guides/conductors, and foreign interpreters (e.g., English and Japanese), to be licensed to ensure the quality of tourism labor force. Also, the Korean government began to provide private hotels with financial supports, and the first civilian-owned airline was introduced. The normalization of diplomatic relations between Korea and Japan was initiated in 1965, encouraging more Japanese visitors to Korea. The International Tourism Company (now Korea National Tourism Organization [KNTO]) and Korea Tourism Association supervised by the Ministry of Transportation's Tourism Bureau were established in 1962 and 1963, respectively. Since then, tourism began to emerge as a staple industry and received significant support from the government (D. Kim, 2001a).

TABLE 1. Summary of Korea Tourism Industry and Education

Classification	1950s-1960s	1970s	1980s	1990s-Current
Government Organization (Overseeing Tourism Industry)	Ministry of Transportation/ Tourism Bureau (1954)	Ministry of Transportation/ Tourism Promotion Division & Tourism Supervision (1979)	Ministry of Transportation/ Tourism Bureau (1981)	The Ministry of Culture and Sports (1994) Ministry of Culture and Tourism (1998)
Policy Goal/Focus	To increase foreign exchange earnings by expanding tourism industry infrastructure	To increase foreign exchange earnings by promoting international tourism	To increase foreign exchange earnings and to enhance quality of life by encouraging domestic tourism	To improve quality of life and to acquire international competitiveness by pursuing a balance between international and domestic tourism
Organization and Law/ Regulation	Tourism Industry Promotion Act (1961) Tourism Employee (hotels and tour guide) License Requirement (1961) Tour Interpreter License Requirement (1962) International Tourism Company (1962) Korea Tourism Association (1963)	Tourism Sciences Society of Korea (1972) Tourism Promotion Funding Act (1972) Tourism Industry Act (1975) Designation of Tourism Community Complexes in Kyungju Bomun (1974) and Jeju Jungmun (1976) Travel Agency License Requirement (1976) Industrial-Education Cooperation Promotional Act (1977)	Korea National Tourism Organization, or KNTO (1982) Tourism Industry Reform Act (1987)	Casino Tourism Promotion Act (1994) Tourism Accommodations Assistance Act (1996) International Convention Industry Promotion Act (1996) Leisure Promotion Act (1998) Korea Academy Society of Culture and Tourism (1998)

Classification	1950s-1960s	1970s	1980s	1990s-Current
Key Events	Designated the first national park, G-Ri Mountain (1967) Exceeded 100,000 foreign visitor arrivals (1968)	Exceeded one billion foreign visitor arrivals (1978)	Hosted the 1986 Asian Games and 1988 Olympics Exceeded two billion foreign visitor arrivals (1988) Overseas Travel Liberalization (1989)	Exceeded three billion foreign visitor arrivals (1991) Designated 'the Year of Visiting Korea' (1994) Exceeded four billion foreign visitor arrivals (1998) Exceeded five billion foreign visitor arrivals (2000) South-North Korea tourism exchange (2000) Designated 'the Year of Visiting Korea' (2001)
Education System	Offered the first tourism program at Kyonggi Women's Junior College (1962) Opened Tourism Employee Training Center (1963) Offered the first four-year tourism program at Kyonggi University (1964) Opened Tour Interpreter Training Center (1968)	Designated Tourism Employee Training Center (1971) Opened Kyungju Hotel School (1977) A total of 4,600 students at 6 four-year universities (1,240 students), 15 two-year college (3,360 students) A total of 91 of tourism educators at post-secondary institutes (1979)	Increased tourism program admission by 3,000 (1981) A total of 14,000 students at 18 four-year university, 8 master programs, 2 doctoral granting institutes and 32 two-year college and 2 vocational high schools (1988)	Increased private institutes for tourism licenses for foreign interpreters, casino dealers, etc. Closed Kyungju tourism employee training center (1999) A total of 174 universities offering tourism programs (2004)

Source: Adapted from the Ministry of Culture and Tourism (2000b).

To ensure labor supply and to improve the quality of the employees working in the tourism industry, the Korean government set up a Tourism Employee Training Center in 1963. Furthermore, the International Tourism Company began training tour interpreters in 1968. During this period, the first tourism program in higher education institutions was offered at Kyonggi Women's Junior College in 1962 with 80 students, and the first four-year bachelor's degree program was offered at Kyonggi University in 1964.

The 1970s

The Korea tourism industry in the 1970s evolved through the government's aggressive promotional strategies and campaigns. The Tourism Promotion Funding Act was passed in 1972 to provide more financial supports and incentives (e.g., tax breaks, low interest rates) for tourism enterprises. Two Tourism Community Complexes, Kyungju Bomun and Jeju Jungmun, were developed in an attempt to contribute to the growth of heritage sites and to encourage the development of tourism in the southern region. Furthermore, the Tourism Sciences Society of Korea was launched in 1972 to conduct academic research about tourism development impacts and quality of tourism education.

In 1978, international arrivals exceeded one billion for the first time, thanks to an influx of tourists from the United States and European countries, as well as a steady increase of Japanese travelers (see Figure 1). Accordingly, more international hotels were constructed, creating a hotel boom throughout the 1970s (Ahn, 1985). As of 1978, there were 35,400 tourism employees and 1,600 hotel rooms (J. Lee, 1980). Responding to the foregoing demand of employees with work experience in the tourism sectors, the Korean government opened designated tourism training centers. The International Tourism Company (now KNTO) in 1977 opened Kyungju Hotel School to train workers specifically employed by deluxe tourist hotels. Also, a travel business license was required for all travel agencies in 1976. As of 1979, tourism programs were offered at 15 two-year colleges with 3,360 students and 6 four-year universities with 1,240 students. Also, 91 faculty members were registered at the Korean Tourism Research Association (J. Lee, 1980).

The 1980s

The Korean tourism industry, in particular, underwent remarkable progress, when the Korean tourism development was pursued to im-

FIGURE 1. Foreign Tourists Arrival and Receipt

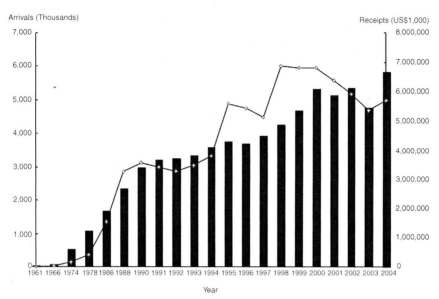

Source: Adapted from KNTO (2004).

prove the Koreans' quality of life and to promote the nation's prosperity. To offset the temporary economic downturn from the late 1970s' oil crisis, various tourism attractions throughout the country were developed at the beginning of the 1980s. Spurred by hosting the 1986 Asian Games and the 1988 Olympic Games, both of which helped raise the nation's international profile as a tourist destination, the Korean government has continually promoted the tourism industry as a vital source for foreign exchange earnings. As of 1989, a total of 20 deluxe hotels for international travelers and 34 first-star hotels were in operation with 20,000 rooms and 36,600 employees.

Furthermore, the 1989 Overseas Travel Liberalization (OTL) ushered the Korean tourism industry into the new era by stimulating Korean's outbound tourism greatly. Before 1989, overseas travel was only permitted to limited vacationers (e.g., married couples, individuals with invitations from friends or relatives abroad) and people for the purpose of government business, private business, and studying abroad. Since the OTL, the Koreans' outbound tourism increased so rapidly that Korea recorded the first tourism deficit in 1991 with US$3.78 million of tourism expenditure as opposed to US$3.43 million of tourism receipt (KNTO, 2004).

Despite the industry's rapid growth and changes, tourism education still lagged far behind until the 1980s, making professional staff recruitment difficult in the tourism industry, owing to the deficiency of its professional status. In 1981, the Ministry of Education allowed an additional 3,000 students for tourism related majors throughout the higher education institutes to stabilize the labor supply for the Korean tourism industry. As of 1988, there were 18 four-year universities offering tourism programs; of which 8 universities granted master's degrees and 2 universities had doctoral programs. Additionally, there were 32 two-year colleges and 2 vocational high schools offering tourism-related programs (Ministry of Culture and Tourism, 2000a).

The 1990s

The 1990s were a period reflecting Koreans' increasing interests in leisure and cultural activities with several momentums that propelled the nation's tourism industry. First of all, the government agency overseeing the tourism industry was changed from the Ministry of Transportation Tourism Bureau to the Ministry of Culture and Sports in 1994, which was renamed four years later as the Ministry of Culture and Tourism. Laws and regulations for the tourism industry were further relaxed, and casino and entertainment businesses were included in the tourism development spectrum and regional tourism planning projects. Specifically, the Korean government promulgated the International Convention Industry Promotion Act in December 1996 in order to promote Korea as an international convention and conference destination. The enactment of this law laid a foundation for future convention and conference business development in Korea.

As the tourism industry flourished, there was a fresh wave of realization about the importance of tourism education and demand for a skilled labor pool. The industry still found a dearth of trained manpower, and hence education and training subsequently became one of the major concerns in the tourism industry. The Korean government, consequently, required all tourism related employees to take job training at a designated training center on a regular basis. There were 10 specialized tourism employee training centers in operation, including two KNTO supervised training centers in Seoul and Kyungju, 4 in four-year universities, and 4 in two-year colleges.

The KNTO's Tourism Employee Training Center was to train low to middle level employees in the tourism industry and to supervise tourism employee license test. This center aimed to provide skilled labor through short-term courses and its main tasks encompassed basic services training, on-the-job training, demonstration training, and special event training. The basic services training is an one-day training required for those who passed tourism employee license tests to focus on service learning and professionalism as a tourism provider. The on-the-job training is designed for all tourism employees for their practical skills and expertise improvement using real-life examples and case studies. The demonstration training is for tour interpreters who want to improve their professionalism and to hone their knowledge and skills on certain subjects. Lastly, the special event training is targeted for special mega events, such as the 2002 FIFA World Cup, to promote tourism employees' professionalism, to increase their language skills, and to enhance service skills among workers employed in transportation, retail, and small- and medium-size tourism enterprises.

However, the tourism employee training requirement mandated by the Tourism Promotion Act was abolished in 1999 in order to give the tourism industry more flexibility in employee training. Consequently, programs at the designated tourism training centers decreased with the demise of the Kyungju center in 1999. On the other hand, private training centers for tour interpreters and casino dealers sharply increased because of the requirement of tourism employee license tests.

As of 2000, a total of 147,982 employees were licensed; of them, 2,889 (2.4%) were employed at managerial levels. There were also 10,999 tour interpreters (7.4%), 81,686 line employees (55%), and 52,408 (35.2%) tour guide/conductors holding a tourism employee license (KNTO, 2001). According to the KNTO, the number of tourism businesses was 5,101 in 1996, 5,936 in 1997, 6,765 in 1998, and 7,706 in 1999, with an annual average growth rate of 17%.

The 2000s

After the decade of economic downturn and several international events, the tourism industry is still acclaimed as a higher value-added business in Korea in the 21st century. A five-day work week also made many Koreans free to enjoy more leisure activities and vacations. Koreans' improved quality of life, increased interest in physical and psychological well-being, and higher income also brought people's attention to travel for their leisure time. The South-North Korean tourism initiation in

2000 opened the new era for Korean peninsular tourism by stimulating inbound and outbound tourist streams. Thanks to North Korea's abundance in natural, historic and cultural resources, a prominent mountain resort, Mountain Geumgang, was designated as a special tourist zone in 2000. Further, co-hosting the 2002 FIFA World Cup and the second Asian Games in 2002 secured the image of Korea as an international travel destination.

According to the Organization for Economic Co-operation and Development (OECD), business classification systems consisted of accommodations, restaurants, airlines, travel agencies, transportations, and leisure-, culture-, and sports-related services; there were a total of 994,000 tourism related enterprises in 2000, an increase of 22% from 1997 in Korea (see Table 2). The number of employees working in the tourism industry increased from 2.37 million in 1997 to 2.64 million in 2000.

As of 2001, 58.9% of the total tourism labor force worked in accommodations and restaurants, 22.4% in transportation, 6.5% in travel agencies and, and 12.1% in leisure-, culture-, and sports-related service sectors. As of 2003, the total number of tourism employees reached 181,788, with 3,021 (1.6%) managerial positions, 13,589 tour interpreters (7.5%), 97,021 (53.4%) line employees, and 68,157 (54%) tour guides/conductors. As of 2004, there were 14,745 licensed foreign tour interpreters and 70,123 licensed domestic licensed travel agencies in

TABLE 2. Korea Tourism Industry by Sector

Classification*	No. of Tourism Enterprises (thousand)				No. of Employees (thousand)			
	1997	1998	1999	2000	1997	1998	1999	2000
Accommodations and restaurants	522	578	601	608	1,402	1,336	1,453	1,556
Air transportation	203	245	220	222	6	16	21	9
Travel agency, transportation related services	22	23	24	26	166	155	164	173
Leisure, culture, and sports related services	87	99	115	121	255	250	285	318
Total	815	889	956	994	2,371	2,280	2,475	2,640

* The table excludes the information about Land/Pipeline transportation and Marine transportation.
Source: National Statistics Office (2000).

Korea. The tourism employee license types and its qualifications, as of 2001, are shown in Table 3.

TOURISM ORGANIZATIONS

The Korean government has supported the tourism industry by designating a central level bureau and self-governing city level agencies. Currently, three main government bodies oversee Korea's tourism planning and policy: the Tourism Bureau of the Ministry of Culture and Tourism (MCT), the Korea National Tourism Organization (KNTO), and the Korea Culture and Tourism Policy Institute (KCTPI).

First, the MCT Tourism Bureau is involved in establishing a national tourism development plan, managing tourism related legislation, operating the Tourism Promotion and Development Fund, controlling and supervising the work of KNTO and KCTPI, promoting the tourism industry, drafting measures on attracting foreign tourists, carrying out tourism promotions, and facilitating cooperation with international bodies and foreign governments.

TABLE 3. Tourism Employee License Types and Qualifications

License Classification		Qualification
Manager Level	General Manager	A minimum of 3-year experience at tourist hotels with a 1st level tourism manager license OR A minimum of 3-year management experience with a special 2nd level tourism manager license
	1st level Manager	A minimum of 3-year experience at any hospitality accommodation with a 2nd level tourism manager license
	2nd level Manager	A minimum of 3-year experience at any hospitality accommodation with a tourism accommodation employee license OR Two-year travel/tourism related college or a four-year university graduates
Employee Level	Front Desk, Rooms, Restaurant, Customer Service Employees	Older than 18 years
	Tour Interpreter	
	Domestic Tour Conductor	

Source: Adapted from KNTO (2001).

Second, the KNTO, as the national tourism organization, is responsible for a number of overseas marketing activities, including promoting destinations, conducting market surveys, supporting the hosting of international conventions, and the development of tourist souvenirs and products in collaboration with local, self-governing bodies and the tourism industry.

Last, the Korea Tourism Research Institute (KTRI) merged with the Korea Cultural Policy Institute (KCPI), to form KCTPI in 2002. In the past, the two institutes had engaged in various consulting activities particularly for government-sponsored research in such areas as culture, arts and the cultural and tourism industry. While continuing to devote itself to research, consulting, and publications, KCTPI has actively expanded its research and policy development linking culture and the arts with the culture and tourism industry (Korea Tourism Research Institute, 2005).

Additionally, there are five tourism-related associations supporting the tourism industry in Korea: Korea Tourism Association, Korea Tourists Hotel Association, Korea Resort Condominium Association, Korea Association of Complex Resort Facilities, and Korea Association of Specialized Travel Agencies. The main responsibilities of those industry associations are to seek tourism development and promotion in their respective areas to support exchanges of useful information among members.

TOURISM EDUCATION

Changes in the higher educational environment are having a tremendous impact on the education process, curricular, learning outcomes and instructional practices (Sigala & Baum, 2003). Especially, education and training are vital to the tourism industry in terms of providing a foundation of knowledge and experience for those who wish to enter the tourism industry as a career and continuing professional development for those already employed in the tourism industry (Horner & Swarbrooke, 2004). The tourism education in Korea, thus, has been developed according to the tourism industry's growth and labor demands. Effective tourism education and training require a co-operative approach, involving partnerships among academic institutions, private enterprises, and governments at different levels, to balance between academic principles and technical knowledge and vocational skills.

Tourism programs at higher education institutions in Korea have been offered over four decades as mandated by the Higher Education Act. The first 4-year undergraduate tourism program was offered at Kyonggi University in 1964. Since then, there has been a substantial increase in the number of universities and colleges offering tourism programs (KNTO, 2000). With regard to curriculum, 4-year universities have focused on tourism principles, theories, and policies, while 2-year vocation colleges have underlined more practical and technical aspects of tourism professions (KNTO, 2004). As of 2004, there were 56 4-year universities and 118 2-year colleges with 8,108 and 31,602 students, respectively, offering tourism-related programs (see Table 4) (KNTO, 2000).

Two-Year College Tourism Programs

Two-year tourism programs in Korea have been a major feeder to the nation's tourism labor force. Generally, the curriculum in these two-year programs consists of three major fields; general requirement (8 credits), major requirement (50 credits), and electives (22 credits), with a total of 80-credit requirement (Park, Hyun, & Ko, 2002). The first year curriculum usually includes general requirement courses and some electives. The second year courses mainly focus on practical knowledge and skills necessary for employment in the tourism industry.

Several challenges facing the two-year tourism programs in Korea need to be addressed. First, there is a lack of cooperation between these programs and the tourism industry in spite of their role as the main supplier to the industry's labor pool. Second, the Koreans' high educational enthusiasm and preference for four-year universities compounded the situation because of the commonly held perception that two-year colleges are for those with lower academic achievement.

TABLE 4. Tourism Education Institutes

Degree/Diploma Granting Educational Institutes	2000[1]		2004[2]	
	# of Schools	Enrollment	# of Schools	Enrollment
4-year university	55	4,088	56	8,018
2-year college	88	38,810	118	31,062
High school	46	3,666	N/A	N/A
Total	199	45,564	174	39,070

[1]Source: Adapted from KNTO (2001).
[2]Source: Adapted from KNTO (2004).

Tourism programs in two-year colleges have become diversified with various concentrations, including foreign language interpretation (e.g., English, Japanese, Chinese, and Russian), tourism/hotel management, airlines and travel agency management, tourism design and art, tourism photography, culinary management, and international conference/convention management (Choi, 1996). Despite the specialization and diversification of program names, however, most of those curricula remain similar without distinctive contents and requirements (see Table 5). Also, there are other obstacles to tackle, such as a lack of qualified faculty, internship opportunities, and decreasing financial support to develop those programs.

Four-Year University Tourism Programs

Tourism programs at four-year universities have expanded rapidly in conjunction with other academic disciplines, thus making the tourism field more comprehensive and broader than before. Like their two-year

TABLE 5. Two-Year College Tourism Programs

	Category	Department/Programs	Post-Graduate Placement
	Travel/Tourism Management	Tourism Management, Airlines, Hotel Management	Hotels, Travel Agencies, Airlines, Duty Free Shops, Condominium, Resorts, Others
	Tourism Foreign Languages	English, Japanese, Chinese, Russian, and others	
	Foodservice/Restaurant Management	Hotel/Restaurants, Culinary (Korean cuisine, Western cuisine, Pastry/Bakery, and others)	Hotels, Airlines, Resorts, Condominium, Restaurants
Others	Event/Convention Management	Convention, Events, Vacation, Leisure Culture, Cultural Assets	Hotels, Airlines, Condominium, Duty Free, Restaurants, Events, Convention/Conferences
	Tourism Information System	Tourism Information, Information Management	Hotels, Travel Agencies, Airlines, Duty Free Shops, Condominium, and others
	Leisure	Tourism Leisure, Leisure Management, Leisure Sports	Leisure Sports, Tourism, and others

Source: Adapted from D. Kim (2001a).

counterparts, four-year university tourism programs have undergone diversification with various specializations in terms of its curriculum (see Table 6).

One of the popular additions to the traditional tourism discipline is foodservice management because of people's increasing interest in restaurant business and management. Recently, foodservice management (often called restaurant management) is becoming an independent program, being separated from the interdisciplinary program structures (e.g., hotel or tourism management). Another example is conference/convention management, which is one of the fastest growing segments in Korea. As international conference/convention centers were opened in metropolitan cities, such as Seoul, Ilsan, Busan, and Daegu, convention and conference management has become popular with a great deal of interest from both the academy and industry. Furthermore, many four-year tourism programs have foreseen the need of curriculum on a variety of emerging sectors within the tourism industry, such as events/festivals, entertainments, and sports.

Graduate Tourism Programs

As of 2000, there were 32 universities offering only a master program and over 20 universities offering master and doctoral programs on tourism (Ministry of Culture & Tourism, 2000b). Specifically, master programs at graduate schools in Korea are classified into two categories; traditional programs and specialized programs. The traditional graduate schools target traditional four-year graduates who want to study an academic discipline and to pursue an academic career. Alternatively, specialized graduate programs are designed for those students who are fully employed and offer classes at nights. Their curricula are strongly based on practical principles and theories appropriate to industry circumstances, while traditional graduate programs are designed to be more research oriented (Cha, 2001).

The number of specialized master graduate programs has increased rapidly nationwide to 154 with 31,399 students, accounting for 11% of the total graduate schools, as of 2000 (S. Lee, 1999). Of them, 32 specialized graduate schools offered a master degree in tourism with 638 students (KNTO, 2000). The popularity of specialized graduate programs appears to continue because of people's desire to continue their education for the professionalism in the level of management as well as academic enthusiasm with the possibility of being faculty at two-year colleges. In spite of the rapid growth of graduate programs, there are

TABLE 6. Sample of Tourism Management Courses Offered at Four-Year Universities

Department/ Program	Course Names
Tourism Management[a]	Principles of Tourism, Tourism Service Manners, Travel Agency Management, Hotel Management, Cultural Tourism, Tourism Law, Tourist Behaviors, Tourism Business, Food Service Industry, Tourism English 1 & 2, Tourism Japanese 1 & 2, Service Industry Management, Tourism Information, International Tourism, Tourism Marketing, Tourism Geography & Resources, Airline Operation, Unification & Tourism, Tourism English Conversation 1-4, Tourism Policy, Travel Agency Internship, Tourism Economics, Overseas Tourism Training 1 & 2, East-West Cultural Tourism, Travel Information System, Field Work, Ocean Tourism
Hotel Management[b]	Principles of Tourism, Tourism Service Manners, Travel Agency Management, Hotel Management, Cultural Tourism, Tourism Law, Tourism Business, Food Service Industry, Tourism English 1 & 2, Tourism Japanese 1 & 2, Service Industry Management, Tourism Information, International Tourism, Tourism Marketing, Hotel & Personnel & Organization, Hotel Catering, Managerial Accounting in Hotel, Hotel Guest Behavior, Hotel Room Management, Hotel Restaurant Management, Hotel & Tourism Service, Convention Industry, Overseas Tourism Training 1 & 2, Hotel English, Hotel Internet Management, Hotel Sanitary Management, Field Work, Hotel Product Strategy, Seminar
Food Service Management[c]	Principles of Cooking, Foodservice Management, Food & Nutrition for Health, Catering Planning and Management, Food & Beverage Purchasing, Food & Beverage Management, Menu Planning & Design, Hotel Restaurant Information Management, Wine & Sommelier, Food Safety, Korean Cuisine Practice 1, 2, & 3, Western Cuisine Practice 1, 2, & 3, Japanese Cuisine Practice, Chinese Cuisine Practice, Bakery & Bread Making Practice, Restaurant Management, Restaurant Franchise Management, Kitchen Management Practice, Hotel Food Service Management Case Study, Food and Culture History, Food Service Product Development, Food Service Cost Control, Restaurant Marketing, Restaurant Design and Layout, Food Manufacturing and Storage, Restaurant Statistics, Consumer Behaviors, Traditional Cuisine Development, Cooking and Wine, Food Coordination, Nutrition

Department/ Program	Course Names
Convention/Event Management[d]	Principles of Event Management, International Convention & Conference Planning, Special Event Management, Hotel Catering Event, Private Event, Event Tourism Management, Cruise Management, Event Finance Management, Event Promotion Management, Recreation Event, Incentive Travel Management, Internet Event, Event Special Skills, Festival Management, Show Business Management, Sports Event, Exhibition/Tradeshow Event, Mass Media Event, Travel Agency Management, Convention Management Services, Convention Planning Practice, Convention Marketing, Convention Business Composition, International Exhibition Management, Convention Economy Principles, Event Planning Management, Catering Planning, Convention and Chinese Culture, Convention Organization Consumer Behaviors, International Conference Interpretation Practice, Food & Wine Preparation Practice, Trade Show/Exhibition Planning Practice, Convention Information Management, Convention English Practice, Convention Finance/Accounting Principles, International Etiquette & Culture, Convention Contracts, E-Convention, Convention Product Development, Convention Communication Principles, International Convention Negotiation, Convention Research Methods, Convention Facility Management, Convention Management Seminar, International Exhibition/Trade Show Case Study

Sources:
[a]Kyonggi University (2005c)
  Kyung Hee University (2005d)
[b]Kyung Hee University (2005c)
  Sejong University (2005b)
[c]Kyonggi University (2005b)
  Kyung Hee University (2005b)
  Sejong University (2005a)
[d]Kyonggi University (2005a)
  Kyung Hee University (2005a)

still arguments regarding the quality of education and over concentration at several universities located in Seoul (Cha, 2001).

The rapid expansion of tourism education jobs in the late 1990s produced a quantum change in the quality of tourism scholarship in Korea. Programs staffed by academics who have not upgraded their skills or who do not have a research orientation are seen to be lagging behind those that pursue research opportunities. Cha and Lee (2001) compared the views on the current curricular issues of specialized graduate tourism programs between academic scholars and industry practitioners. Results of the study indicated that there were clear discrepancies on what tourism education at graduate schools should be emphasized between academic faculty and industry professionals. Specifically, academic professors emphasized more research methodology and information technology than industry experts, while industry participants underlined more tourism policy and regulation issues. Even though Korean universities are producing a large number of doctoral graduates in tourism, concerns have been raised that many of these people need to be more qualified for teaching tourism programs.

Virtual (Cyber) Tourism Programs

The new educational providers have risen in order to fill the undeniable demand for open, flexible, distance, and life long learning as well as to pursue profits. Virtual universities are based on the cyberspace frequently operated by traditional academic settings (i.e., colleges or universities). Stamps (1998) argued that the structure of future universities would be either fully or partially virtual and consist of a network of links with suppliers, leaving universities to concentrate on their core activity: research and teaching.

As the advent of cyber-based education has gained its popularity due to its increased employability of students and functional effectiveness (S. Kang, Jeon, Jeong, & Bang, 2002), in 1996, technology assisted education was proposed with the popularity of rapidly available distance education, cyber training, and simulated educational resources in Korea. Existing manpower with significant work experience is challenged to establish career paths in the tourism industry. Therefore, the development of on-line programs was a welcome addition to the traditional education channel in that this new medium can improve the knowledge of current and potential employees as an alternative venue for continuing and life long learning experience, especially for non-traditional students. Cyber universities are expected to grow rapidly as a new learning venue in the future education environment. Particularly, tourism employees usually work hectic schedules that make their regular training and learning experience limited. In that sense, cyber education can resolve these challenges by being available immediately regardless of time and space. As of 2004, 17 cyber universities existed, of which 8 universities have offered tourism related majors (Cha, 2001).

INDUSTRIAL-EDUCATION COOPERATION

Industrial and education cooperation was mandated by the Industrial-Educational Cooperation Promotional Act in 1977, which required education programs and the industry to collaborate with each other in creating hands-on experience opportunities for students. Under this law, students attending a two-year college or four-year university majoring in tourism/hospitality management were required to work at tourism related enterprises for 1 to 2 months during summer or winter breaks.

The creation of industrial-educational cooperation, or also called 'cooperative vocational education' or 'occupational education,' was intended to strengthen an active relationship between industry and education programs to meet the business challenges and create professional opportunities for students. These programs encompassed such different practices as internships, work experience, supervised occupational experience, field practice, work based learning, whose definitions vary depending on situations and scholars (K. Kang & Lee, 2003). Students can gain experience for their career and employment interests as well as training opportunities by demonstrating knowledge, techniques, skills, and abilities (aptitudes) in the real world. Alternatively, tourism businesses can take advantage of these temporary employment opportunities in detecting future perspective employees. From the educators' point of view, they can benefit from the cooperation by gaining insight about curriculum development, exploring funding sources, and establishing networks for students' future employment opportunities. However, like their counterparts in two-year colleges, the issue of lack of systematic industry-education cooperation should be addressed with four-year university tourism programs.

Figure 2 shows the number of students participating in tourism industrial-education cooperation programs from 1988 to 1998. Despite this requirement, not all students completed their hands-on experience. Even worse, a sharp decrease of participants since 1998 can be ascribed

FIGURE 2. Tourism Industrial-Educational Cooperation Participants

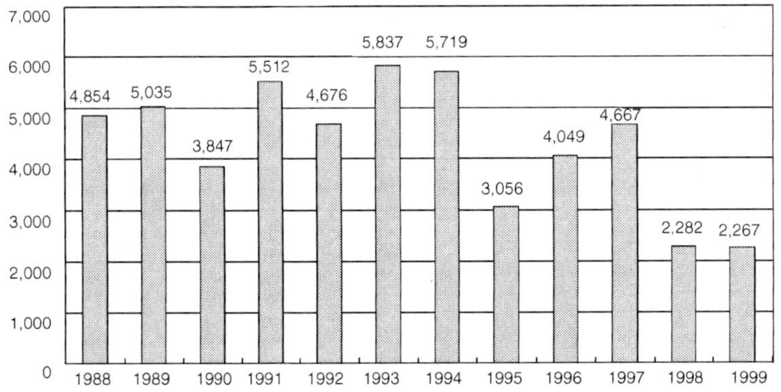

Source: Adapted from KNTO (2001).

to the impact of the 1997 financial crisis that resulted in a high unemployment rate because many hospitality businesses had suffered and tried to reduce the number of regular employees.

THE FUTURE OF TOURISM EDUCATION

As tourism education has matured and become increasingly recognized as a legitimate academic field of study, the Korean tourism education has evolved to achieve dual goals; generating future employees contributing to the development and expansion of the tourism industry, and establishing the status of tourism as a prominent research oriented discipline. There are several issues for Korean educators to consider in paving future directions for fruitful results to achieve these goals. Tourism education programs should strive to provide pathways for the future when current and potential employees can integrate their knowledge and skills to project themselves into a higher level of professionalism. No matter what, the status of tourism education in the future is unlikely to change unless both industry and academia recognize and appreciate the value of developing highly skilled and competent tourism managers (Sigala & Baum, 2003). The following three suggestions are made to address the concerns and challenges facing the tourism education and to guide the disciple to better serve its stakeholders in the fast changing tourism environment.

Curriculum Improvement

Most current tourism curricula have been developed with operational concepts and knowledge, and little attention is given to specific skill or technique development. Even though there is a law requiring all tourism major students to gain some level of practical experience, it has not been strongly enforced in reality. Not many educational programs incorporate practical training into their curricula in a systematic way due to lack of resources or difficulty of finding industry partners. Therefore, students are mostly instructed in the classrooms, and experience on practical skills is definitely lacking, which can hamper their employability and delay their career advancement after graduation.

Partnership with the industry should be actively sought to bring first-hand expertise and knowledge into the traditional instructions (Sigala & Baum, 2003). The emphasis on internship, a viable means of co-operative partnership among students, educators, industry professionals and governments, is a must to rectify the possible problems facing the tourism industry in Korea. A lack of technical skills and working experience definitely have taken its toll on future tourism employees at their initial career stage by wasting time on obtaining fundamental skills and knowledge that can be learned earlier. Without a rigid requirement for internships, practical training or work experience, the quality of the workforce in the future will suffer more considering the growing competition and increasing travelers' savvy knowledge and experiences. Another solution may be the involvement of industry professionals in classrooms that could substantially enhance the learning experience of tourism students (Cho & Schmeltzer, 2000).

Another problem which needs to be addressed in curriculum reform is that few students, after spending four years of studying tourism, are committed to the tourism industry for their career partly due to unrealistic career expectations (Cha, 2001; D. Kim, 2001a). Traditionally, service employees have been working under a less desirable working environment with long hours and repetitive tasks. Many employees have intentions to quit their job or leave the industry when they are offered a better salary package from a different industry. Therefore, preparing students to face the reality at the early stage of their education may lessen any reality shocks about the nature of the job, work conditions, and human relations that they may encounter after graduation (Chung & Ji, 2000; S. I. Kim, 2001b; Park et al., 2002).

Academic resources, such as library and classroom materials, need to be updated on a regular basis to reflect the unique nature of the tourism industry in Korea as well as comprehensive changing trends of the global tourism market. Translated textbooks published in western countries (mainly US and UK) are frequently used in classrooms, which do not reflect specific Korean cultures, values, and circumstances. This may result in confusion among students when they apply their knowledge and skills into daily tasks in reality. An organized commitment and efforts should be made to publish more updated textbooks and other literature that can be used in classrooms.

The globalization of the tourism industry is creating a need for more focus on transnational cross-cultural issues in tourism. Particularly, one of the issues to be addressed in conjunction with this trend is an emphasis on foreign language training. In future, Chinese visitors are expected to increase rapidly in the next decades because of its geographic proximity and China's rapid economic growth, and consequently, a need for Chinese speaking employees is rapidly growing. Although current students are required to take foreign language classes, the hours or credits are not enough to master a language. Therefore, educators should come up with alternative or supplementary methods of preparing their students for better communication skills with their international customers.

Training Employees in the Tourism Industry

The human resource oriented nature of the tourism industry differentiates it from other economic sectors. This unique nature has direct consequences for the delivery of education and training (Baum, 2001). Development of quality human resources is critical to the future health of tourism sectors affected by trends in globalization and fierce competitiveness (Little & Watson, 2004). New market niches, such as nature tourism, eco-tourism, and adventure tourism, are constantly flourishing in response to travelers' changing demands. The spread of information technology also has changed the way of doing business by tourism providers and of making decisions by customers (Costa, 2004; D. Kim, 2001a). Therefore, today's workforce must be equipped with new skills to match the rapid pace of transformation characterized by greater use of information technology (D. Kim, 2001a).

In spite of the rapidly changing business environment, professional education and training of tourism employees have a relatively short history in Korea. The unavailability of skilled labor and a lack of continuing training have placed limitations on the level of desirable and consistent in service quality. Most of all, there is a need of commitment for resources and professional guidance to develop the much needed 'service orientation' philosophy and skills.

Traditionally, training and education were important to gain employment in tourism, but after that, it played little role in the worker's actual career. Education and training, however, are vital to current employees in that it helps them keep up with changes occurring in today's business environment, make staff feel valued, help reduce staff turnover, and make sure that staff who are promoted to supervisory or managerial positions can perform efficiently. To resolve this challenge, the tourism industry enterprises should consider forming partnerships with education providers. The development of jointly designed and delivered degrees and the sharing of resources are the most evident collaborative activities that can lead to efficient development of teaching material and great accumulation of knowledge and expertise for both future and current tourism employees (Sigala & Baum, 2003).

Government Support and Policy Formation

Tourism education is highly dynamic, influenced by the wider political, economic, social, and environmental climates. Tourism education policy must be developed with consultation between both the tourism industry and education stakeholders so that clear and coherent education policies can be generated. If tourism education is implemented with little policy guidance, then there will be a constant conflict between education providers and the tourism industry and environment, as each seeks to satisfy its own interests. Policies can definitely help to give a focus and direction to present and future tourism education (Amoah & Baum, 1997).

The Korean government should facilitate and assist the efforts exerted by tourism education institutions. The Industrial-Educational Cooperation Promotional Act needs to be revised or enacted with a proper authority to ensure mutual cooperation. The government may consider providing financial incentives or rewards for tourism enterprises who participate in the partnership. Government also should make an effort to secure research funds, setting-up training facilities, equipment, and strategic plans for developing quality teaching environment. Furthermore, tourism professional bodies have played a leading role in continuous development of both training and education. Partnership with those professional organizations like the American Hotel and Lodging Association, which has run a well structured comprehensive training program for the US hospitality sector for a number of years, should be constantly pursued for mutual benefits.

CONCLUSIONS

This paper presents an overview of Korea tourism industry and tourism education over the past four decades and to suggest future directions for the Korea education system in the 21st century. A number of changes to tourism education and the people who teach it have occurred as the tourism industry has matured and become recognized increasingly as a legitimate academic field of study (McKercher, 2002). Tourism education in Korea enjoyed remarkable growth throughout the 1990s and is expected to become more popular throughout the 2000s. Nevertheless, several issues should be addressed about the sustainability of the tourism industry's growth and prosperity. During this process, all stakeholders–private and public sectors alike–should strive to harmonize tourism education more effectively to make the tourism industry flourish further. By doing so, Korea's tourism education will prepare students with a broader disciplinary foundation and a balanced knowledge and skill for the global tourism era.

REFERENCES

Ahn, O. (1985). A study on the approach of the curriculum in tourism department of Junior College. *Korea Tourism Research*, 9(1), 3-34.

Amoah, V. A., & Baum, T. (1997). Tourism education: Policy versus practice. *International Journal of Contemporary Hospitality Management*, 9(1), 5-12.

Baum, T. (2001). Education for tourism in a global economy. In S. Wahab & C. Cooper (Eds.), *Tourism in the Age of Globalization* (pp. 198-212). London: Routledge.

Cha, S. B. (2001). A comparison of views on the curricula issues of special tourism programs in graduate school between academy and industry. *Journal of Korea Culture and Tourism*, 3(2), 193-202.

Cha, S. B., & Lee, D. S. (2001). A comparative study of stakeholders' perceptions on tourism specialized graduate education process. *Consumption & Culture Study*, 4(3), 107-117.

Cho, W., & Schmeltzer, C. (2000). Just in time education: Tools for hospitality managers of the future? *International Journal of Contemporary Hospitality Management*, 12(1), 31-36.

Choi, K. (1996). A study on the cooperative education of tourism related departments of Junior college. *The Journal of Tourism Studies*, 8(4), 263-285.

Chung, J., & Ji, K. (2000). The tendency to study necessity of tourism education to target citizens and society. *Tourism Management Research*, 7(1), 229-254.

Costa, J. (2004). The Portuguese tourism sector: Key challenges for human resources management. *International Journal of Contemporary Hospitality Management*, 16(7), 402-408.

Horner, S., & Swarbrooke, J. (2004). International cases in tourism management: Case 26 Tourism education and training (pp. 261-273). London: Elsevier Butterworth Heinemann.

Kang, K., & Lee, J. (2003). A study on the model and program development of work-based experience for the Junior College in Korea. *The Journal of Vocational Education Research*, 22(2), 43-72.

Kang, S., Jeon, I., Jeong, K., & Bang, J. (2002). *K-12 cyber education development*. Seoul, Korea: Korea Education Development Center.

Kim, D. (2001a). *Specialization of human resources in tourism sector*. Seoul, Korea: Tourism Research Institute.

Kim, S. I. (2001b). *Integration of biodiversity and tourism: Korean case study*. Seoul, Korea: UNEP's Biodiversity Planning Support Programme.

Korea Tourism Research Institute. (2005). *Welcome to the homepage of Korea Culture and Tourism Policy Institute*. Retrieved May 5, 2005, from http://www.kctpi.re. kr/english/e-index.html

KNTO. (2000). *Annual tourism report*. Seoul, Korea: Korea National Tourism Organization.

KNTO. (2001). *Planning for the Activation of Tourism Education Programs*. Seoul, Korea: Korea National Tourism Organization.

KNTO. (2004). *Annual tourism report*. Seoul, Korea: Korea National Tourism Organization.

Kyonggi University. (2005a). *Convention management curriculum*. Retrieved September 5, 2005, from http://www.kyonggi.ac.kr/organ/content/view.asp?oMID=10691&organID=1069&menuID=2

Kyonggi University. (2005b). *Food service management curriculum*. Retrieved September 5, 2005, from http://www.kyonggi.ac.kr/organ/content/view.asp?oMID=10681&organID=1068&menuID=2

Kyonggi University. (2005c). *Tourism management curriculum*. Retrieved September 5, 2005, from http://www.kyonggi.ac.kr/organ/content/view.asp?oMID=10651&organID=1065&menuID=2

Kyung Hee University. (2005a). *Convention management curriculum*. Retrieved September 5, 2005, from www.khu.ac.kr/m4/s1/f5_2.htm

Kyung Hee University. (2005b). *Food service management curriculum*. Retrieved September 5, 2005, from www.khu.ac.kr/m4/s1/f5_3.htm

Kyung Hee University. (2005c). *Hotel management curriculum*. Retrieved September 5, 2005, from http://www.khu.ac.kr/m4/s1/f5_1.html

Kyung Hee University. (2005d). *Tourism management curriculum*. Retrieved September 5, 2005, from http://www.khu.ac.kr/m4/s1/f5_1.html, http://dasan.sejong.ac.kr/%7Ehoteldpt/

Lee, J. (1980). A study on the long-range forecasting the demand and supply policy of Korea tourism manpower. *Korea Tourism Research, 4*(1), 64-85.

Lee, S. (1999). *A study on the improvement of industrial-education cooperation system for tourism employees*. Unpublished doctoral dissertation, Kyonggi University, Seoul, Korea.

Little, J. D., & Watson, S. (2004). Developing graduate managers for hospitality and tourism. *International Journal of Contemporary Hospitality Management, 16*(4), 408-412.

McKercher, B. (2002). The future of tourism education: An Australian scenario. *Tourism and Hospitality Research, 3*(3), 199-210.

Ministry of Culture and Tourism. (2000a). *Annual report on tourism trends*. Seoul, Korea: Ministry of Culture & Tourism.

Ministry of Culture and Tourism. (2000b). *The 2nd tourism development planning*. Seoul, Korea: Tourism Culture and Tourism Policy Institute.

National Statistics Office. (2000). *Korea tourism industry by sectors*. Retrieved April 21, 2005, from http://kosis.nso.go.kr/

National Statistics Office. (2001). *Korea major economic index*. Retrieved April 23, 2005, from http://kosis.nso.go.kr/

OECD. (2002). *National tourism policy review: Republic of Korea*. Organization for Economic Co-operation and Development. Retrieved June 8, 2005, from http://www.oecd.org/dataoecd/43/49/33649881.pdf

Park, S., Hyun C., & Ko, K. (2002). A study on practical tourism education program in two-year colleges: Focusing on customized training program. *Korea Tourism Policy Research, 8*(3), 201-217.

Sejong University. (2005a). *Foodservice management curriculum.* Retrieved September 5, 2005, from www.sejong.ac.kr

Sejong University. (2005b). *Hotel management curriculum.* Retrieved September 5, 2005, from http://dasan.sejong.ac.kr/%7Ehoteldpt/

Sigala, M., & Baum, T. (2003). Trends and issues in tourism and hospitality higher education: Visioning the future. *Tourism and Hospitality Research, 4*(4), 367-376.

Stamps, D. (1998). The for-profit future of higher education. *Training, 35*(8), 22-29.

World Bank (2003). Korea–Transition to a knowledge-based economy. Retrieved June 1, 2005, from www.worldbank.org/korea

Australian Tourism Education:
The Quest for Status

Philip L. Pearce

SUMMARY. An appraisal of Australian tourism education is undertaken by pursuing its historical development and the key issues of teaching locations, generic skills and graduate attributes, educator competence, human resource planning and how to assess performance. It is argued that Australia, when considered as a case study in the global context of higher tourism education, occupies a distinctive and relatively successful niche. The distinctiveness derives from both its late entry into the field and the status-oriented context in which it has grown. The success is characterised by a strong research-education nexus and the consolidation rather than loss of the degree offerings over time. *[Article copies available for a fee from The Haworth Document Delivery Service: 1-800-HAWORTH. E-mail address: <docdelivery@haworthpress.com> Website: <http://www.HaworthPress.com> © 2005 by The Haworth Press, Inc. All rights reserved.]*

KEYWORDS. Tourism education, status quest, consolidation

INTRODUCTION

Australia, with a population of just over 20 million people in 2004, is home to a diverse multicultural population clustered largely around the

Philip L. Pearce is Foundation Professor of Tourism, School of Business, James Cook University, Townsville, Queensland, 4811, Australia (E-mail: philip.pearce@jcu.edu.au).

[Haworth co-indexing entry note]: "Australian Tourism Education: The Quest for Status." Pearce, Philip L. Co-published simultaneously in *Journal of Teaching in Travel & Tourism* (The Haworth Press, Inc.) Vol. 5, No. 3, 2005, pp. 251-267; and: *Global Tourism Higher Education: Past, Present, and Future* (ed: Cathy H. C. Hsu) The Haworth Press, Inc., 2005, pp. 251-267. Single or multiple copies of this article are available for a fee from The Haworth Document Delivery Service [1-800-HAWORTH, 9:00 a.m. - 5:00 p.m. (EST). E-mail address: docdelivery@haworthpress.com].

doi:10.1300/J172v05n03_11

251

Eastern coast of the continent. In 2003, Australia received almost five million international visitors who accounted for thirty percent of the total tourism expenditure. It is forecast that international tourism will continue to grow at about 3-5 percent annually while domestic tourism will provide a stable, but only marginally expanding, base (Boundy, 2004). There are over 100,000 small and medium size enterprises which comprise the sector (Bolin & Greenwood, 2001).

Australia in 2004 is also home to thirty-nine universities, which are recognised and funded predominantly by the Commonwealth Government. Importantly, universities are not the only component of higher, or post-secondary, education. There are also state and federally funded colleges of technical and further education. Typically these institutions, over 100 in 2004, are diploma, not degree granting, bodies. Some of them, but certainly not all, play a role in tourism and hospitality training. Their role in tourism education is largely in operational rather than advanced managerial education and they are not involved in research and research training of tourism students. The focus of this review is on the university tourism education sector with less attention to the technical and further education institutions.

The concept of academic status in universities and in areas of study is an important consideration in locating and framing tourism education in Australia and beyond (Becher, 1989; Fuchs, 1992; Pearce, 1995). This theme will be explored in further detail in the following sections.

THE HISTORY AND RISE
OF AUSTRALIAN TOURISM EDUCATION

Australian universities can be divided into four clusters. The first cluster consists of six institutions, each based in a different state and specifically in the capital city of that state. These universities were established in the nineteenth century and were heavily influenced by British cultural and educational practices. These universities served the small pre-World War II population exclusively until an Australian National University was created in the 1950s. This new institution was quickly followed by other new arrivals and together they can be defined as the research culture oriented universities of the 1960s and 1970s. They comprise a second cluster for the purposes of this appraisal. This new wave of institutions provided Australian students with additional opportunities to study traditional disciplines in both the largest cities and in major regional centres. As well as the prevailing British influences shaping Australian universities, the institutions of the 1960s and 1970s were also influenced by an influx of North American academics and there were some creative efforts to structure faculties and courses in innovative ways. A total of thirteen universities were added to the original six in this post World War II expansion. Not all of these universities were developed at exactly the same time but together they represented a coherent response to the educational needs of the rising population of baby boomers in post World War II Australia (see Figure 1).

The third cluster of Australian universities did in fact all come into existence at the same time–specifically in 1987 or at least shortly after that date. The Commonwealth Government, like its counterpart in the United Kingdom, created 17 new universities out of the 20 or so institutes of technology and advanced education colleges which had been the second of the three-tier post secondary system. This amalgamation and upgrade of the institutes and colleges paved the way for the existing third-tier institutions–the local training and technical colleges–to become the new second tier of education with a specific trade and skills focus. An account of the Australian education scene in the 1990s therefore can be summarized as six universities in cluster one, thirteen uni-

FIGURE 1. The Provision of Tourism Education in Australian Universities

CLUSTER ONE: Traditional city Universities Nineteenth century origins	Location	University	Providence of Named Degrees in Tourism in 2004
	Sydney	U. of Sydney	·
	Melbourne	U. of Melbourne	·
	Adelaide	U. of Adelaide	·
	Brisbane	U. of Queensland	√ (after amalgamation in 1987)
	Perth	U. of Western Australia	·
	Hobart	U. of Tasmania	√ (after amalgamation)

Sources (Universities and web pages):
   University of Sydney (2004)–*http://www.usyd.edu.au/*
   University of Melbourne (2004)–*http://www.unimelb.edu.au/*
   University of Adelaide (2004)–*http://www.adelaide.edu.au/*
   The University of Queensland (2004)–*http://www.uq.edu.au/study/studyarea.html?area=bus_law*
   University of Western Australia (2004)–*http://www.uwa.edu.au/*
   University of Tasmania (2004)–*http://www.utas.edu.au*

FIGURE 1 (continued)

CLUSTER TWO: Phase II Research Universities 1950s-1960s-1970s origins	Location	University	Providers of Named Degrees in Tourism in 2004
	Townsville	James Cook U.	√
	Brisbane	Griffith U.	√
	Armidale	U. of New England	-
	Sydney	Macquarie U.	-
		U. of New South Wales	√
	Canberra	Australian National U.	-
	Melbourne	Monash U.	√
		La Trobe U.	√
	Geelong	Deakin U.	√
	Adelaide	Finders U.	√
	Perth	Murdoch U.	√
	Wollongong	U. of Wollongong	√
	Newcastle	U. of Newcastle	√

Sources:
  James Cook University (2004)–*http://www.icu.edu.au/flbca/public/business/tourism.shtml*
  Griffith University (2003)–*http://www.griffith.edu.au/academicprogramsandcourse/*
  University of New England (2004)–*http://www.une.edu.au/*
  Macquarie University (2004)–*http://www.mq.edu.au/*
  University of New South Wales (2004)–*http://www.unsw.edu.au/*
  Australian National University (2004)–*http://www.anu.edu.au/*
  Monash University (2004–*http://www.monash.edu.au/pubs/ugrad/buseco.html*
  La Trobe University (2004–*http://www.latrobe.edu.au/handbook/lawman/tourism_courses.htm*
  Deakin University (2004)–*http://www.deakin.edu.au/courses/documents/undergrad/brochures/Business.pdf*
  Flinders University (2004)–*http://www.flinders.edu.au/courses/ugrad/*
  Murdoch University (2004)–*http://handbook.murdoch.edu.au/courses/*
  University of Wollongong (2004)–*http://www.uow.edu.au/*
  University of Newcastle (2003)–*http://www.newcastle.edu.au/study/australian/index.html*

versities in cluster two and seventeen new universities in cluster three. Over time, these origins, while known to the people in the university sector, have diminished in the public consciousness. The distinctions do persist, however, in some of the alliances and attitudes within Australian universities. This historical record partly accounts for where tourism courses are located and where they are conspicuously absent.

A small fourth cluster can also be noted as a way of completing this historical framework. In the 1980s and 1990s, a small group of three private universities started their operations in Australia. Additionally there are two private hospitality/hotel schools, the latter with specific cluster two affiliations.

An examination of Figure 1 reveals that of the six universities in cluster one, the cluster which includes Australia's oldest universities, only two now teach tourism and importantly this tourism teaching is actually a consequence of university-college amalgamations in 1987. In cluster two–the newer research universities–nine out of thirteen institutions do teach tourism, while in cluster three sixteen out of seventeen institutions are involved in tourism education. Even in the smaller fourth cluster of

CLUSTER THREE: Post 1987 Universities	Location	University	Providers of Named Degrees in Tourism in 2004
	Darwin	Charles Darwin U.	√
	Rockhampton	Central Queensland U.	√
	Brisbane	Queensland U. of Technology	-
	Sunshine Coast	U. of Sunshine coast	√
	Toowoomba	U. of Southern Queensland	√
	Lismore	Southern Cross U.	√
	Canberra	U. of Canberra	√
	Albury	Charles Sturt U.	√
	Melbourne	U. of Victoria	√
		Royal Melbourne Institute of Technology	√
		Swinburne Institute of Technology	√
	Adelaide	U. of South Australia	√
	Sydney	U. of Western Sydney	√
		U. of Technology Sydney	√
	Perth	Edith Cowan U.	
		Curtin U.	√
	Ballarat	U. of Ballarat	√

Sources:
Charles Darwin University (2004)–*http://eagle.ntu.edu.au/NTR/Apps/coursere.nsf/CDU_pw/AreasInterest/ EE8EE3E460DCD92F69256DE6000BC1D3?OpenDocument*
Central Queensland University (2004)–*http://www.cqu.edu.au/pages/ugprgmslist_business.html*
Queensland University of Technology–*http://www.qut.edu.au*
University of Sunshine Coast (2004)–*http://www.usc.edu.au*
University of Southern Queensland (2004)–*http://www.usq.edu.au*
Southern Cross University (2004)–*http://www.scu.edu.au/courses/course_desc.php?spk_cd+3004110*
University of Canberra (2004)–*http://www.uc.edu.au/courses/index.cfm?action=browse&type=course&coursegroup=01*
Charles Sturt University (2004)–*http://www.csu.edu.au/cgi-pub/course/getcourse?nationality=Australia&top=On+ Campus&two=Undergrate&three=All&submit.x69&submit.y=10&submit=Submit*
University of Victoria (2004)–*http://www.vu.edu.au/Courses/Handbooks/BUSINESS/index1.asp*
Royal Melbourne Institute of Technology (RMIT) (2004)–*http://www.rmit.edu.au/browse/Study%20at%20RMIT%2F2005% 20Program%20Lists/*
Swinburne Institute of Technology (2003)–*http://domino.swin.edu.au/cd31.nsf/07921ddf50528dleca256768003fbbda/ 563c3e9d0653395cca256b050002c18e?OpenDocument*
The University of South Australia (2004)–*http://www.unisa.edu.au/study/progcourses/default.asp*
University of Western Sydney (2004)–*http://handbook.uws.edu.au/hbook/COURSE_INDEX.ASP#uC03*
University of Technology Sydney (2004)–*http://www.uts.edu.au/div/publications/bus/ug/index.html*
Edith Cowan University (2004)–*http://handbook.ecu.edu.au/ECUCourseList.asp?Page=53&Filter=&hb=1&fac=0&field=2*
Curtin University (2004)–*http://www.curtin.edu.au*
University of Ballarat (2004)–*http://www.ballarat.edu.au/courseguide/display/cgi?ID+39*

private institutions three out of five participants offer tourism options. Clearly tourism teaching is widespread but not evenly spread through the institutional clusters.

The impetus for developing specifically Australian tourism education came from three forces. It is the interplay of these forces and their consequences which has produced the pattern described above and featured in Figure 1. The first force originated in a tourism industry initiative to develop a tourism program similar to that at the University of Hawaii. The industry lobby group of that time, the Australian Tourism Industry Association, approached a number of cluster one universities in an effort to establish a tourism school. In the competitive, status driven environment of the state capital institutions rooted in English origins, tourism was not, in the mid-1980s, seen as sufficiently academi-

FIGURE 1 (continued)

CLUSTER FOUR: Private institutions: 1980s-1990s ongoing	Location	University	Providers of Named Degrees in Tourism in 2004
	Gold Coast Blue Mountains (via Sydney) Sydney Perth Sydney	Bond U. Blue Mountains Hotel School International College of Tourism and Hotel Management U. of Notre Dame Australian Catholic U.	√ (degree conferred by U. of New England) √ (degree conferred by Macquarie U.) √ - (Hotel Management only)

Sources:
Bond University (2004)–*www.bond.edu.au*
Blue Mountains Hotel School (2004)–*http://www.hotelschool.com.au/courses/courseindex.html*
International College of Tourism & Hotel Management (2004)–*http://www.icthm.edu.au*
University of Notre Dame (2004)–*http://www.nd.edu.au/curriculum/degrees/marketing/indices/all.shtml*
Australian Catholic University (2004)–*http://www.acu/edu.edu.au/course_areas/Business-and-Informatics/index.cfm*

cally serious and status-enhancing to justify action (cf. Becher, 1989). The industry approaches to start a new degree program in Australia were rejected. The industry lobby group turned its attention to one of the cluster two universities, specifically James Cook University, located in a tourism relevant region and with some existing research interests in tourism. On this occasion, the reception was much more welcoming and the first Chair of Tourism was established in the late 1980s and one of the first research-oriented managerial style degrees was developed.

A second force, larger in scale and of considerable import, was also at work. Many of the recently upgraded institutes of technology and colleges of advanced education had existing hospitality and hotel management courses. The new freedoms created by becoming a university enabled many of these cluster three universities to augment their existing offerings by either specifying tourism majors or developing full tourism degrees. Two of the former colleges were attached to, or amalgamated with, an existing cluster one (University of Queensland) and an existing cluster two (Griffith University) university with the consequence that these two universities also acquired a ready-made tourism capacity. Later, the University of Tasmania also developed tourism education through this amalgamation approach. Clearly, the world of higher education in tourism was changing quickly.

Six other cluster two universities, monitoring these trends also identified an opportunity to increase their student numbers and hence their budgets for the larger purpose of their research and prestige profile by joining the quest for tourism programs. Inside a decade, tourism studies in Australia had moved from being rejected as a style of university development by the older institutions to being fully embraced by the newer institutions. The cluster one universities, to adopt a sporting metaphor, were caught flat-footed. With no previous interests in tourism, they had no ability to capitalize on existing staff and facilities. Within a decade, institutions in the same cities had largely occupied the territory of tourism. Only the cluster one universities of Queensland, and later Tasmania through the amalgamation process, were able to make a tourism statement.

These historical manoeuvres and forces have led to a rich set of undergraduate offerings in tourism. Most institutions have also developed postgraduate coursework programs. Doctoral level programs exist in most universities but tend to be stronger in the former cluster one and two universities, such as James Cook, Queensland, and Monash. Nevertheless, two of the larger institutions in tourism in Australia–Southern Cross and Victoria University–are also active in research-based higher degree programs. At the undergraduate level, tourism degrees in Australia are typically called Bachelor of Tourism, Bachelor of Tourism Management, or Bachelor of Business (Tourism) with some specialist labels, such as Ecotourism and Cultural Tourism, also appearing.

BROADER ISSUES

The appeal of reviewing tourism education in one country is the ability to identify trends and issues relevant to other settings thus creating synergies and potentially offering solutions. A consideration of the broader issues in Australian tourism education can focus on five themes: the proliferation of campuses and teaching locations in the present decade, the generic skills and graduate attributes shaping curriculum design, the development of teaching skills and competence amongst educators, human resource planning and employment issues in Australia, and the complex task of assessing tourism education.

Teaching Locations

The locational information presented in Figure 1 concentrated on the main campus of each institution. This emphasis is in fact only a part of the contemporary educational scene in Australian tourism offerings. Many universities now have multiple campus sites and tourism may be offered at several but not all of these locations. For example, Central Queensland University offers its tourism degree in two regional cities, as does the University of Southern Queensland. Additionally, several regional universities have educational centres or partners in the capital cities and offer some or all of their degrees in these locations. Further, a number of institutions have offerings in Asia, including tourism majors and Masters degrees in Singapore, Malaysia, Thailand and China. James Cook University, for example, has full tourism undergraduate and Masters (by coursework) degrees at both its Cairns and Townsville campuses as well as feeder or affiliate tourism operations in Sydney and Singapore with the possibility of further links with China. This is not atypical of the bigger programs, such as Griffith University, Southern Cross University, and Victoria University.

The Commonwealth Government in Australia has been sensitive to the issue of quality and consistency of multi-campus and particularly international degrees provided by Australian institutions. There are a number of checking mechanisms to review the adequacy of lecturing staff, consistency in materials, and the quality of student work. Such quality assurance schemes are important in influencing senior university decision-makers on program expansion and multi-campus teaching. For the individual academics there may be expanded and demanding workload issues in coordinating one subject in four or five locations with a suite of lecturing staff depending on the supply of teaching materials, directions, and monitoring or marking assignments. This expansion is of course driven by money, but again issues of reputation and status are important as senior administrators and educators view profitable operations which diminish the prestige of the university as arguably less desirable than those which perform moderately well financially but prosper in the research and prestige stakes. There may well be a phasing out of these multiple locations, particularly internationally, as institutions respond to quality appraisals and rationalise their campus diversity and minimise cross campus repetition.

Generic Skills and Graduate Attributes

In reviewing Australian tourism education, Wells (1996) provided samples of tourism content. Almost a decade later, there are only a few additions to Wells' list (see Table 1).

The expected addition of some new topics in tourism degrees is consistent with the dynamic nature of tourism. Further, a more widespread

TABLE 1. Content Areas in Australian Tourism Degrees

PRIMARY	ADDITIONAL
Nature of Tourism (Tourism Systems)	E-marketing
Historical Development of Tourism	Cultural Tourism
Determinants and Motivations of Tourism	Interpretation
Statistical Measurement and Dimensions	Ethics
Significance of Tourism and Its Impacts	Cross-Cultural Studies
Component Sectors	Heritage and Tourism
Marketing	Sociology of Leisure
Physical Planning and Development	
Organisation (Government, Policy)	
Finance	
Tourism Law	
Tourism Practicum	
Tourism Management	
Computer Applications	
Tourism Transport	
Special Interest Tourism	
Conventions, Events, Meetings	
Ecotourism	
International Tourism	

Adapted from Wells (1996) and websites of Australian Tourism universities (as shown in Figure 1).

trend across the country has been attention not just to the content of tourism degrees but to the qualities of graduates. These abilities and skills have been variously referred to as generic skills, graduate attributes, and transferable skills. They can be defined as:

The abilities, capacities and knowledge to function as a sophisticated professional in an information rich society. (Pearce, 2002, p. 21)

In the Australian context, the Commonwealth Government provided each university with a mandate to develop a list of generic skills according to their location and unique offerings. The graduate attributes or skills may therefore be slightly different from institution to institution but tend to include the following–critical thinking and problem-solving, working with others, communication, numeracy, information technology awareness, life long learning orientation, social and cultural awareness and civic responsibility. For many tourism programs, the task of building these skills into the content subjects specified in Table 1 and then providing an assessment of at least some of these graduate abilities is an ongoing and critical issue in Australian tourism education. Despite the difficulties of this task, there is certainly a challenge here to all educators to think about exactly what students are gaining in an enduring long-term sense from content-based subjects and courses.

Educator Competence

In the early days of tourism education, not just in Australia, there was often a desperate search to recruit tourism educators. New tourism staff were sometimes cajoled into teaching tourism from adjacent subject areas such as hospitality or marketing, a few chose to focus their pre-existing economics, psychology or geography skills on the tourism phenomenon, while others transferred to an educational career from business or government. In contemporary recruitment and staff development, a newer discipline-based cohort of young tourism PhD scholars are now entering the educational market place. Such well-qualified individuals are the new face of tourism education in Australia. There are, however, some testing issues for such new tourism educators. In particular, most of the new wave of tourism graduates will have both an undergraduate and higher degree in tourism. They are therefore required to confront the disciplinary details of particular content areas which have formed tourism study–such as economics, geography, sociology, marketing, psychology–without having formally studied that discipline. There may well be a necessary bridging process to assist the full development of such educators. Such a process may consist of both close mentoring and guides to the literature so that the tourism-discipline links are accessible yet detailed. The criteria for success in this educating the educators in disciplinary subtleties can be extracted from a general principle of understanding reported by Ramsden (1992):

> When we talk about a student (educator) understanding something (parts of a discipline), what we are really saying is that he or she is capable of relating to a concept or topic in the way that an expert in that subject does. (p. 171)

Following these criteria, it is likely that historical and contextual reviews of disciplines and the preoccupations they have may be of particular benefit to tourism educators seeking to familiarise themselves with the dauntingly large underlying territories of tourism.

Human Resources Planning

One of the outstanding features of Australian tourism education implicit in Figure 1 is the proliferation and maintenance of a large number of tourism programs. Bushell and Robertson (1993) identified twenty-two universities offering twenty-six bachelors degrees while the present appraisal amounts to thirty institutions with at least one named tourism degree. Clearly, it would appear that the muted mutterings by academics that there are too many Australian degrees and courses has not been well founded, and ongoing consolidation rather than over-saturation characterises the current situation.

There is no grand master plan in the Australian higher education sector for the required or desirable number of tourism graduates. Riley, Ladkin, and Szivas (2001) argued that there are considerable complexities in trying to develop such overarching "manpower" planning efforts and proposed that research directed at understanding individuals' career choices is at least as valuable as determinations based on tourism forecasts. The current scenario in Australia for managerial level tourism education is to let the universities determine their own emphases, resources and support for tourism education with the employability of the students ultimately influencing the fate of the courses.

One of the potential reasons why Australian tourism education has continued to flourish is that graduates from tourism degree programs have not had to compete with large numbers of graduates in fields such as recreation, parks management, and leisure. While there are some qualifications and programs in these areas, they are much less developed and prominent compared to, for example, parks and recreation programs in the United States or leisure studies in the United Kingdom and Europe. Tourism graduates have, therefore, been able to move into a world of employment in Australia that is freer than in some other countries. Figure 2 depicts a range of employment positions pursued by Australian tourism graduates. It highlights three major sectors of employment—the commercial sector, the education and training sector, and the public and facility management sector. The employment positions adjacent to one another are more closely related than those which are further apart suggesting possible areas where employees may readily transfer jobs. The figure which has been used both in a promotional and analytical sense is termed the Tourism Wheel of Fortunes.

FIGURE 2. The Tourism Wheel of Fortunes

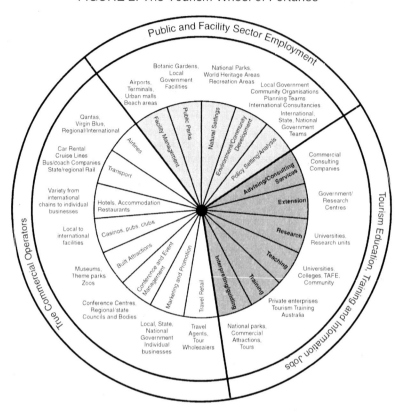

Some Australian university programs highlight employment prospects for their students in select parts of Figure 2, while others are more generic in their educational programs and the destination of graduates. The more specialist programs, such as those in cultural tourism and ecotourism and those with an emphasis on guiding and interpretation, are directing would-be employees to quite select wedges in the wheel. An analytical use of this description of graduate destinations can be envisaged; and while studies have not been done, there is potential to examine outcomes at the single institutional level and across institutions. Additionally, the way graduates move around the wheel in terms of career development is also worthy of research attention. There are also graduates who are not employed in any of the job positions described in the wheel–examples might be retail management or real estate sales and marketing–and questions of why and how people decide to leave or enter tourism employment are also worthy of specific study (cf. Riley, Ladkin, & Szivas, 2001).

ASSESSING TOURISM EDUCATION

Attempts to assess tourism education at the university level in Australia easily fall prey to the status predilections of the assessor. If employment is the criteria, one array of judgments can be made both on the system as a whole and on individual institutions, assuming that reliable data are available in this area. Certainly, many institutions promote their tourism degrees with the rich allure of future tourism jobs in an expanding tourism world. If educational connections to the tourism commercial world are the criteria, then the awards of tourism prizes and the interplay among educators, business leaders, and students become the prominent hallmarks of success. Further, if the international profile of the university is the chosen criteria, then the research profile of staff and higher degree students as well as international student recruitment and alumni activity become the defining factors. It is clear from this outline that unidimensional appraisals and claims for superior performance need to be treated with caution as components rather that the totality of performance.

As Ramsden (1992) and Faulkner, Pearce, Shaw, and Weiler (1995) have pointed out, there is not a necessary link between any of these criteria and what graduates can actually do. Successful tourism education can be defined in multiple ways, but it may include taking in moderate performing students and teaching them a great deal. The contrast here is in accepting high performing high school students and not teaching them very much–the question to be asked is which one is the superior tourism education program?

Two studies reporting on images of Australian tourism education programs and Australian researchers are noteworthy. Like most research studies, there are some issues of sampling and context, but as measures of specific variables they provide some insights. Hsu and Yeung (2003) reported that three Australian tourism education programs are well recognized in the larger Asia Pacific region–James Cook University, Griffith University and Southern Cross University. The sample for this study was based on attendance at an academic conference in Macau; but it does capture the scale, international outreach, and researcher prominence of the nominated institutions. As specified earlier, this kind of evidence does not mean that there are not excellent or high-quality offerings at other institutions when other criteria are used. A second criterion, the research productivity of staff in major tourism journals, has been collated by Ryan (in press). In this assessment, the most published tourism academics in the journals are at James Cook University, Griffith University, and the University of Queensland. Nevertheless, there are active researchers at most Australian institutions; and when monographs and industry publications are also considered, there is a strong argument that many Australian education programs are supported by a researcher-educator model.

Australian tourism programs, like other educational units in contemporary universities everywhere, need to establish clear visions of what they want to achieve and how to measure that success. It is unlikely that any institution will have the resources in the Australian context to be an international leader in research education, as well as an extensive industry networking unit, and additionally be a major provider of commercial sector graduates. Australian tourism education programs would do well to seek their status rewards in those domains where they have historical skills and contextual advantages rather than striving for all possible meritorious but resource demanding targets. The quest for status has been a defining element in the history of Australian tourism education in universities and is likely to be a continuing force as global education possibilities and new technologies create further educational options in tourism.

REFERENCES

Australian Catholic University. (2004). *Course areas–Business and infomatics* [Online]. Available: *http://www.acu.edu.au/course_areas/Business-and-Infomatics/index.cfm*

Australian National University (2004). [Online]. Available: *http://www.anu.edu.au/*

Becher, T. (1989). *Academic tribes and territories. Intellectual enquiry and the culture of disciplines.* Milton Keynes, U.K.: The Society for Research into Higher Education and the Open University Press.

Blue Mountains Hotel School. (2004). *Course overview–Undergraduate programs* [Online]. Available: *http://www.hotelschool.com.au/courses/courseindex.html*

Bolin, P. R., & Greenwood, T. (2001). *Tourism businesses in Australia: A profile of the size and geographic distribution of tourism related businesses.* Canberra: Bureau of Tourism.

Bond University. (2004). [Online]. Available: *http://www.bond.edu.au*

Boundy, K. (2004). *Australian tourism futures*. Keynote address presented at the Tourism Futures Conferences, Townsville, Australia.

Bushell, R., & Robertson, R. W. (1993). *Credit transfer practice in tourism and hospitality programs*. Report prepared for the Australian Vice-Chancellors' Committee, Credit Transfer Project.

Central Queensland University. (2004). *Undergraduate programs–Business* [Online]. Available: *http://www.cqu.edu.au/pages/ugprgmslist_business.html*

Charles Darwin University. (2004). *Courses and programs–Area of study–Tourism* [Online]. Available: *http://eagle.ntu.edu.au/NTU/Apps/coursere.nsf/CDU_pw/AreasInterest/EE8EE3E460DCD92F69256DE6000BC1D3?OpenDocument*

Charles Sturt University. (2004). *Courses at Charles Sturt University on Campus–Undergraduate–All* [Online]. Available: *http://www.csu.edu.au/cgi-pub/course/getcourse?nationality=Australia&top=On+Campus&two=Undergraduate&three=All&submit.x69&submit.y=10&submit=Submit*

Curtin University. (2004). [Online]. Available: *http://www.curtin.edu.au*

Deakin University. (2004). *Course guides–Business & management* [Online]. Available: *http://www.deakin.edu.au/courses/documents/undergrad/brochures/Business.pdf*

Edith Cowan University. (2004). *2004 on-line handbook* [Online]. Available: *http://handbook.ecu.edu.au/ECUCourseList.asp?Page=53&Filter=&hb=1&typ=1&fac=0&field=2*

Faulkner, B., Pearce, P., Shaw, R., & Weiler, B. (1995). Tourism research in Australia: Confronting the challenges of the 1990's and beyond. In B. Faulkner, M. Fagence, M. Davison, & C. Craig-Smith (Eds.), *Bureau of Tourism Research, Tourism Research and Education in Australia, Proceedings from the Tourism and Educators Conference, Gold Coast (1994)* (pp. 3-25). Canberra: Bureau of Tourism Research.

Flinders University. (2004). *Courses & Programs–Undergraduate courses–Bachelor degrees* [Online]. Available: *http://www.flinders.edu.au/courses/ugrad/*

Fuchs, S. (1992). *The professional question for truth: A social theory of science and knowledge*. Albany, NY: State University of New York.

Griffith University. (2003). *Academic programs & courses–Study options–Business & commerce–Undergraduate program* [Online]. Available: *http://www.griffith.edu.au/academicprogramsandcourses/*

Hsu, C., & Yeung, M. (2003). Perceived rankings of hospitality and tourism journals and schools. In K. Chon, & I. Yang (Eds.), *Conference Proceedings of First APAC-CHRIE Conference "Hospitality, Foodservice and Tourism Research and Education: 'The Asian Waves'"* (pp. 529-537). Hong Kong: The Hong Kong Polytechnic University.

International College of Tourism & Hotel Management. (2004). *Academic programs–Tourism programs* [Online]. Available: *http://www.icthm.edu.au*

James Cook University (2004). Available: *http://www.jcu.edu.au/flbca/public/business/tourism.shtml*

La Trobe University. (2004). *Undergraduate handbook 2004–Faculty of law & management–School of tourism & hospitality* [Online]. Available: *http://www.latrobe.edu.au/handbook/lawman/tourism_courses.htm*

Macquarie University. (2004). [Online]. Available: *http://www.mq.edu.au/*

Monash University. (2004). *Undergraduate course guide 2005–Course description & career opportunity–Business & economics* [Online]. Available: *http://www.monash. edu.au/pubs/ugrad/buseco.html*

Murdoch University. (2004). *Handbook 2004–Courses–Hospitality management & tourism services (B Com)* [Online]. Available: *http://handbook.murdoch.edu. au/courses/*

Pearce, P. L. (1995). *Issues in Australian tourism research.* Report presented at World Tourism Trends to the Year 2000: Research Catalyst Workshop, University of Western Sydney, Sydney, Australia.

Pearce, P. L. (2002). The Curriculum Reform and Trends in Hospitality Education in Australia. In *Proceedings of Hospitality Education International Conference* (pp. 119-141). Taipei: National Taiwan Normal University.

Queensland University of Technology. (2004). [Online]. Available: *http://www.qut. edu.au*

Ramsden, P. (1992). *Learning to teach in higher education.* London: Routledge.

Riley, M., Ladkin, A., & Szivas, E. (2001). *Tourism employment analysis and planning.* Clevedon: Channel View Publications.

Royal Melbourne Institute of Technology (RMIT). (2004). *Study at RMIT–Why study at RMIT* [Online]. Available: *http://www.rmit.edu.au/browse/Study%20at% 20RMIT%2F2005%20Program%20Lists/*

Ryan, C. (in press). The ranking and rating of academics and journals in tourism research. *Tourism Management.*

Southern Cross University. (2004). *Course information 2005–Bachelor business in tourism management* [Online]. Available: *http://www.scu.edu.au/courses/course_ desc.php?spk_cd+3004110*

Swinburne Institute of Technology. (2003). *Courses–Course information–Bachelor of business (tourism & management)* [Online]. Available: *http://domino.swin.edu.au/ cd31.nsf/07921ddf50528dleca256768003fbbda/563c3e9d0653395cca256b050002c18e? OpenDocument*

The University of Queensland. (2004). *Programs & courses, study areas–Economics, business, law & tourism* [Online]. Available: *http://www.uq.edu.au/study/studyarea. html?area=bus_law*

The University of South Australia. (2004). *Study at Uni SA–Programs & courses* [Online]. Available: *http://www.unisa.edu.au/study/progcourses/default.asp*

University of Adelaide. (2004). [Online]. Available: *http://www.adelaide.edu.au/*

University of Ballarat. (2004). *Student services–Course guide services–Business* [Online]. Available: *http://www.ballarat.edu.au/courseguide/display/cgi?ID+39*

University of Canberra. (2003). *Courses–Course description–Browse by level* [Online]. Available: *http://www.uc.edu.au/courses/index.cfm?action=browse&type= course&coursegroup=01*

University of Melbourne. (2004). [Online]. Available: *http://www.unimelb.edu.au/*

University of New England. (2004). [Online]. Available: *http://www.une.edu.au/*

University of New South Wales. (2004). [Online]. Available: *http://www.unsw.edu.au/*

University of Newcastle. (2003). *Study options for undergraduate Australian students–Course information* [Online]. Available: *http://www.newcastle.edu.au/study/ australian/index.html*

University of Notre Dame. (2004). *Course information* [Online]. Available: *http://www.nd.edu.au/curriculum/degrees/marketing/indices/all.shtml*

University of Southern Queensland (2004). [Online]. Available: *http://www.usq.edu.au*

University of Sunshine Coast (2004). [Online]. Available: *http://www.usc.edu.au*

University of Sydney (2004). [Online]. Available: *http://www.usyd.edu.au/*

University of Tasmania (2004). [Online]. Available: *http://www.utas.edu.au*

University of Technology Sydney. (2004). *UTS handbook 2004–Faculty of business–Undergraduate courses* [Online]. Available: *http://www.uts.edu.au/div/publications/bus/ug/index.html*

University of the Sunshine Coast. (2004). *Undergraduate programs–Program overviews* [Online]. Available: *http://www.usc.edu.au/Students/CoursesPrograms/UndergradPrograms/Overviews/*

University of Victoria. (2004). *Victoria University 2004 handbooks online–Faculty of business & law* [Online]. Available: *http://www.vu.edu.au/Courses/Handbooks/BUSINESS/index1.asp*

University of Western Australia. (2004). [Online]. Available: *http://www.uwa.edu.au/*

University of Western Sydney. (2004). *Academic courses–Undergraduate courses* [Online]. Available: *http://handbook.uws.edu.au/hbook/COURSE_INDEX.ASP#uC03*

University of Wollongong. (2004). [Online]. Available: *http://www.uow.edu.au/*

Wells, J. (1996). The tourism curriculum in higher education in Australia 1989-1995. *Journal of Tourism Studies*, 7(1), 20-30.

Index

Aletheia University (Taiwan), 174
Alpine tourism industry, 41
Apprenticeship training, 47
Articulation, in Canadian tourism
    education, 14-16
ASEAN Tourism Agreement, 205
Asia Cooperation Dialogue (ACD)
    Tourism Business Forum,
    205-206
Asian Wave, 157-158
Associate degree programs
    in Hong Kong, 145-146
    in South Korea, 237-238
    in Taiwan, 170-172
    in Turkey, 95-102
Australia
    about, 251-252
    tourism education in
        assessing, 263-264
        history of, 252-257
        issues in, 257-263
Austria
    future challenges of tourism
        education system in, 58-59
    tourism education in, 46-49
    tourism industry in, 49-52
    vs. Switzerland's educational
        system, 57-58
Axworthy, Lloyd, 8

Bagan Declaration, 206
Ben-Gurion University (Israel), 72
    tourism education program of,
        74-76
Birmingham College of Hospitality,
    Tourism and Creative
    Studies, 33

Block transfers, Canadian education
    and, 14-15
Bournemouth University (Israel), 78
British Isles. See Ireland; United
    Kingdom

Canada
    alliance building in tourism
        industry in, 9-11
    articulation in, 14-15
    loss of research talent in tourism
        industry in, 20-22
    National Manpower Training
        Strategy report, 11-14
    National Training Act (1981) of,
        8-9
    tourism and hospitality programs in,
        15-16
    tourism education councils in, 19
    tourism education in
        articulation in, 14-16
        future of, 23-24
        in 1960s, 3-4
        in 1970s, 5-8
        in 1980s, 8-14
        in 1990s, 14-15
        Ontario's experience in, 4-5
        present day, 18-23
    tourism industry in, 2-3
Canadian Employment and
    Immigration commission
    (CEIC), 8-10
Canadian Hospitality Institute, 10-11
Canadian Tourism Commission
    (CTC), 18,20-23
Canadian Tourism/Hospitality
    Advisory Committee on
    Human Resources, 10

Canadian Tourism Human Resource
    Council (CTHRC), 16-19
Central School of Tourism (Israel), 65
Champlain College, 78
China
    opportunities in tourism in, 159-160
    tourism higher education in
        curricula in, 125-126
        distribution of schools in,
            120-122
        history of, 118-120
        mechanisms for running schools
            and programs for, 122
        objectives for, 122-124
        problems and challenges of,
            127-131
        program hierarchy for, 120
        program setup for, 124-125
        scale of, 120
        textbooks and teaching materials
            for, 126-127
        trends and prospects for,
            131-134
    tourism in, 159-160
China National Tourism Administration
    (CNTA), 118-119,160
Chinese Culture University (Taiwan),
    172-174
Chulalongkorn University (Thailand),
    199
Competitiveness, Porter's diamond of,
    42-43
Cooper, Simon, 20
The Council. *See* Canadian Tourism
    Human Resource Council
    (CTHRC)
Curricula
    in China, 125-127
    future developments, in Hong
        Kong, 158-159
    revisions, in Turkey, 108-109
    in Taiwan, 188-190,192-195
    in Thailand, 217-218

for Turkish associate degree
    programs, 99-101
Cyber tourism programs. *See*
    E-learning

DACUM (Developing a Curriculum)
    system, 4-5
Division of continuing Education and
    External Studies (Technion)
    (Israel), 63
Dublin College of Catering, 28
Dvir school (Israel), 65

Economic Cooperation Strategy
    (ECS), 206
Eilat College (Israel), 72
E-learning
    in Hong Kong, 162-163
    in South Korea, 242
England. *See* United Kingdom
Entrepreneurs, in tourism industry,
    41-42
European Centre for the Development
    of Vocational Training
    (CEDEFOP), 29
European Hotel Diploma
    (EURHODIP), 28-29

Failte Ireland, 34-35
Farleigh Dickenson University, 79
Four-year programs. *See*
    Undergraduate programs

Graduate programs. *See* Postgraduate
    programs
Great Britain. *See* United Kingdom
Guangwei, He, 160

Haifa University, 64,71,78
Haking Wong Technical Institute
    (HWTI), 140,142

Hebrew University (Israel), 78
Higher education. *See* Tourism
     education
Higher Education Funding Council for
     England (HEFCE), 33
Hong Kong
     e-learning in, 162-163
     tourism higher education in
          associate degree programs,
               145-146
          future developments for,
               156-164
          history of, 139-148
          overview of funding for,
               148-156
          postgraduate programs, 147-148
          top-up degree programs, 146-147
          undergraduate programs, 142-145
          vocational-based programs,
               139-142
     tourism in, 138-139
Hong Kong Institute of Vocational
     Education, 142
Hong Kong Polytechnic, 140-142
Hong Kong Technical College, 142
Hospitality and tourism education. *See*
     Tourism education
Hotel Association of Canada (HAC), 19
Hsing Wu College (Taiwan), 172,174
Human resources development, in
     Thailand, 220-222

INDECORE (Industry Developed Core
     Curriculum), 4,12-13
Ireland
     Institute of Technology (IT) system
          in, 34
     internationalization of tourism
          education in, 35-37
     tourism education in, 34-35
Israel
     about, 62
     academic programs in tourism and
          hospitality in 2000 in, 76-80

Ben-Gurion University's program
     for tourism education, case
     of, 74-76
early efforts to develop academic
     programs for tourism
     industry in, 71-74
future challenges for tourism
     industry in, 86-87
history of tourism education in,
     62-66
"millennium revolution" in tourism
     education in, 66-71
shifts in tourism programs since
     2000, 80-84
tourism industry and academia
     relations in, 84-86

Johnson and Wales University, 80
Junior colleges, in Taiwan, 170-172.
     See also Associate degree
     programs

Korea. *See* South Korea

Lausanne Hotel School, 28,67
Learning and Teaching Support
     Network (LTSN) (UK), 33
Life style entrepreneurs, 42
Long-distance learning. *See* E-learning

Master degree programs. *See*
     Postgraduate programs
Ming Chuan College (Taiwan), 173,175

National Centre for Tourism Studies
     (University of Limerick), 34
National Kaohsiung Hospitality
     College (NKHC) (Taiwan),
     29,178,188-190

National Training Act (1981)
(Canada), 8-9
New tourism and, 43-44
Nova Southwestern University, 78

Ontario Hostelry Institute (OHI),
5-8,13
Organization for the Academization of
the Hospitality and Tourism
Industry in Israel (OAHTI),
72-74

Pizam, Abraham, 74
Pollock, Anna, 221
Polytechnic tourism education, in
Austria, 48
Porter's diamond of competitiveness,
42-43
Postgraduate programs
in Hong Kong, 147-148
in South Korea, 239-242
in Turkey, 106-108
Prince of Songkla University (PSU)
(Thailand), 199-200
Public choice theory, 45

Republic of Korea. *See* South Korea
Research. *See* Tourism research

Sandwich-style instruction, 178-179
Scottish Hotel School, 29,33
Shanghai Institute of Tourism, 118
Shannon College of Hotel
Management, 34
Singapore Hotels Association
Technical Education Center
(SHATEC), 29
South Korea
about, 226
tourism education in, 236-242

cyber programs, 24
four-year university programs,
238-241
future of, 244-247
graduate programs, 239-242
industrial-educational
cooperation for, 242-244
two-year college programs,
237-238
tourism industry in
history of, 226-235
organizations in, 235-236
Switzerland
future challenges of tourism
education system in, 58-59
history of tourism in, 52-53
labor market in, 54
supply side of tourism market in, 54
tourism education in, 54-57
types of tourism in, 53
vs. Austria's educational system,
57-58

Tadmor School (Israel), 64-65,80
Taiwan, tourism education in
academic institution evolvement in,
186-191
name changes and, 186-188
teaching faculty and, 190-191
curricula for, 188-190,192-196
development of, 172-186
future development trends in, 192
issues in, 191-192
overview of, 168-172
tourism research and, 195
Tamkang College (Taiwan), 173-174
Thailand
human resources development in,
220-222
tourism higher education in
current status, structure,
characteristics and trends of,
209-219
development and evolution of,
199-206

future developments for,
219-222
from 1996-1999, 207-209
tourism in, 198-199,201-206
Tourism Canada, 9-10
Tourism education, xiii-xiv. *See also*
specific country
externalities of, 45
internationalizing, 29-30
origins of, 28-29
Tourism education councils (TECs)
(Canada), 19
Tourism industry. *See also* specific
country
entrepreneurs in, 41-42
introduced, 40-41
"new tourism" in, 43-44
structural changes in, 41-46
studies of development of higher
education in, 90
Tourism Industry Association of
Canada (TIAC), 18
Tourism research
lack of, in Canada, 20-22
in Taiwan, 195
Travel industry. *See* Tourism industry
Turkey
higher education system in, 92-94
studies of tourism education in,
90-91
tourism development in, 91-92
tourism education in, 94-95
associate degree programs for,
95-102
auditing and certifying programs
in, 110
collaboration and, 110-111
curricula revisions for, 108-109
four-year degree programs for,
103-106

funding of, 111-112
future developments for,
108-112
postgraduate programs for,
106-108
staff certification for, 109-110
tourism graduates in
keeping, 103
placement of, 102
Two-year college programs. *See*
Associate degree programs

Undergraduate programs
in Hong Kong, 142-147
in South Korea, 238-239
in Thailand, 207-219
in Turkey, 103-106
United Kingdom
internationalization of tourism
education in, 35-37
tourism education in, 31-33
University of Derby, 79
University of Limerick, 34
University of Nevada, Las Vegas,
79-80

Virtual tourism programs. *See*
E-learning
Vocational-based programs
in Austria, 47-48
in Hong Kong, 139-142

Wei, He Jian, 160
Westminster College (London), 28

BOOK ORDER FORM!

Order a copy of this book with this form or online at:
http://www.HaworthPress.com/store/product.asp?sku= 5857

Global Tourism Higher Education
Past, Present, and Future

—— in softbound at $29.95 ISBN-13: 978-0-7890-3282-9 / ISBN-10: 0-7890-3282-1.
—— in hardbound at $49.95 ISBN-13: 978-0-7890-3281-2 / ISBN-10: 0-7890-3281-3.

COST OF BOOKS _____

POSTAGE & HANDLING _____
US: $4.00 for first book & $1.50
for each additional book
Outside US: $5.00 for first book
& $2.00 for each additional book.

SUBTOTAL _____

In Canada: add 7% GST. _____

STATE TAX _____
CA, IL, IN, MN, NJ, NY, OH, PA & SD residents
please add appropriate local sales tax.

FINAL TOTAL _____
If paying in Canadian funds, convert
using the current exchange rate.
UNESCO coupons welcome.

❏ BILL ME LATER:
Bill-me option is good on US/Canada/
Mexico orders only; not good to jobbers,
wholesalers, or subscription agencies.

❏ Signature _____

❏ Payment Enclosed: $_____

❏ PLEASE CHARGE TO MY CREDIT CARD:

❏ Visa ❏ MasterCard ❏ AmEx ❏ Discover
❏ Dîner's Club ❏ Eurocard ❏ JCB

Account #_____

Exp Date_____

Signature_____
(Prices in US dollars and subject to change without notice.)

PLEASE PRINT ALL INFORMATION OR ATTACH YOUR BUSINESS CARD

Name

Address

City   State/Province   Zip/Postal Code

Country

Tel   Fax

E-Mail

May we use your e-mail address for confirmations and other types of information? ❏Yes ❏No We appreciate receiving
your e-mail address. Haworth would like to e-mail special discount offers to you, as a preferred customer.
We will never share, rent, or exchange your e-mail address. We regard such actions as an invasion of your privacy.

Order from your **local bookstore** or directly from
The Haworth Press, Inc. 10 Alice Street, Binghamton, New York 13904-1580 • USA
Call our toll-free number (1-800-429-6784) / Outside US/Canada: (607) 722-5857
Fax: 1-800-895-0582 / Outside US/Canada: (607) 771-0012
E-mail your order to us: orders@HaworthPress.com

For orders outside US and Canada, you may wish to order through your local
sales representative, distributor, or bookseller.
For information, see http://HaworthPress.com/distributors

(Discounts are available for individual orders in US and Canada only, not booksellers/distributors.)

Please photocopy this form for your personal use.
www.HaworthPress.com

BOF06